International Business in China

KV-051-255

International Business Series

Academic Editor: Alan M. Rugman, University of Toronto

27 NO

-4 FE

-2

13

29 N

16

THE LIBRARY
UNIVERSITY OF
WINCHESTER

KA 0239989 X

International Business in China

Edited by Lane Kelley
and Oded Shenkar

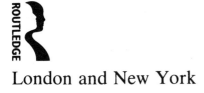

London and New York

KING ALFRED'S COLLEGE
WINCHESTER

650.0951
KEL
0239989X

First published 1993
by Routledge
11 New Fetter Lane, London EC4P 4EE

Simultaneously published in the USA and Canada
by Routledge
29 West 35th Street, New York, NY 10001

Reprinted 1994

© 1993 Editorial selection Lane Kelley and Oded Shenkar, individual
chapters to their authors.

Typeset in Times by J&L Composition Ltd, Filey, North Yorkshire
Printed and bound in Great Britain by
Antony Rowe Ltd, Chippenham, Wiltshire

All rights reserved. No part of this book may be reprinted or reproduced
or utilized in any form or by any electronic, mechanical, or other means,
now known or hereafter invented, including photocopying and recording,
or in any information storage or retrieval system, without permission in
writing from the publishers.

British Library Cataloguing in Publication Data
A catalogue record for this book is available from the British Library

Library of Congress Cataloging in Publication Data
has been applied for.

ISBN 0-415-05345-5

Contents

List of contributors

John Frankenstein is Director of CitiCorp Doctoral Program and Senior Lecturer at the Asian Management Research Centre of the University of Hong Kong Business School.

Mark Barnard is International Programs Officer at the College of Tropical Agriculture and Human Resources of the University of Hawaii at Manoa.

Oded Shenkar is Head of the International Business Program at the Faculty of Management at Tel-Aviv University, and Professor at the Department of Management, University of Hawaii at Manoa.

Stephen Thomas is Chairman of the Department of Political Science, University of Colorado, Denver.

Ronald C. Brown is Professor at the School of Law, University of Hawaii at Manoa.

Sylvain R. Plasschaert is Professor of Finance, I-V. Leaven and UFSIA (Antwerp) at Brussels, Belgium.

K.K. Seo is Professor at the Financial Economics Institution, University of Hawaii at Manoa.

Aspy P. Palia is Professor at the Department of Marketing, University of Hawaii at Manoa.

Paul W. Beamish is Professor and Director of the Centre for International Business Studies at the University of Western Ontario, London, Canada. He is also the Editor-in-Chief of the *Journal of International Business Studies*.

Lorraine Spiess is the President of China Trade Consultants. She was formerly Executive Director of the Canada–China Trade Council.

Mee Kau Nyaw is Professor of Organization and Management at the Chinese University of Hong Kong.

Simcha Ronen is Professor at the Faculty of Management and Chairman of the Organization Behavior Program, Tel-Aviv University.

Kam-Hon Lee is Professor of Marketing at the Chinese University of Hong Kong.

Thamis Wing-Chun Lo is Lecturer at the Department of Marketing, Chinese University of Hong Kong.

Gao Guopei is Professor and Dean at the Faculty of International Business Management, University of International Business and Economics, Beijing.

Richard W. Brislin is Research Associate at the East–West Center, University of Hawaii at Manoa.

C. Harry Hui is Lecturer at the Department of Psychology, Chinese University of Hong Kong.

1 Toward the year 2000

Some strategic speculations about international business in China

John Frankenstein

> *What do foreigners least understand*
> *about doing business in China?*
>
> *That the economy is under State control,*
> *and thus the State can legitimately intervene*
> *in any deal at any time under any pretext.*
> Chinese trade lawyer, Beijing, summer 1988
>
> *Politics in command.*
> Mao Zedong

Any attempt to estimate the nature and scope of China's international business at the end of the present decade is, by necessity, an adventure in speculation. The world events of 1989–90 remind us that Haldane's observation about the universe – that it is stranger than we can imagine – applies to history as well. The business strategist and political-risk analyst must go beyond economics to an understanding of the salient factors that drive the Chinese system and an awareness of the key signposts can provide the basis of an informed estimate of macro-risks.

ECONOMICS: A QUICK LOOK

Before we specify those factors, however, we should not ignore the macroeconomic forecast. Let us assume that Chinese foreign trade growth will fall in the 6–10 percent range for the next decade. Using the official figure for total two-way trade in 1989 of US$111.6 billion – a 440 percent increase over 1978's figure and 7 percent of China's GNP – as the base, we come up with a rough estimate for total trade in 1999 that falls between US$200 billion and US$290 billion. In other words, simple mathematics suggests that Chinese trade could increase by a factor of two or three by the end of the decade.[1]

Furthermore, we should not ignore what the Chinese leadership has been saying about the future of the Chinese economy. In the late 1970s, as Deng Xiaoping and the reformers of the time took charge, the call was for realizing the "Four Modernizations" (of the economy, agriculture, science and technology, and defense), of doubling major economic aggregates by 1990 and quadrupling them by the end of the century. While at first blush those goals seemed unattainable, those set for 1990 appear to have been reached.

The goals set out in the late 1970s continue to be those of the Chinese leadership in the early 1990s as well. Communist Party General Secretary Jiang Zemin, speaking at Chinese national day in 1989, remarked that GNP had doubled over the past decade, and that the "problem of feeding and clothing the population has been basically solved." The next step would be to double GNP again by the year 2000. The strategy: "[D]ependence on scientific and technological progress and continuous rise in labor productivity. We shall strictly control the growth of the population, raise its quality, and pay attention to the preservation of the ecologic environment." On the foreign investment side, the Chinese Ministry of Foreign Economic Relations and Trade (MOFERT) has projected that total realized foreign investment will increase two or three times by the year 2000 (from a total of US$15.4 billion to over US$40 billion).[2]

As the decade of the 1980s has shown, the macro growth suggested by Chinese officials and by our rough calculation is attainable; obviously there is a potential for increased foreign business. But these estimates have such a broad range that they are really not very useful, except to indicate the forecaster's uncertainty. The uncertainty is warranted.

In the Chinese case, the economic forces that drive international trade are subordinated to the political imperative. The political events of the summer of 1989 appear to have rewritten the script of the reforms initiated under Deng Xiaoping in 1979. While the leadership speaks of continuing the reforms, policies appear to differ substantially from those of the last ten years: recentralization, priority to the inefficient state sector and even hints of recollectivizing agriculture. Certainly, politics has reemerged as the arbiter of China's future – the transition struggle appears to be underway – and the outlook is for protracted struggle. Thus is is with the Chinese political scene that we have to start, for once again, politics are in command.

SOME POLITICAL BASICS

Seemingly puzzling policy oscillations mark the development of the People's Republic of China (PRC) since 1949. The bureaucratic, Stalinist 1950s ended in the turmoil and massive famine of the Great Leap Forward; the brief period of reform and reconsolidation that followed in the 1960s concluded with the world turned upside down in the catastrophic Cultural Revolution. The transitional 1970s were equally tumultuous: Lin Biao's failed *coup d'état* in 1971, China's change of course and the Nixon visit in 1972, the deaths of the major players of the Revolution, Mao, Zhou Enlai and Zhu De, and the overthrow of the Gang of Four – Mao's widow and other radicals – in 1976. And in 1979 came the resurrection, after spells in the wilderness, of Deng Xiaoping. The 1980s saw the implementation of what appeared to be massive reforms in all spheres of Chinese life under the general rubric of "The Open Policy"; that phase ended dramatically as the Party bureaucrats cracked down not only in Tiananmen Square, but all over China.[3]

In one sense, the reform period appears to have been quite unusual, particularly if one concentrates on China's relative openness to the outside world during the decade of the 1980s. From another perspective, however, we can see that the period is part of a larger pattern of swings from one policy extreme to another. In fact, these oscillations are not random and inexplicable; rather they are the result of the Chinese leadership's attempts to grapple with the problems of modernization and are products of the interaction between political constants from the past and political cycles from the present.

CONSTANTS[4]

All Chinese rulers have been faced with one crucial problem: how to rule a large country with a large population from a single place. The first Emperor of the Qin dynasty offered a solution which has persisted for more than 2,000 years: authoritarian, bureaucratic centralism.

The Qin's organizational solution brought with it certain operating principles. One was a tradition of the absolute and arbitrary power of the ruler, power that was invested in the ruler's person, power that was unchecked by institutions. The ideology of the Mandate of Heaven – that one ruled because of one's superior virtue – meant that opposition to power was by definition unrighteous and thus illegitimate: there is, in the Chinese political tradition, no meaningful concept of a "loyal opposition." The traditions of Confucianism, which stressed that correct behavior and thought would lead to a properly ordered society and that it was the responsibility of the properly educated to set an example and to lead the less fortunate to that society, only reinforced this not always benevolent authoritarianism.

Thus control, the power to compel, is a key value in the Chinese system. Furthermore, the political perspective is inward-looking: time and time again Chinese leaders would sacrifice or ignore external dangers and threats to deal with internal challenges: in the mid-nineteenth century the Qing dealt with the Taiping and Nian Rebellions before attempting to cope with Western imperialism; in the 1930s, Chiang Kaishek cut deals with the Japanese so he could concentrate on exterminating the Communist movement; in the 1960s, Mao, with the Americans in Vietnam threatening China's southern border and the Russians building up nuclear forces to the north, turned against his own party in the Cultural Revolution; and, indeed, the Chinese leadership reacted at Tiananmen in the summer of 1989 as the world looked on aghast. We will recognize that these traditions, reinforced by a passion for order and a fear of *luan*, or disorder, together with the equally strong Chinese obsessions with secrecy and unanimity (Chinese political norms abhor factions which, of course, exist everywhere) have strong resonances with the later traditions of Leninism.

MORE QUESTIONS: MODERN CYCLES

The disasters of the nineteenth and twentieth centuries – the Opium War of 1839–42 and the subsequent "Century of Humiliation" – raised some additional and inter-related questions for China's rulers. The most salient issue was how to restore China's greatness. Here, ultimately, a fierce nationalism and determination to avoid foreign interference carried the day. Two other related and persistent questions emerged as well: how to deal with the West, and how to transform China's society.

The West was, after all, the source of both China's political and economic humiliation and, through modern technology, her possible salvation. The Self-Strengthening Movement of the mid-nineteenth century came up with two recipes. One was "Self-Reliance," a term which could mean anything from autarchy to enmeshment with the outside world. The other was the formulation, "Chinese learning for fundamentals, Western learning for use" – in other words, China would take what might be useful from the West but at the same time maintain Chinese values. For the Self-Strengtheners and the imperial regime that supported them, Chinese values meant the continuation of the Confucian and dynastic traditions; ultimately the social, economic and political imperatives of industrial technology would collide with these orthodoxies.

The matter of transforming Chinese society is equally complex and indeed, closely related to the issue of dealing with the West. As the nineteenth century ground to a close, the declining political capacity and inappropriateness of the imperial system was laid bare. Attempts at reform failed; revolution – the wholesale replacement of elites – became the only alternative. With this came concerns about transformation. Most modernizers agreed that the problems were rooted in China's past – intellectuals of the May 4 movement such as Hu Shih and Lu Xun ridiculed "feudalism" and called for its destruction. Some modernizers called for science and democracy – others, more radical, such as Mao Zedong, called for the creation of a new socialist man.

Understanding these issues is not just an exercise in historicism. The success of revolution did not mean that these issues disappeared: indeed, late twentieth-century Chinese fears of Western influence compromising Chinese values, now cast in the Sino–Leninist vocabulary of "spiritual pollution" and "bourgeois liberalism" are the latest replay of the Self-Strengtheners' dilemma. When Chinese intellectuals in the 1980s condemned feudalism they were not only condemning the past but also its persistence in the rule of China by its "New Class." And as we have seen since the summer of 1989, that "New Class" has more than reasserted itself.

But not only did these issues persist, but new and equally vital questions emerged. Whose vision – Sun Yatsen's, Chiang Kaishek's, Mao Zedong's, Liu Shaoqi's, Deng Xiaoping's – was correct? Which road should China follow? Because all of these revolutionaries were dedicated nationalists, the context took on a special edge; the attempts to answer these questions has led to continuous turmoil.

READING THE TEA LEAVES

One useful way to understand these modern dynamics has been to posit, as Dorothy Solinger suggests, a three-line struggle between transformative "Maoist" radicals at one extreme, flexible "pragmatists" at the other, and a centralizing tendency of statist bureaucrats who, above all, value control and who pit "stability" of the system against the putative disorder (*luan*) that would ensue if the Party were not there. One tendency or faction at the extremes may temporarily carry the day (usually in coalition with another group against the third), but the political pendulum eventually returns to the bureaucratic center.[5]

A related view, drawing on Western understandings of organizations, suggests that the variations are the outcome of political elites correcting – and over-correcting – the unintended consequences of policies. Because communication within the system is inadequate and the information incomplete and often erroneous, incremental decisions made at the top to rectify problems only make things worse, and thus a complete change of direction becomes the only solution.[6]

Another interpretation, which pits the extremes of the political spectrum against each other, is the somewhat more conventional view of the developments in the People's Republic as a two-line contest between "socialist" and "developmental" values. Here the debates are over the nature and degree of centralization and planning, the appropriateness of material incentives (as opposed to the egalitarian "iron rice-bowl" of guaranteed employment, whether Party "reds" or State "experts" should guide the economy, and how investment should be allocated between heavy industry, light industry, and agriculture.[7]

Not surprisingly, when foreign economic relations become an issue, overseas links tend to be favored by the more "liberal" tendencies and regarded with suspicion, if not rejected, by the more conservative or "radical" lines. But political matters remain central to these two- or three-line debates. In the Chinese setting, policy is instrumental – what ultimately counts is who wins and dominates, who maintains control. This is not to say that policy outcomes are unimportant or trivial. But political outcomes are even more important. In the Hobbesian Chinese political game there are real winners and real losers, and losers often don't make it back into the arena.

THE DENG REFORMS: 1979–89

With this background in mind, then, a brief review of the goals and accomplishments of the reforms is appropriate, for they provide the setting which drew – or allowed – the attention and participation of international business in China's development. They also form the background of the current political scene in the People's Republic.

International respectability

The greatest accomplishment of the reforms was the reestablishment of the international legitimacy of the People's Republic. While that relegitimation process began with the understandings reached between Mao and Nixon in the early 1970s, under Deng it reached a high point. No longer was Beijing the capital of "Red China," the country of blue ants, the model of totalitarian excess. Instead, the international community welcomed China into the fold: one saw a dramatic expansion of diplomatic relations, increasing participation in international organizations – China even applied to the GATT – and, as we have noted above, an increase in foreign trade. Furthermore, China moderated its disputes with former adversaries: Sino–US relations were normalized, trade agreements were signed and party-to-party relations restored with the USSR, culminating in Gorbachev's dramatic if upstaged visit to Beijing in the summer of 1989, and even relations with Taiwan eased.

Indeed, as trade and investment with the island increased, and as Hong Kong, recovering its natural niche in the political economy of the Pacific as an entrepôt for the China trade, became more and more linked to the economy of southern China, there was talk in the late 1980s of a "Greater Chinese" economy. The Taiwan–Mainland trade, most of it routed through Hong Kong, has grown enormously, even if the very tenuous political progress toward some kind of understanding that had been made over the preceding decade has recently been compromised. In 1988 that trade was in the US$2–3 billion range, making the Mainland Taiwan's fifth largest trading partner; informal estimates including invisibles, mainly Taiwanese tourism, suggest the total may have reached US$6 billion. For the first half of 1989, total Taiwan–Mainland merchandise trade reached just over US$2 billion, up about 55 percent over the previous period, with Taiwan running a substantial surplus of US$1.4 billion.[8] Taiwan investments in the Mainland have surged too – many in Fujian, the home province of many Taiwanese, although there are reports of Taiwanese investment in sites as varied as Guangdong and Beijing; according to MOFERT, Taiwanese investment at the end of 1989 reached a total value of US$1 billion.[9]

Hong Kong has become the leading source of investment in the PRC, mostly in Guangdong: for instance, in 1988 China signed 5,890 foreign investment contracts valued at US$5.18 billion – Hong Kong firms concluded over 4,500 of these, with a total value of US$3.4 billion (66 percent of the total). Here, Hong Kong investors are trying to cope with both a very tight labor market and continuing competitive wage pressures. The upshot is that perhaps as many as 2.5 million workers in Guangdong work in Hong Kong-invested enterprises; when we consider that the industrial workforce in Hong Kong itself is around 800,000, we can get a better sense of the territory's integration with China.[10]

Indeed, as the 1980s came to a close there was a foreign investment boom. Comparing the thirty-month period January 1987–June 1989 to the preceding seven *years*, the number of signed contracts grew by 400 percent; their value was up over 67 percent. Furthermore, foreign business people reported that over the decade Chinese business practices and conditions improved considerably. This is not to say that all was smooth sailing, but there was the perception that decisions were being made more quickly, that political inference was declining and that a more regularized, less arbitrary, climate was evolving. In short, foreigners were learning how to survive, cope and succeed in China, and the Chinese business bureaucrats were learning how to function in the larger international environment.[11]

Internal efforts

But none of this could have happened without internal reform as well. The ideology of the regime moderated: the chief contradiction, it was said, was no longer political, but rather economic, between inadequate and lagging production and high and increasing social demand. A "household responsibility system" was introduced in the agricultural sector, ending twenty years of collectivization, and not only bringing back markets but also small-scale tenant farming (with the state as landlord). In the industrial sector, investment emphasis shifted to light industry. And while the central planning apparatus remained in place, there was wholesale decentralization of decision-making, down to the factory and locality. Private and collectively-owned enterprises outside the plan were encouraged – these would soak up unemployment (finally acknowledged to exist under Chinese socialism), "enliven" the economy, and provide goods and services not available from the bureaucratic and subsidized state sector.

Furthermore, there were attempts to reform the roles of the state and the party. The state apparatus was streamlined, and party authority diminished. The factory manager, the "expert," now responsible not only for production but also planning, distribution and marketing, was to be in charge; the Party secretary, formerly the *de facto* boss, was to be limited to, as one factory manager told me, "*sixiang gongzuo*" – "thought work." Thus the promise was the depoliticalization of life, social relaxation. Indeed, there was a wholesale reevaluation of Mao (70 percent good, 30 percent bad, although some Chinese might reverse those percentages) and the past. The Cultural Revolution, the great negative example against which Deng could hold up his reforms, was termed "The Ten Lost Years"; there were reports that the then Party General Secretary Hu Yaobang spoke of "twenty lost years," and a government official, at a private meeting in Beijing in 1988, spoke of "thirty lost years" – the entire span of the PRC from 1949 to 1979! In short, the "radical tendency" of Chinese politics was delegitimized.

The economic and social results of the reforms could not be questioned. Superficial observation on the streets, in the markets and in the countryside suggested great changes in the standard of living: more color, more goods, more houses and more construction. Economic data from the official State Statistical Bureau backed up these impressions, as shown in Table 1.1.

Table 1.1 The economic reforms: 1978–89[12]

	1978	1989	% annual change
Gross national product (billion yuan)	684.6	1,567.7	7.8
Total foreign trade (billion US$)	20.6	111.6	16.6
Grain (million tons)	304.7	407.45	2.7
Televisions (million)	0.51	24.85 [1988]	47.5
Refrigerators (million)	0.028	7.4 [1988]	74.7
Bicycles (million)	8.54	41.22 [1988]	17.1
Per-capita income – rural (yuan)	134	424 [1986]	15.5
Per-capita income – urban (yuan)	614	1,329 [1986]	10.1

Dilemmas of reform

But there were some inherent contradictions and unintended consequences to the reforms. First of all, the reforms relied on old means to accomplish new ends. The aims of the reforms were, shall we say, a kinder, gentler China, a depoliticized and debureaucratized China of laws, not men, a China responsive to the broad economic needs of the population. And indeed, a multiplicity of laws and regulations has emerged in the political, social and economic spheres. It would be difficult to say that a body of law, based on practice, has developed: the system tends to be deliberately untransparent, with many, sudden and unannounced changes in implementing regulations, which, in any case, are often held to be state secrets not for circulation. But a commercial code is slowly evolving.

The reforms as a whole, however, were decreed from the top and pushed through not by public debate but rather on the basis of Deng's personal prestige and power. To be sure, the aim was not even a simulation of bourgeois democracy – the regime reiterated again and again that the reforms were based on the Four Cardinal Principles: following the socialist line, proletarian dictatorship, leadership of the Communist Party, and Marxism–Leninism–Mao Zedong thought. But they engendered both economic progress and social relaxation. Even victims of the anti-intellectual campaigns of the 1950s and 1960s began to speak out again, and newer, bolder voices began to be heard.

Thus began a continuing play between people speaking out and the government cracking down. A "Democracy Wall," complete with big character posters, flourished in Beijing from 1979–80. But the campaign for "socialist spiritual civilization" closed it down, and its major participants vanished into the Chinese Gulag; perhaps more menacing was Deng's subsequent extra-legal move to remove the Chinese Constitutional guarantee of the right to put up big character posters. Other campaigns against "bourgeois liberalism" and "spiritual pollution" followed – while conventional analysis suggested that the "conservatives" among the elite were the prime movers, Deng supported them all.[13]

Unintended consequences

Thus the fine line – a particularly fine line in China – between social relaxation and social disorder began to be breached. At the same time, the reforms had some unwelcome and surely unintended economic consequences as well. Inflation surged – never to the hyper-levels that helped bury the Guomindang in the 1940s – but still to the point that there were runs on banks in late 1988 as city dwellers, mostly state employees on fixed salaries, saw the value of their savings erode. Indeed, the inflation masked the apparent progress reflected in the numbers above. As the State Statistical Bureau put it in a preliminary report on 1989:

> According to a survey carried out in nineteen cities, the real income of 35.8 percent of the families there dropped because of inflation, but *owing to a change in consumer psychology*, most families managed to balance their books with a slight surplus. However, there was a considerable drop in per capita income of low-income families [emphasis added].[14]

Inequalities between regions and professions emerged as well – the coastal provinces boomed while the interior languished. And on a more personal level, urban professionals saw their incomes surpassed by those of taxi drivers, waitresses in hotels catering to foreigners and street peddlers. After decades of enforced poverty, the Chinese took the slogan "To get rich is glorious" seriously – perhaps too seriously. More than one foreign observer was struck by the spread of a grasping, money-seeking mentality that was a far cry from the "serve the people" sloganeering of previous periods, or even what passes for normal, competitive business ethics in the West.

The atmosphere fed corruption. Fake commissions and "agent's fees" became standard fare in contracts. And the use of personal connections and "the backdoor" insured that high officials and their children reaped most of the benefits and blocked others from getting even the crumbs. A Chinese friend speaking privately in the late 1980s expressed his bitterness at the situation by remarking that in the early days of the revolution everybody ate cabbage but now the people still ate cabbage while the cadres eat meat – even as he lamented his inability to cash in fully on the relative boom times he saw around him. Another expressed shock upon reading, for the first time, Orwell's *Animal Farm* – how, he demanded, could an Englishman writing forty years ago have known so much about contemporary China?[15]

Response of the system to crisis

The inflation and popular response to it in the fall of 1988 plus concern (official and otherwise) over corruption brought about an austerity program and new slogans calling for, in typical campaign style, two apparently contradictory policy lines: "deepening the reforms and rectification of the economy." The slogan appeared to mask a growing division within the leadership over the direction China was taking – "rectification of the economy" suggested a return to more conservative practices. The language itself was worrisome: in the Chinese context, "rectification" is a loaded term, and implies that not only do *things* have to be put right, but also that the way one *thinks* about them has to be corrected.[16]

In short, by the fall of 1988 the bureaucratic tendency was gathering steam. And thus we can see that the massive demonstrations that occurred all over China in the spring and summer of 1989 were twin symptoms of a political and economic crisis that had been building for some time, and the kind of ferment that rapid economic change and development can bring.

The summer of 1989: the leadership under attack

The summer events in Beijing and elsewhere in China have been dramatically reported. All contain testimony to the hopes and the fears of the people in Tiananmen Square, the contagion that was on the streets before that night, and the psychological devastation, despair and hatred that followed. One cannot deny that the Chinese leadership's legitimacy and competence was under attack – the formation of autonomous student and (more dangerous) worker organizations, the brief emergence of a press free from censorship, the open distribution of funds from Hong Kong and elsewhere all ran counter to the imperative of control.[17]

Three days after the crackdown, banners calling for the leadership's resignation still had not been pulled down in some sections of the city. Reliable private reports in 1990 indicate that despite the arrests and attempts at repression and intimidation (not only the executions but also the writing and rewriting of "self-examinations" of one's behavior and attitudes), a sullen mood remains in the capital, there are vague expectations of further action, and anger at the government seems to be widespread – even to the point that Chinese speak the latest round of bitterness in front of other Chinese they don't know.

Indeed, the way the Chinese political elites reacted to the situation sparked by the demonstrations appeared to respond almost perfectly to the imperatives of Chinese political culture. Under pressure and in crisis the leadership retreated behind the veils of "The Center" (*Zhongyang*), "The Party"; anonymous statements and decrees stressing unity and control and decrying factionalism were issued. The imperative of power was shown as Party General Secretary Zhou Ziyang, accused of splitting the party, was stripped of his position in a display of political expediency that overwhelmed both Party norms and Party rules. And to back up this political lesson, the Army, exercising the ultimate authority, seized control of Beijing. In disregard of the reformist pledge to establish a rule of law, a "White Terror" (as Beijing residents called it) targeted a wide range of dissidents and common citizens who had the misfortune of being in the wrong place at the wrong time. For many the outcome was dire: arrest, abuse, and, for some, execution.

Reestablishment of control

The political crackdown and the economic rectification – primarily a drastic squeeze on credit and reemergence of planning – that preceded it have accomplished some short-term goals. Control has been reestablished. Inflation dropped dramatically. But there have been short-term costs: the deflation and the economic slowdown that was the result did not end in any economic shake-out: indeed, the squeeze has been on the private and collective sectors, while inefficient state enterprises have received massive subsidies just to keep them barely afloat, thereby worsening the Chinese government deficit. As production and sales have fallen, and as the availability of working capital has been reduced, there are increasing reports of unpaid receivables, idle (but paid) workers, debt failures and other signs of economic difficulty. The immediate outlook indeed, goes beyond deflation to recession and stagflation. But recent reports of loosening credit – an example of the kind of "corrective" management made difficult by problems in the policy information feedback loop – fuel fears that the funds may go to the more politically powerful rather than to the more economically efficient and thus not really contribute to the solution of China's economic problems.[18]

Few problems resolved

There are long-term costs as well. While the June events reestablished control, few of the problems that were the catalyst for the Tiananmen demonstrations have been truly resolved. The political succession issue is unsettled. That Jiang Zemin, a former Shanghai Party boss without a national constituency, was named Party Secretary and was designated by Deng as his successor only indicates that a compromise was forced; surely Jiang must be aware of the fates of other "Number Twos" – Liu Shaoqi, Lin Biao, Hu Yaobang and Zhou Ziyang.

Chinese elites have been alienated. Many of China's best and brightest have been driven abroad (some escaping by an underground railroad despite nation-wide manhunts); others, already in foreign countries, have elected to stay away. The opposition has been radicalized. And, very significantly, the support of Overseas Chinese that the Beijing government used to enjoy has been lost.

Other elements darken the picture. Population growth appears to be out of control, with a dynamic all its own. Despite record harvests over the past decade, an agricultural crisis looms. One solution, whispered in the press and economic journals, goes by the code words "regaining economies of scale" and "new collective economy" – the analyst must ask whether this might be the stuff of a rural cadre's worst dream, recollectivization?

THE REFORMS UNDER ATTACK

Indeed, since the June events and the reemergence of the bureaucratic solution, virtually every aspect of the Deng Reform program has come under fire. The rhetoric of class struggle and of foreign enemies has reemerged. Price reform, a crucial element in moving the economy forward, was frozen under the austerity program of 1988 and is still suspended. Wage reform, linking pay and performance, has been compromised first by continued subsidies and second by an imposed, forced savings plan that requires workers to accept part of their pay in government bonds. The contract system in industry, the analog to the rural responsibility system, has been compromised by a return to planning and recentralization. And the collective and private sectors that were supposed to enliven the economy have not only been the victims of the credit squeeze but have come under attack for alleged tax evasion, promoting inequalities and "inappropriate profits." Thus the outlook is for austerity and recentralization. "Comrades," Party boss Jiang Zemin said in late 1989

> [should] . . . together with the people, live frugally for some years.
> . . . [W]e should lay stress on a proper degree of centralization,
> gradually increase the proportion of state financial revenues in the
> national income, and increase the proportion of state revenues
> controlled by the central government.[19]

STRIVING FOR CONTROL: THE REGIME UNDER SIEGE

What then of the present short-term outlook? The situation one faces in the early 1990s is of a political elite at the center that has returned to the bureaucratic practices of the 1950s. The language of official statements suggests that the regime feels itself to be under siege. In his governmental work report delivered to the National People's Congress in March 1990, Li Peng, the man who ordered martial law in Beijing last summer made that clear:

When we are confronting pressure from abroad and difficulties at home, preserving the country's stability is a matter of paramount importance. Every citizen of the PRC must treat the hard-won political situation of stability and unit *as he treasures his own life* [emphasis added].

Indeed, Li pointed out in a now common formulation, "Political and social stability is the prerequisite" if economic progress is to continue.

Jiang Zemin, the Party Secretary General had sounded similar statements the previous year upon the fortieth anniversary of the founding of the People's Republic. His remarks are worth quoting at length; they contain elements which reflect the underlying currents that drive the Chinese political system.[20]

Jiang began by suggesting a plot inspired from abroad, the aim of which is not only to overthrow the Communist Party but also to infringe on Chinese sovereignty. He characterized the June events as having been

stirred up by hostile forces, both internal and external, [which aimed at] overthrowing the Chinese Communist Party's leadership and subverting the socialist system, at turning China into a bourgeois republic, and reducing it once again to a dependency of the Western capitalist powers.

Against this background, what part does the current Chinese leadership see for foreign business? A necessary, but "supplementary role" in the state-dominated economy:

In China's economic growth we shall persist in taking public ownership as the main body and developing diverse economic sectors, bringing into play the beneficial and necessary supplementary role of the individual economy, the private economy, Chinese–foreign joint ventures, cooperative enterprises and foreign-owned enterprises. . . . This doesn't mean in any way weakening or eliminating the position of public ownership as the main sector. . . . Large and medium-sized enterprises under public ownership are the mainstay of China's socialist modernization.

[Our policy toward other sectors] is, first to encourage them to develop vigorously within limits specified by the state; and second, to strengthen management and guidance over them by economic, administrative [*codewords for Party and state political regulation*] and legal means so as to give effect to their positive role and to restrict their negative aspects that are harmful to socialist economic development.

In other words, Socialist learning for fundamentals, Western learning for use.

Thus the June 1989 events were the pivot for a return to statist, conservative policies. Will the center be able to carry through and what are some of the possible long-term effects?

China is, of course, a huge country, and what is decreed in the capital may be realized differently in different parts of the country. Indeed, the rampant regionalism spawned by the decentralization of the reform-decade continues. The scope of that dilemma was summed up in early 1989, as the bureaucratic noose was tightening, by a State council official who said that "We are living in the worst of two possible worlds, where central directives are no longer effective and the free market is distorted by all sorts of restrictions." A CITIC official added, "The central government is trying to get a grip on the economy, but at the local level everyone just wants to protect what they've got."[21] A contact who visited his native village near Xiamen in Fujian Province in late 1989 came back to report that the June events and the crackdown appeared to have little effect – even direct trade (we might call it smuggling) between Taiwan and Xiamen was being carried out openly. And Hong Kong business people report commercial relations across the border to the special economic zones, and Guangdong Province had essentially returned to "business as usual" by the end of 1989.

BUSINESS AS USUAL? BACK TO THE BASICS

Thus, when writing this in early 1990, the outlook for international business in China is mixed. Certainly from an internal perspective and for the short term, it is back to the basics of the China trade. Certainly one of the basics that indeed never changed, even in the decade of reform, was a basic trade strategy that emphasized technology transfer for import substitution and for exports, and that attempted to minimize debt.

Initially, we will have to recognize that the bureaucratic environment which had started to erode in the 1980s is back. Accordingly, we can expect Chinese trade and investment intentions to be spelled out in economic plans, and we know that these plans stress a return to the basic infrastructural and heavy industrial preferences of the past and a policy of promoting both import-substitution and exporting industries. Imports will be cut. With the demise of the "liberal" Zhao Ziyang, one can also expect a reemphasis on sectoral rather than regional development – Zhao's "trickle West" strategy of allowing the coastal provinces and economic zones to take the lead is on the shelf. We can further expect bureaucratic caution and increased regulation.

THE COMMONPLACES OF THE CHINA TRADE

Thus it should be clear that what we might call the commonplaces of the China trade will still remain in place:

- Know why you're in China. Does being in China make sense strategically, even if the aims of your Chinese stakeholders (partners, customers) are different from yours?
- Know the plan. it will tell you what the Chinese want, and will indicate where and how foreign exchange will be allocated and whether your project is apt to be approved.
- Remember that business in China is based on personal relations and guanxi. As a US technology manager based in Beijing remarked to us in a survey we conducted in 1988, "Personal relations are everything."
- Be prepared for complexity and ambiguities. Chinese partners may not know what the rules are; in the re-politicized environment, bureaucrats may be unwilling to make decisions. Business deals are apt to be complex in any case, involving intense negotiations over price, always the key factor, availability of foreign exchange, some kind of counter-trade and the transfer of technology, with all of that trade's complexities of regulation.

But if these factors constitute a not very happy short term, what about the external environment and the longer term? It should be clear that longer term will depend heavily on the resolution of the succession issue in China. The issue is not really whether the political contest will continue – it will – but rather how confined it will be. If, as we have suggested, the current regime appears to feel that it is under siege, then it seems reasonable to go further and advance that the environment is volatile.

In any event, the regime must know that a single spark can start a prairie fire, and a reasonable (and therefore probably incorrect) forecast will be to suggest slow cycles of repression followed by periods of relaxation during which the citizenry will test the boundaries of what's possible. When the survivors of China's first generation of revolutionary leaders, such as Deng Xiaoping, go to meet Marx and Mao, it could be that those boundaries will be stretched farther than anyone can foresee today. Other future and extreme worries should include the potential for the resurgence of extreme regionalism; the possibility of a political intervention by the armed forces should civil authority fail; and for famine and other population-based calamities or natural disasters of an extent to which the state, already stretched to its limits, cannot effectively respond to.

What do the political models we have briefly discussed suggest? The return of the kind of revolutionary enthusiasm and frantic mass movements favored by the "Radical Tendency" seems unlikely given the delegitimization of that disposition and the absence of a truly charismatic leader in the emerging leadership generation. While there is a rekindling of interest in Mao's writings and visitors to Shaoshan (Mao's birthplace) are increasing, one suspects that this *Mao Zedong re* (a Chinese phrase best translated as "Mao Zedong fad") is as much inspired by distaste for the current leadership as it is by fond memories of Mao himself. This sense is reinforced by other evidences of the trend, which include the issuance of a collection of Cultural Revolution songs on a *karaoke* "sing-along" video-laser disc.

The contest to come, then, will be between those who favor the bureaucratic solution and those who are not threatened by change. But power has its own logic in China, and we can look forward to increased attempts to assert control. Whether these efforts will ultimately bring in the Army as a major policy player is uncertain; a worst case scenario might, however, include increasingly repressive attempts by the center to regain control that only stimulate regional reaction and efforts to establish more distinct regional autonomy. As we contemplate this outlook, we should also remember that while the peasantry, 80 percent of the population, are crucial to fundamental political change in China – that's why recollectivization is so problematic – China is also a Third World country, and thus what happens in the cities, particularly the capital, is tremendously important.

But we should not overlook the capacity of the current group of

Chinese leaders to make adjustments in their own program, nor should we overlook the infinite capacity of political elites (not only in China) to say one thing and do another. After all, once their personal power is assured, and once some convenient scapegoats (living or dead) are found, the survivors in the current group could change course once again. In the late 1980s the people in power were "all for reform." Deng Xiaoping himself would be a good role-model: a devoted enthusiast of Mao and the Great Leap, he also oversaw some of China's harshest mass repressions, including the Anti-Rightist campaign of the 1950s; later he would reemerge as the pilot of China's new course. In any case, many observers appear to have overlooked something in Deng's over-quoted remark that the color of the cat matters little; what counts is whether the cat catches mice. But to catch mice well, the cat must have sharp teeth and quick, strong claws.

EXTERNAL FACTORS: BEYOND GREATER CHINA

But if China's internal situation does not appear promising, there are other factors in China's external environment that also have to be dealt with. Of these, probably the most important will be the continued growth of China's Pacific Rim neighbors during a period of Chinese economic difficulty, thereby widening the regional socio-economic gap. Even if the most rosy predictions come to pass for China, Taiwan and Korea will have far surpassed the People's Republic. For instance, current estimates of Taiwan's GDP per capita put the figure US$9,000; one Taiwan analyst privately suggests that the figure is at least 20–40 percent higher because of the "unofficial" (unreported and thus tax-evading) underground economy on the island. Similarly, Korea is rapidly heading toward advanced economic standing, with a 1988 per capita income of about US$3,500, more than ten times that of China's.

Thus regional disparities are bound to increase. How China can compete in such a situation is a matter to ponder. Furthermore, investment from Taiwan and Korea that might have gone to China may go elsewhere. For instance, private contacts in the Pacific Rim trade advise that some Taiwan investment is going to Vietnam.

But there are other events on the horizon of which we must take account. One is symbolized by the date 1992, the emergence of a single European market (SEM). While many difficulties with the achievement of this European ideal remain – European monetary union, a seeming requirement for a single market, and the astonishing reemergence of Eastern Europe – the lure of Europe will divert players away from China. Some of these will be marginal in any case, but the heavy hitters, particularly those from Japan and the US, may simply find better returns there and thus reduce their participation in the difficult Chinese environment. In short, 1992 may spell significant opportunity costs for the PRC.

The next events are likewise symbolized by two dates: 1997 and 1999, the recovery by China of irredentia torn from the motherland by Western imperialism. The return of Macao at the end of the century will write *finis* to 500 years of European enclaves on the coast. But it is the return of Hong Kong that poses the greatest problems.

There are those in the Chinese leadership for whom 1997 does not mean opportunity, but rather the end of the Opium War. Regardless of what one may think about the "One-Country, Two-Systems" rubric under which Hong Kong is being returned to China (and certainly such a concept runs counter to China's "One-Country, One-System" traditions), the absorption of Hong Kong will not be easy. The city-state's standard of living is at advanced industrial levels and, economically and from the standpoint of infrastructure, is one of the most sophisticated cities in the world, requiring sophisticated management of a kind not readily apparent north of the current border. Hong Kong *laissez-faire* economic traditions are, of course, at direct variance with China's.

Still, as we have noted above, the Hong Kong and Chinese economies are tightly linked. Not only is Hong Kong China's largest trading partner and investment source, but China is also Hong Kong's largest investor. Hong Kong remains the base of China operations for many foreign firms. But the exodus of many of the territory's best and brightest, spurred by a decline in confidence in the future, is troublesome,[22] and wrangling over Hong Kong's Basic Law and the refusal of the Chinese to commit meaningfully to the continuation of the freedoms now enjoyed there does not promote trust.

There are other factors in China's external environment which, if they do not have an immediate business impact, will have long-term effects on China's political setting. The evolution of the Southeast Asian security situation is important: here we are concerned not only with the settlement of conflicts in Cambodia and between China and Vietnam, but also how the question of America's bases in the Philippines is resolved and the resultant forward American security posture. That outcome could affect American positions in Korea and

Japan and lead to a greater political and security role for Tokyo than currently is the case. The Korean peninsula remains a potential hot spot. And just how the CIS, China's nuclear neighbor to the north and west, resolves the problems engendered by *perestroika* and *glasnost* are far beyond our scope here.

What we have outlined above thus can only be taken as indicators and signposts we are apt to encounter in China's uncertain future. From the perspective of early 1990 the immediate outlook is not promising. For the short term a conservative trade policy will be in place. Even if the "liberal" tendency reemerges, we know from past experience that China's foreign economic relations will develop slowly and to China's, not the outside world's, drumbeat.

But we also know that China is more than a group of aging revolutionaries seeking some kind of final justification. We know that verdicts are reversed. June 1989 and its aftermath was the first act in the uncertain drama of transition. The analyst who understands the deep currents that propel the Chinese system can, if not predict, at least understand whatever course China might take. Just the same, most China watchers would ruefully admit that no matter how much we might study and prepare, China will always surprise us.

POSTSCRIPT: NEW PLANS, NEW THEORIES, OLD PATTERNS

Since the above was written, Chinese political and economic cyclical patterns have played themselves out once again. In the immediate post-Tiananmen climate, plans for continued and increased state planning and controls were published. But by the end of 1992, at the 14th Party Congress, the regime was calling for the development of a "socialist market economy." What happened? Politics remained in command. And economic reality got in the way.

The Eighth Five-Year Plan and the Ten-Year Plan

The Eighth Five-Year Plan (1991–5) and a broader Ten-Year Plan (1991–2000) that were to guide the economy to the end of the millennium were announced in December 1990. The plans were a move away from Zhao Ziyang's coastal development, "trickle West" focus and played conservative themes of sectoral "balance" and "coordinated development" of infrastructure, basic industries and agriculture. The poorer inland provinces would be allowed to develop their own enterprise zones, complete with the usual set of incentives (tax breaks, etc.) to attract foreign investment. But, following "essential" and "correct guiding principles", "public ownership" – that is, the inefficient state enterprises – would remain the core of the economy; the emphasis would be on transforming existing enterprises, not creating new ones. Foreign investment and technology were allowable if they improved "China's ability of self-reliance." According to the plans, a GNP growth rate of around 6 percent would be "sufficient."[23]

And at the same time, "social development" would be emphasized – this clearly was a nod toward rebuilding the Party and its prestige. Some initial moves in this direction included the resurrection of the PLA martyr Lei Feng, a bad memory of the 1960s.

However, in a speech elaborating on the plans, Chinese Prime Minister Li Peng spoke of promoting exports and developing the coastal zones further: "Practice has proved that our country's policy for establishing special economic zones and opening cities and belts along the coast to the outside world is correct."[24] Thus not only did the plans appear to be contradictory, calling for both strengthened central planning and further market reform, technical transformation and new enterprises, but there seemed to be subtly expressed differences among the leadership. These contradictions reflected the behind-the-scenes maneuvering of elite factions. They also pointed up the dilemma facing China's leadership post-Tiananmen: the desire for future economic development and for strengthened political control. Indeed, they are caught in the same trap as the nineteenth century "self-strengtheners." The authoritative *Far Eastern Economic Review* summed up the view of many observers by the title of its report on the plans: "Policy in paralysis."[25]

Beijing: Irrelevant?

Some of the steps taken by the central regime in 1990–1 included cutbacks on rural credit and increased subsidies to the state sector. But the results were mixed. The state sector continued to stagnate. Out in the provinces, particularly in the south, where Beijing's writ tended to be honored more in word than by deed, economic development continued unhindered by the Center's desire for a slower growth rate. Indeed, in the so-called "Greater China" economic space, the economy kept growing by well over 10 percent prompting fears by some of overheating and inflation. We do not have the space to develop the story in all its detail, but in January 1992 Deng Xiaoping made a visit to the Shenzhen Special Economic Zone. And he saw that it was good, and said, "Let there be development of this kind for 100 years."

Deng's blessing took the lid off. During 1992 China reintroduced some price reform measures, cut red tape, freed up imports and exports, opened new trade and development zones, allowed foreign investment in state enterprises, started to rationalize foreign exchange swap markets and promoted new private sector initiatives, including the establishment of stock markets. On the foreign trade side, 1992 was a banner year. "Greater China" interdependence continued to develop: PRC investments in Hong Kong reached new heights, property speculation in coastal China took off, Taiwan investment and trade flows increased, and, in Hong Kong, Mainland China, Taiwan and Hong Kong interests pooled their capital to form joint investment companies. Major trade disputes, particularly those with the US, reached some kind of tentative settlement, and China's GATT application appeared to inch forward.[26] In the prevailing boom-town atmosphere, memories were short: when Deng first visited Shenzhen in 1984, he had chillingly termed the SEZ only an experiment.

By the end of the year, the regime had to acknowledge that economic development had gathered such momentum that some of the positions staked out earlier had effectively been reversed. In his report to the 14th Party Congress in October 1992, Party chief Jiang Zemin noted that the growth rates called for in the 8th Five-Year Plan would be revised upward (from 6 percent to 8–9 percent) to reflect the reality of "the situation at home and abroad." The report also called for the establishment of a "socialist market economy," and the continuation of economic reform on a broad front, thus allowing differential regional development so that "Guangdong and other areas where conditions are ripe to basically achieve [*sic*] the goal of modernization in 20 years." In addition, the authority to engage in foreign trade and overseas investment will be further devolved to more enterprises and to scientific institutes. At the same time, Jiang said, China should increase imports and "make more use of foreign resources and advanced technology." The promise of all this Jiang ascribed to Deng Xiaoping, "the chief architect of our socialist reform." Indeed, Deng is to be elevated to the highest rank of the Marxist pantheon, that of theoretician, for "formulating the theory of building socialism with Chinese characteristics."[27]

The numbers behind the shifts

Figures from the first six months of 1992 indicate the size of the boom. Estimates are that GNP grew by more than 12 percent, with industrial production up by 18 percent; most of this growth came from the private and collective sectors. Over the same period, total Chinese two-way trade reached an approximate total value of US$82 billion, well on the way to the estimates put forward at the beginning of this chapter. Foreign investors put US$3.4 billion into the country – a 130 percent increase compared to 1991, and pledged US$14.7 billion, more than three times the amount for the same 1991 period. Retail sales grew by 14 percent, a mark of the reality of a consumer market in China (indeed, this was evident to any traveller in China's cities in 1991 and 1992), and a reflection of the growth of annual per capita income in China from about RMB350 in 1979, the first year of the reforms, to about RMB1400 in 1991. But perhaps the most significant number of all didn't have to do with investment, sales, or income: Chinese statistics released on the eve of the Party Congress revealed that by mid-1992 there were 22.6 million self-employed entrepreneurs in China – 14 years before there had been virtually none.[28]

Conclusion: Toward the year 2000

On the surface the Chinese economic and foreign trade outlook appears attractive, on the up-swing of the political cycle. The powerful mix of the new entrepreneurial class and the interests of bureaucratic entrepreneurialism, operating in a decompressing economic environment, will bring new pressures for further reform. The successful China trader will move quickly to take advantage of this window. Just the same, attention must still be paid to the "commonplaces of China business": the need for patience and the requirement of having sound financial arrangements in place, plus a strategy based on meeting China's needs – technology transfer, capital inflows and export potential.

The successful China trader will also keep an eye on political signposts: the outcome of short-term political maneuvering as the shakeout from the 14th Party Congress continues (many senior cadres were sent into retirement), and longer-term power plays as the elite position themselves for the post-Deng era. Looking further ahead, there are sure to be uncertainties which will affect trade and investment. What will the Center do when the inflation cycle reaches its next peak (perhaps as early as 1993)? And the 1997 reversion of

Hong Kong to PRC control does not promise to be smooth. Although the territory's booming entrepôt trade is crucial for south China's prosperity, the PRC authorities have chosen to play political hardball – Chinese bluster over a proposed new airport for the territory and modest steps to increase the representative quality of the colonial administration (to name just two issues) have shown Beijing's true Leninist nature. Jiang Zemin's report may suggest economic liberalization, but politically, the regime's colors are still nailed to the mast of the Four Basic Principles. In sum, the potential for swings in the larger policy arena remains. It is the outcome of elite power games, far more than plans or speeches on scraps of paper, that will determine China trade in the year 2000.

NOTES

1 However, one might properly raise some questions about the estimate. In the 1980s, Chinese foreign trade grew much faster. According to official Chinese statistics, Chinese foreign trade grew at the astonishing annual rate of 40 percent during the decade of the economic reforms decreed by Deng Xiaoping (1979–89), even though it slowed dramatically at the end of the period, to 25 percent for 1987–8 and to 8.6 percent for 1988–9; we would note the later decline comes from a major devaluation (around 25 percent) of the renminbi (RMB) against the US dollar in 1989. We should also note that the trade was starting from a very low level, which biases the growth rate. Furthermore, these calculations use the early 1990 official exchange rate of 4.7 RMB = US$1, when, in fact, a more proper value might be the "gray" swap market rate of about 7 RMB = US$1. One factor would raise the estimate, the other lower it; the point is that even with conservative assumptions one ends up with an extremely broad range. Finally, we should note that despite the growth, China's trade is small, given the size of the country: for 1988 Hong Kong's two-way trade was valued at about US$103 billion; Taiwan's, US$110 billion; Thailand's US$35.7 billion, and Japan's, US$460 billion. For the sources of these figures see "Report on social and economic growth in 1989," *China Daily*, Business Weekly section, p. 3, and *Asia 1990 Yearbook, Far Eastern Economic Review*, Hong Kong 1989, pp. 6–9.

2 For a comprehensive account of the reforms see Harry Harding, *China's Second Revolution: Reform After Mao*, Brookings Institution, Washington, DC, 1987; A. Doak Barnett, "China's modernization: development and reform in the 1980s" and Robert F. Dernberger, "Economic policy and performance" in *China's Economy Looks Toward the Year 2000*, Vol. 1: *The Four Modernization*, US Congress, Joint Economic Committee, 1986. See also Jiang Zemin, "Speech at the meeting in celebration of the 40th anniversary of the founding of the People's Republic of China," *Beijing Review*, October 9, 1989, pp. 11–24. The projections for foreign investment are contained in "Hong Kong still to be top investor," *China Daily*, March 28, 1990.

3 In the interest of strict accuracy, we can date the end of the ascendency of the reformers from the fall and winter of 1986 when conservatives blocked the discussion of political reform at the sixth Plenum of the Twelfth Central Committee. Student demonstrations that winter resulted in the dismissal of then Party Secretary Hu Yaobang; thus "martyred," his death in the spring of 1989 became the rallying point for the student demonstrations that ultimately were put down at Tiananmen Square. See Immanuel C.Y. Hsu, *China Without Mao*, Oxford University Press, 1990, pp. 218ff.

4 Much of the discussion here draws on the work of Lucian Pye. See in particular his *The Dynamics of Chinese Politics*, Oelgeschlager, Gunn & Hain, 1981; and *The Mandarin and the Cadre*, University of Michigan Center for Chinese Studies, 1988.

5 See Dorothy Solinger, *Chinese Business Under Socialism: The Politics of Domestic Commerce, 1949–1980*, University of California Press, 1984.

6 This view is presented, with considerably more elaboration, in Peter N.S. Lee, *Industrial Management and Economic Reform in China, 1949–1984*, Oxford University Press, 1987, Chap. 1, "The theoretical framework: the policy-making process in China," pp. 1–20.

7 See Suzanne Ogden, *China's Unresolved Issues: Politics, Development, and Culture*, Prentice-Hall, 1989, especially Chap. 8, "Economic development: the conflict between socialist and developmental objectives," pp. 258–301.

8 Lincoln Kaye, "Netting a quick profit," *Far Eastern Economic Review*, November 16, 1989, pp. 68–9.

9 There is great fascination about Taiwan on the Mainland. Li Peng devoted several paragraphs to Taiwan in his March 1990 "Work report" in which he stressed both reunification and Mainland investment opportunities. In the late 1980s there was an astonishing flood of reports concerning Taiwan–PRC economic relations – investments, purchases, trade missions – from both Taiwan and PRC sources. For a sample see Li Jiaquan, "More on reunification of Taiwan with the mainland," *Beijing Review*, January 16, 1989, pp. 26–30; "Regulation clears way for Taiwan investors", *China Daily*, July 7, 1988, p. 1; "Mainland fifth for ROC trade," *Free China Journal*, January 9, 1989; "Commentary on Taiwan investments on Mainland" [*Zhongguo Xinwenshe*: China News Agency], Foreign Broadcast Information Service, January 4, 1989, p. 77; "*Liaowang* on trade across Taiwan Strait," Foreign Broadcast Information Service, January 11, 1989, p. 63; "Taiwan businessmen invest in Fujian," *Beijing Review*, April 18, 1988, p. 24; "Billion-dollar trade with mainland may be tip of undocumented iceberg," *Free China Journal*, January 11, 1988; "CETRA urges establishment of more active ROC–Mainland trade policy," *Trade Opportunities in Taiwan*, April 11, 1988. See also Mitchell A. Silk, "Reaching across the water," *China Business Review*, November–December 1988, pp. 10–15. For the Taiwanese investment figure, see "Hong Kong still to be top investor," *China Daily*, March 28, 1990, p. 2.

10 The investment figures are drawn from *The Chinese Economy in 1988 and 1989*, Central Intelligence Agency, August 1989; the employment figures are from the American Consulate-General, Hong Kong, *Foreign Economic Trends: Hong Kong*, October 1989.

11 For the investment data, see Richard Brecher, "The end of the wonder

years," *China Business Review*, January–February 1990. For a summary of Chinese business environment issues, see John Frankenstein, "Doing business in China," in *Global Business Management in the 1990s*, Robert Moran (ed.), Beacham Publishing, 1990.

12 The data here comes from official Chinese statistics cited in a variety of sources. The 1989 numbers come from *China Daily* (February 26, 1990); figures for 1979 and 1988 are cited in "Major economic indexes," *China Reconstructs*, October 1989, pp. 40ff; 1986 figures are from *China: Economic Performance in 1987 and Outlook for 1988*, Central Intelligence Agency, May 1988.

13 Harding, *op. cit.*, pp. 187ff.

14 See *China Daily*, February 26, 1990, Business Weekly section, p. 3.

15 Private reports.

16 See, for instance, the usage in "Zhao Ziyang Report to CPC 3rd Plenary Session," *China Daily Report*, Foreign Broadcast Information Service, October 28, 1988, pp. 13–20.

17 There has been voluminous reporting of the events. Some of the most vivid accounts have appeared in the *New York Review of Books*, particularly Orville Schell, "China's spring," June 29, 1989; Fang Lizhi and Orville Schell, "Letters from the other China," Roderick MacFarqhar, "The end of the Chinese revolution," July 20, 1989; and Merle Goldman, "Vengeance in China," November 9, 1989. For a useful synopsis of the events, see "China," *Asia 1990 Yearbook*, Hong Kong 1989, published by the *Far Eastern Economic Review*.

18 There have been numerous reports in the press on these subjects. For a good wrapup of these and other post-Tiananmen difficulties, see Richard Brecher, "The end of investment's wonder years," *China Business Review*, January–February 1990.

19 Jiang, op. cit.

20 Jiang, op. cit.

21 Cited in Julia Leung, "Energy crisis shuts factories in China," *Wall Street Journal*, January 6, 1989, p. A6; Adi Ignatius, "Defiant managers: local enterprises are sabotaging China's attempt to cool economy," *Asian Wall Street Journal Weekly*, January 23, 1989, p. 3.

22 For a discussion of this issue see Christopher Hunt, "Relentless brain drain imposes a heavy toll on Hong Kong business," *Asian Wall Street Journal Weekly*, March 19, 1990, p. 1; "Hong Kong's human resource challenge," *China Business Review*, January–February 1990, pp. 44ff.

23 See "Communiqué of the 7th Plenary Session of the 13th Central Committee of the Communist Party of China," *Beijing Review*, January 7–13, 1991, pp. 27–9; "Keynotes of the Eighth Five-Year Plan (1991–1995)," *Beijing Review*, January 14–20, 1991, pp. 8–10.

24 See "Chinese premier on guidelines of the 10-Year Plan", *Beijing Review*, December 24–30, 1990, p. 17.

25 Tai Ming Cheung, "Policy in paralysis," *Far Eastern Economic Review*, January 10, 1991, pp. 10–11.

26 For a summary of the 1992 reforms, see "Boom time for China profits", *Asian Business*, October 1992, pp. 28–34.

27 The official *China Daily* printed the English text of Jiang's report under the headline "Jiang Zemin's report: Deng blazes path to socialism",

October 13, 1992, p. 4. Jiang defined "socialist market economy" as one in which "market forces, under the macro-economic control of the State, serve as the basic means of regulating the flow of resources" and one which is "responsive to changing relations between supply and demand".

28 By way of comparison, only twenty years ago, in 1973, there were about the same number of Party members – 28 million – as there are entrepreneurs now (1992 Party membership stands at 51 million). We don't know how many entrepreneurs are also Party members, but it is probably safe to assume that as a group the entrepreneurs are more dynamic than the many time-servers and poorly educated cadres who make up so much of the Party.

2 Variations in the economic development of China's provinces

An exploratory look[1]

Mark Barnard and Oded Shenkar

Since Deng Xiaoping's ascension to power, reform has been the key word guiding China's development. Initial experiments, initiated during the Third Plenum of the Eleventh Central Committee in December 1978, were confined mainly to the rural areas. Their success has set in motion a reform process which has gradually encompassed urban areas as well.

In October 1984, the "Decision of the Chinese Communist Party Central Committee on reform of the economic system" was adopted. This document set the stage for an expansion of the reforms to urban areas. It sought to decentralize the urban economy by reducing the government's role in the management of economic enterprises. The government's role has been redefined to provide guidance rather than mandatory planning, delegate more autonomy and decision-making power to the enterprise and its managers, gradually allow price reform based upon market forces, establish a linkage between remuneration and productivity, and further encourage international economic cooperation, including foreign direct investment.

The present paper provides a preliminary look at the impact of the economic reforms on the various provinces, autonomous regions, municipalities, special economic zones (SEZs), and coastal cities. The data presented includes regional figures on gross industrial output and enterprise profits and taxes, wages and cost of living as well as foreign trade, including foreign direct investment.

One of the most important by-products of the reforms has been the accentuation of differences among the various provinces and regions. This development marks a radical deviation from previous Chinese policies, including the long-cherished themes of self-sufficiency and egalitarianism. These variable development trends and their implications are the focus of this chapter.

ECONOMIC TRENDS

Gross industrial output

Figure 2.1 shows the regional variations in the average gross industrial output value per staff and worker. As expected, the coastal cities rank high on this measure, along with Hubei province; while western provinces rank low, along with Jiangxi, Jilin and Heilongjiang.

Profits and taxes

A disparity in the average profits for large and medium-sized enterprises throughout the various regions is apparent in Figure 2.2. Surprisingly, Gansu, Hubei, and Heilongjiang have high average profits. Hubei's exceptional performance may be explained in terms of its relatively high per capita gross industrial output (not presented here), but this is not the case for Gansu and Heilongjiang.

Wages

Surprisingly, Figure 2.3 shows wages for staff and workers to be high in the western provinces of China which are typically under-developed. The municipalities of Beijing, Tianjin and Shanghai, and the province of Guangdong are also high, as expected. The coastal cities portray a large variation in wage levels, showing that development in these key areas has progressed at an uneven pace. The SEZs rank high, except for Shantou which is lagging behind its counterparts.

Cost of living

Percentage increase in the cost of living also varies as shown on Figure 2.4. With the exception of Ningxia, the western provinces, though having high wage levels, are experiencing only a moderate cost of living increase, probably because inflationary pressures associated with price deregulation are weaker there than in Guangdong, Zhejiang, and Beijing.

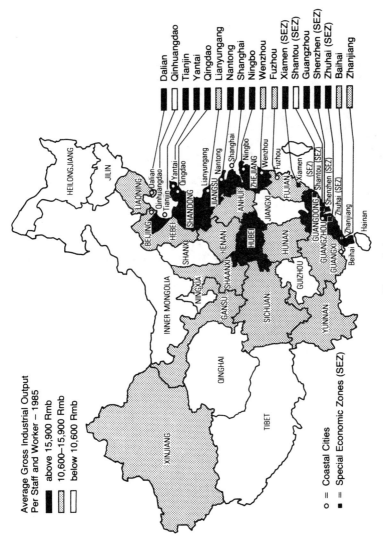

Average Gross Industrial Output
Per Staff and Worker – 1985

■ above 15,900 Rmb
▨ 10,600–15,900 Rmb
□ below 10,600 Rmb

○ = Coastal Cities
■ = Special Economic Zones (SEZ)

Dalian
Qinhuangdao
Tianjin
Yantai
Qingdao
Lianyungang
Nantong
Shanghai
Ningbo
Wenzhou
Fuzhou
Xiamen (SEZ)
Shantou (SEZ)
Guangzhou
Shenzhen (SEZ)
Zhuhai (SEZ)
Baihai
Zhanjiang

Figure 2.1

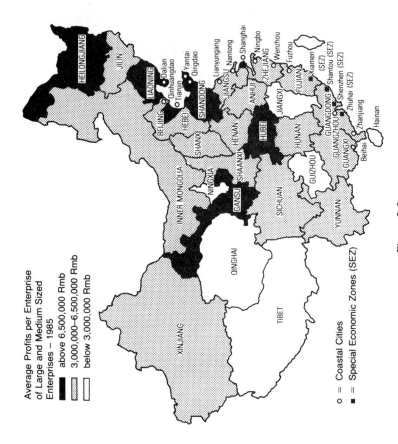

Average Profits per Enterprise
of Large and Medium Sized
Enterprises – 1985

■ above 6,500,000 Rmb
▨ 3,000,000–6,500,000 Rmb
☐ below 3,000,000 Rmb

o = Coastal Cities
■ = Special Economic Zones (SEZ)

Figure 2.2

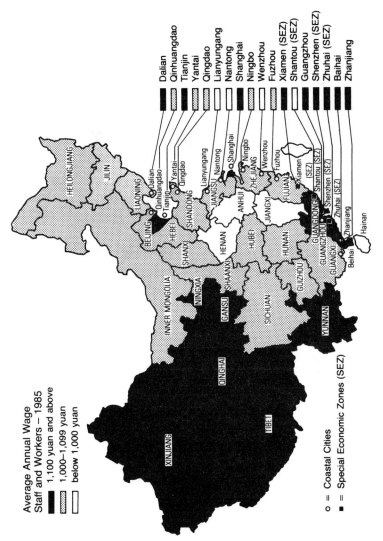

Average Annual Wage
Staff and Workers – 1985

■ 1,100 yuan and above

▨ 1,000–1,099 yuan

□ below 1,000 yuan

o = Coastal Cities

■ = Special Economic Zones (SEZ)

Dalian
Qinhuangdao
Tianjin
Yantai
Qingdao
Lianyungang
Nantong
Shanghai
Ningbo
Wenzhou
Fuzhou
Xiamen (SEZ)
Shantou (SEZ)
Guangzhou
Shenzhen (SEZ)
Zhuhai (SEZ)
Baihai
Zhanjiang

Figure 2.3

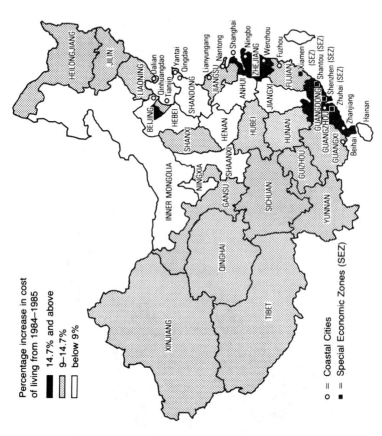

Percentage increase in cost
of living from 1984–1985

■ 14.7% and above
▨ 9–14.7%
☐ below 9%

o = Coastal Cities
■ = Special Economic Zones (SEZ)

Figure 2.4

INTERNATIONAL TRADE AND INVESTMENT

Exports and imports

As expected, areas high in both exports and imports (Figures 2.5 and 2.6) are almost exclusively concentrated along China's coast, although Shanxi and Ningxia have medium import levels while Xinxiang has a medium level of both imports and exports.

Joint ventures

Foreign investment has been concentrated in few of China's coastal cities, along with Beijing and Qinghai (Figure 2.7). Over 50 percent of Hong Kong joint venture investment has been made in the SEZs, most notably Shenzhen which borders the Territory, while Japan and the US have invested 43 percent and 49 percent respectively in the coastal cities, and only 4 percent and 8.4 percent in the SEZs (Figures 2.8–2.10). Both Japan and the US have over 50 percent of their total investments in the municipalities of Beijing, Shanghai, and Tianjin (57 percent and 67.6 percent respectively) while Hong Kong has only 24.3 percent of its investments in these municipalities.

THE EVOLUTION OF REGIONAL VARIATIONS

Aguignier (1988) suggests that imbalances are a key feature of the economic geography of China, and that these imbalances have been a constant concern of the Chinese. With the introduction of economic reforms, imbalances surfaced again as a central issue in China. Coastal cities, special economic zones (SEZs), key industries, and some provinces have been given or exploited their relative advantages in economic and human resources or geographical location to further their own development, leaving the Chinese hinterland lagging behind.

The 1984 Decision foresaw the possibility that the economy would develop unevenly in different areas. Though guaranteeing that all members of society would see an improvement in their prosperity, the Decision did not promise "absolute egalitarianism or that all members of society become better off simultaneously at the same speed." Thus it has been suggested that "only when some regions, enterprises and individuals are allowed and encouraged to get better off first through diligent work can there be a strong attraction and inspiration to the majority of people" (*Beijing Review* October 29, 1984, p. xii.

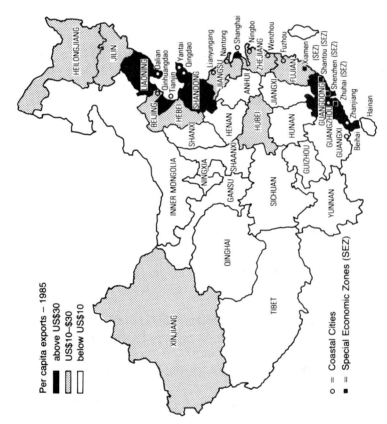

Figure 2.5

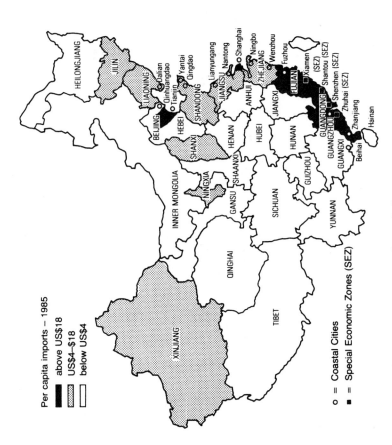

Per capita imports – 1985

above US$18
US$4–$18
below US$4

o = Coastal Cities
■ = Special Economic Zones (SEZ)

HEILONGJIANG

JILIN

LIAONING
Dalian
Qinhuangdao
Tianjin
Yantai
Qingdao

BEIJING
HEBEI
SHANDONG
Lianyungang
Nantong
JIANGSU
Shanghai

SHANXI
HENAN
ANHUI
Ningbo
ZHEJIANG
Wenzhou

NINGXIA
SHAANXI
HUBEI
JIANGXI
Fuzhou
FUJIAN
Xiamen (SEZ)

GANSU
SICHUAN
HUNAN
GUANGDONG
Shantou (SEZ)
GUANGZHOU
Shenzhen (SEZ)

INNER MONGOLIA
GUIZHOU
GUANGXI
Zhuhai (SEZ)
Zhanjiang

QINGHAI
YUNNAN
Behai
Hainan

TIBET

XINJIANG

Figure 2.6

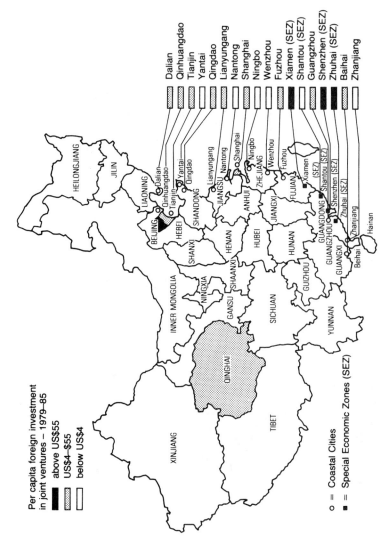

Figure 2.7

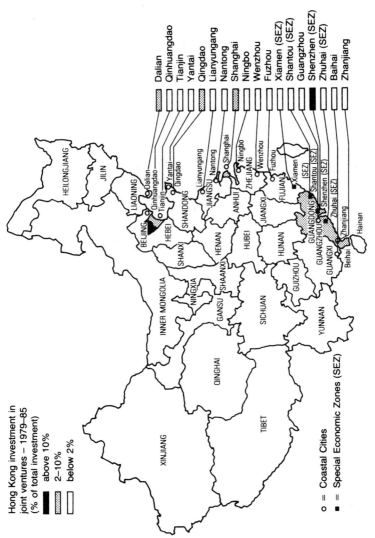

Hong Kong investment in
joint ventures – 1979–85
(% of total investment)

■ above 10%

▨ 2–10%

□ below 2%

| Dalian |
| Qinhuangdao |
| Tianjin |
| Yantai |
| Qingdao |
| Lianyungang |
| Nantong |
| Shanghai |
| Ningbo |
| Wenzhou |
| Fuzhou |
| Xiamen (SEZ) |
| Shantou (SEZ) |
| Guangzhou |
| Shenzhen (SEZ) |
| Zhuhai (SEZ) |
| Baihai |
| Zhanjiang |

o = Coastal Cities

■ = Special Economic Zones (SEZ)

Figure 2.8

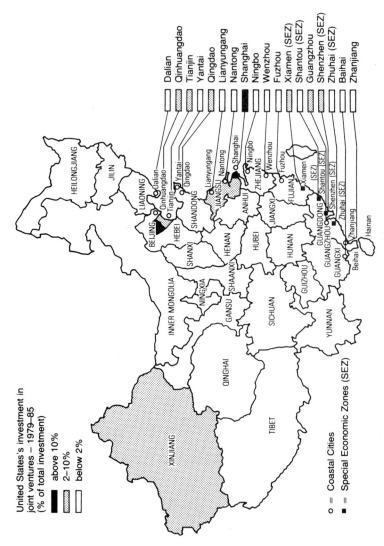

United States's investment in
joint ventures – 1979–85
(% of total investment)

■ above 10%
▨ 2–10%
☐ below 2%

o = Coastal Cities
■ = Special Economic Zones (SEZ)

Dalian
Qinhuangdao
Tianjin
Yantai
Qingdao
Lianyungang
Nantong
Shanghai
Ningbo
Wenzhou
Fuzhou
Xiamen (SEZ)
Shantou (SEZ)
Guangzhou
Shenzhen (SEZ)
Zhuhai (SEZ)
Baihai
Zhanjiang

Figure 2.9

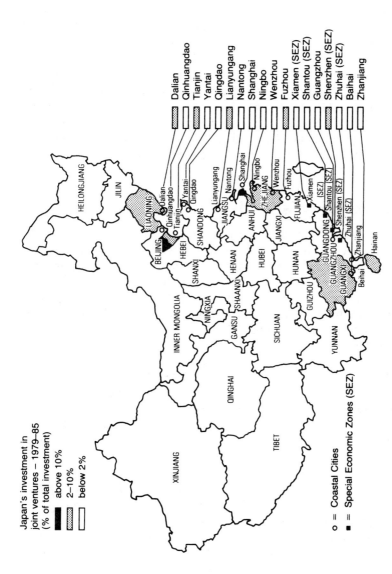

Japan's investment in
joint ventures – 1979–85
(% of total investment)

■ above 10%
▨ 2–10%
☐ below 2%

o = Coastal Cities
■ = Special Economic Zones (SEZ)

Dalian
Qinhuangdao
Tianjin
Yantai
Qingdao
Lianyungang
Nantong
Shanghai
Ningbo
Wenzhou
Fuzhou
Xiamen (SEZ)
Shantou (SEZ)
Guangzhou
Shenzhen (SEZ)
Zhuhai (SEZ)
Baihai
Zhanjiang

HEILONGJIANG
JILIN
LIAONING
Dalian
Qinhuangdao
BEIJING
Tianjin
Yantai
HEBEI
Qingdao
SHANDONG
INNER MONGOLIA
SHANXI
Lianyungang
SHAANXI
HENAN
JIANGSU Nantong
Shanghai
ANHUI
Ningbo
HUBEI
ZHEJIANG
Wenzhou
NINGXIA
GANSU
JIANGXI
Fuzhou
QINGHAI
SICHUAN
HUNAN
FUJIAN
Xiamen (SEZ)
GUIZHOU
GUANGDONG
Shantou (SEZ)
TIBET
XINJIANG
GUANGZHOU
Shenzhen (SEZ)
YUNNAN
GUANGXI
Zhuhai (SEZ)
Beihai
Zhanjiang
Hainan

Figure 2.10

The centralized budget in pre-reform days ensured that most financial resources were turned over to the central government and disbursed from there. This allowed the state to determine the allocation of fiscal resources, preventing direct relation between the amount of income of a province and the amount it could expend (Aguignier 1988). With the adoption of economic reforms, the government has forfeited much of its budgetary control. With the introduction of taxes, provinces, municipalities, autonomous regions, and even individual enterprises gained more control over income and expenditure. The state has therefore less funds to invest as these sub-areas keep a portion of the profit to invest independently of the central government. Rich regions thus have more money to invest, while poor regions can no longer rely on the central government to make up the difference.

IMPLICATIONS OF REGIONAL VARIATIONS

One reason why growing inequality is a cause for concern is inflation. Empowered with increased autonomy, provincial authorities pressured banks to provide loans, thus increasing inflationary pressures. In an effort to increase the price of materials they controlled, provincial authorities have set up barriers in order to stop these materials from being exported out of their borders (*Far Eastern Economic Review*, October 13, 1988, p. 96 and October 27, 1988, p. 38).

Another problem which stemmed from the regional attempts to hold on to valuable resources, was the creation of shortages which hampered production in other provinces. This resulted in the creation of a unique "barter" system, in which provincial authorities and individual enterprises trade a given resource only when the other party can supply a valuable resource to that province or enterprise.

The increasingly unequal distribution of income has brought significant dissatisfaction among workers in less well-to-do regions. The problem has been addressed as early as 1986, when Deputy Premier Tian Jiyun acknowledged that "now there is a looming gap in incomes of employees in different trades and industries. Incomes at some private enterprises are excessively high . . ." (Noronov, 1988, p. 130). The *Beijing Review* (December 8, 1986, p. 21) recently stated that "China's economy has developed rapidly but not geographically evenly. The coastal region, with its well-established industry and easy access to the world, has moved far ahead of the central and western regions." Unequal distribution of income is also being blamed in part for the rise in lawlessness in China (*Far Eastern Economic Review*, October 27, 1988, p. 40).

The development of the "red-eye disease" (Chinese term for envy) became a prime concern not only for ideological reasons. The Chinese authorities were not equipped to deal with the implications of differential wages, e.g. migration. Selivanova (1987) pointed out that inter-provincial migration has increased from 30 million in 1982 to 40 million in 1985. This increased migration draws people mostly to coastal areas, special economic zones and to cities that have a higher than national average rate of construction and commercial activity. In Beijing, over 49 percent of the migrants in 1985 came in search of jobs.

China's leadership still seems to continue to emphasize the key economic zones and coastal regions. The more modern factories already in these areas are likely to attract more overseas investment and are better equipped to continue to develop and produce for export. Perhaps the Chinese leadership is correct in predicting that the development of these regions will "eventually stimulate and assist economic development in the central interior as well as the least-developed Far Western areas" (*Far Eastern Economic Review*, March 24, 1988, p. 58). The question is whether those in the less well-to-do areas will wait patiently for that to happen.

NOTE

1 This chapter was first published in *GeoJournal*, 21(1/2) (May/June 1990), pp. 177–92. Reprinted with permission.

REFERENCES

Aguignier, Philippe, "Regional disparities since 1978." In S. Feuchtwang, A. Hussain and T. Pairault, (eds), *Transforming China's Economy in the Eighties*, Vol. II. "Management, industry and the urban economy," Westview Press, 1988.

Central Committee of the Chinese Communist Party. Decision of the Central Committee of the Communist Party of China on Reform of the Economic Structure, *Beijing Review*, October 29, 1984.

China International Economic Consultants, Inc. *The China Investment Guide 1986*. 3rd Edition. Longmans, 1986.

Delfs, Robert, "Run for election, but do not expect to win," *Far Eastern Economic Review*, March 24, 1988.

do Rosario, Louise, "China's price pirates," *Far Eastern Economic Review*, October 13, 1988.

Noronov, R., "The Chinese working people's living standards," *Far Eastern Affairs*, February 1988.

Office of Leading Group of the National Industrial Census under the State Council (ed.), Industrial Census 1985 (large and medium-sized enterprises) People's Republic of China. Economic Information & Agency, Hong Kong 1988.

Salem, Ellen, "Things fall apart, the centre cannot hold," *Far Eastern Economic Review*, October 27, 1988.

Selivanova, E., "Economic reform and population migration in the PRC," *Far Eastern Affairs*, September 1987.

State Statistical Bureau, China Urban Statistics 1986. Longmans and China Statistical & Consultancy Service Centre, Hong Kong 1987.

State Statistical Bureau, "Economic growth in different areas," *Beijing Review*, December 8, 1986.

State Statistical Bureau," Statistical yearbook of China (1981–1985)," Economic Information & Agency, Hong Kong 1981–1986.

3 Chinese enterprise management reforms in the post-Tiananmen era
The view from Liaoning Province

Stephen Thomas[1]

Although management reforms in the People's Republic of China have come a long way since 1978, many of these reforms have been partially reversed following the events in Tiananmen Square in June 1989. The political stalemate at the national level has put new management reforms on hold. Managers facing an economic slow-down are instead preoccupied with meeting payrolls, paying for materials, and collecting overdue accounts receivable.

In order to gain more understanding of management reforms as viewed by enterprise managers, I conducted research in China's Liaoning Province, concentrating on the industrial cities of Shenyang and Dalian, during May and June of 1990. Liaoning Province, located in the northeastern part of the People's Republic, is one of the most heavily industrialized provinces in China. Within sixty miles of Liaoning's capital, Shenyang, there are five major industrial cities with populations of over one million: Fushun, the "coal city"; Benxi, "the iron-and-coal city"; Liaoyang, "the chemical-fiber city'; Anshan, "the steel city"; and Panjin, "the crude-oil city."

NATIONAL POLICY CONTEXT FOR LIAONING PROVINCE MANAGEMENT REFORMS

Enterprise management reforms in China began with a decision by the Third Plenum of the Chinese Communist Party Central Committee in December 1978 to carry out a major reform of the Chinese economy. Urban enterprise reform began in earnest with the October 1984 Chinese Communist Party Central Committee policy decision on "China's economic structure reform." One of the most important reforms of Chinese state enterprises has been the director responsibility system. The director responsibility system has enlarged enterprise autonomy and has increased the power of enterprise directors to make changes that can increase efficiency, productivity, and profitability.

Significant management reforms took place between 1984 and 1989. In the efforts to reform Chinese state enterprises, managers were made the key link between the government and the factory and its workers. The most important reforms in the role of managers in Liaoning state enterprises occurred in 1986, when their relationship to the state was set out in a contract (*chengbao*). The contract specified the goals that managers were to attain and the new autonomy and powers that they were granted to achieve these goals.

Even with the reforms from 1984 to 1989, managers were still expected to balance a set of competing and sometimes contradictory requirements both from the central government and from the workers and purchasers of the factory goods. Managers were simultaneously asked: to increase productivity, efficiency, and profit, while at the same time hiring and retaining as many workers as possible; and to abide by state-set prices for inputs and products, while at the same time becoming more sensitive to free market forces.

Before 1978, enterprises had been run by Communist Party bureaucrats who often knew relatively little about management techniques. After 1978, and particularly since 1984, factory managers increasingly are individuals such as engineers who know about the actual production aspects of the enterprise. There has also been an effort to provide managers with educational upgrading through training programs, such as the Dalian Management Training Center for Industrial Science and Technology Management (with SUNY Buffalo and the United States Department of Commerce) in Liaoning Province, the Beijing National Training Center, and other programs set up by the Chinese Enterprise Management Association. Managers have in addition been sent overseas for advanced study. It was planned that by 1990 all enterprise managers would have undertaken some form of management training (Warner, p. 84).

Another aspect of the reforms was that whereas before 1984 a manager was often the Party secretary, or took orders from the Party secretary, after 1984 the manager was not usually the Party secretary and was not obligated to follow his or her advice. Despite the reforms, managers still did not act totally alone, such as has been the case in the Soviet factory manager system. Post-reform Chinese managers did, however, enjoy greatly broadened powers to manage their factories with a minimum of worker or Party input.

At the same time, economic reforms took place within the context of constraints from both pre-1984 and macroeconomic factors, together with uncertainties about political support from the government for continuing economic reforms. Pre-existing economic constraints included the fact that most large state-owned enterprises in Liaoning were developed by the Chinese central government in Beijing and continued to be under national or provincial ownership and control. Enterprise managers therefore have had to serve the policy goals of the national and provincial governments, such as providing employment for as many Chinese workers as possible and producing the quantity and type of goods specified in the central economic plan. Politically, managers have still had to follow central government policy shifts, regardless of their economic consequences for the enterprise.

LIAONING PROVINCE ENTERPRISE MANAGERS

Almost all medium and large enterprises in Liaoning are under national or provincial economic control. The remainder are under municipal control. Currently, for most national and provincial enterprises in Liaoning, 80 percent of enterprise profits and 75 percent of foreign exchange earnings are turned over to the central or provincial government.

Liaoning Province has about 10 percent of the capital investment for all of China. Many of the state enterprises in the province have sought after and gained foreign investment or technology, but exports constitute no more than 10 percent of the output of enterprises where I interviewed managers.

Over 100 enterprises in the northeast, out of 214 large enterprises nation-wide, are under the new *shuangbao* (double guarantee system), where the government guarantees to provide production inputs and also guarantees to purchase the outputs. This is a very important commitment during a time of economic downturn, but it has tied the enterprises closely back under the control of central planning mechanisms. Central or provincial government ownership has also meant that managers are appointed by the state, serve on the basis of a national system of *changbao* (management contract), and are given about the same management latitude regardless of the enterprise.

I interviewed managers of five large national or provincial enterprises, one medium-sized enterprise, and one smaller collective. My selection of subjects was based in part on a suggested list provided by the then US Consul General in Shenyang, Eugene Dorris, and his Political and Economic Officer, Steve Fox. The suggested enterprises had managers who were thought to be reform-minded.

Working from the list and from other sources of guidance, I interviewed managers at the following factories:

1 Gold Cup Auto Factory (one of the largest truck manufacturers in China)
2 Northeast China Pharmaceutical Factory
3 Shenyang Non-Ferrous Metal-Rolling Plant
4 Shenyang Steel-Rolling Mill
5 Shenyang Hardware Casting Factory (a small turnaround cooperative)
6 Pneumatic Drill Factory of Shenyang
7 Shenyang Water-Pump Factory

The interviews were conducted through a Chinese interpreter (although I speak passable Chinese) and were rather free-ranging. I cannot claim that my sample is necessarily representative of Liaoning Province enterprises, or of China in general. Nevertheless, many of my findings are similar to those of other American researchers who have interviewed enterprise managers during 1989–90 in different parts of China (see "Chinese enterprise reform: a factory-level perspective," presented by Dr Kevin O'Brien at the 1990 American Political Science Association, and a draft paper based on summer 1990 interviews with Beijing and Shanghai enterprise managers submitted by Dr Margaret Pearson).

The managers interviewed are among the best known to the American Consulate, and are also among the most supportive of management reforms. In May of 1990, as many as one-third wanted to renegotiate their *chengbao* (management contracts) with the state; and some were reported even to be considering refusing to renew their *chengbao* with the state when the three-year contract period ended in late 1990.

The major issues were the pricing of products and how to pay workers. The major goal for future reform, in the opinion of US Consul Officer Steve Fox, was to "break the iron rice-bowl" by basing worker bonuses on the performance of the factory, of the workshop, and, as much as possible, of the individual worker.

Again according to Steve Fox, capital for state enterprises was being allocated politically, and enterprises were still being asked to retain employees when they closed. When enterprises were consolidated, as was done in the case of Gold Cup Auto (formerly sixty-five factories), they still had to retain employees. Consequently, much of China's current unemployment is due not to reform policies, but to job losses by temporary workers, or to losses by workers in cooperative or collective enterprises (particularly in township enterprises) that have been closed down. Nevertheless, Liaoning faced a 5 to 8 percent unemployment level, similar to national levels, that has necessitated a policy of no firings. Instead, the policy has been to set up sideline enterprises for some of the 30 to 40 percent redundant labor in most state enterprises.

There are over 7,000 enterprises in the Tyesyi District in Shenyang, and many have triangle debts, cash-flow problems, and credit problems. The major problems for many managers right now, therefore, are to find funds for meeting payrolls and purchasing material inputs, and to avoid bill collectors. The Liaoning government set up a barter-trade market in April 1990 to swap excess out-of-plan output for debts. Many enterprises are only able to continue by borrowing from the People's Bank of China or from the government.

Another option for helping financially troubled enterprises is to permit the leasing by foreigners of whole enterprises from the Ministry of Foreign Economic Relations and Trade (MOFERT). This leasing arrangement would allow foreign businesses to keep any profits generated through reorganization, but only to repatriate those profits if products could generate foreign exchange in the world market.

Liaoning Province is more dependent than many areas on the price of raw materials, and therefore would be helped by continued price reforms in some areas, and hurt in other areas. In terms of increased prices for raw materials, many of Liaoning's coal, iron ore, mangesite, boron, talc industries, and oil fields, most of which are now losing money and require subsidies, would be helped by increases in prices of raw materials. Liaoning factories, on the other hand, could be hurt if their raw material inputs, including energy, were to increase greatly in price.

Liaoning state enterprise managers are the real reformers, according to Steve Fox. Generally they would prefer to have bankruptcies and factory closings, even if workers have to be paid their wages for no work, because that would leave more capital for the more successful factories. Also, there could be continued consolidation of failing factories under the management of successful factories, such as has occurred with Gold Cup Automotive and the Shenyang Steel-Rolling General Mill.

Gold Cup Automotive Company

I interviewed the Chairman and President, Mr Zhao Xiyou, a well-known reformer. The Gold Cup Automotive Company is a provincially-owned factory that is one of China's largest truck producers. The factory began before 1949 as a repair facility, became a truck assembly plant in the 1960s, and then by the 1970s moved into actual manufacturing of trucks. Expansion began in 1984, as part of the new reforms, when sixty-five different factories were consolidated into the Shenyang Truck Factory. This plant became the Gold Cup Automotive Company when one of its truck models won the national Gold Cup award for quality. Its 6,000 employees produced over 30,000 trucks of different kinds in 1989, at a cost of about 16,000 RMB (about US$3,480) per truck. Production was projected at 40,000 in 1990, most as part of the state plan.

Company President Zhao was appointed by the state and works on the basis of a *chengbao* (contract) that lays out five areas of director responsibility:

1 profits
2 new product research and development (technical transformation)
3 product quantity
4 product quality
5 total income of the enterprise

Chairman Zhao approves of the contract system, but felt that it needed additional measures, such as allowing managers to link responsibility to income, and permitting factory managers more control over their factories. He mentioned one example of micro-managing from above: state regulations specify even the price of the dinner for a guest banquet. He also mentioned that the factory must receive permission to carry out technical transformation costing over 1 million renminbi (RMB) (US$217,000), unless a company has a joint venture with a foreign firm. Mr Zhao was in the process of trying to negotiate a small joint venture. The five managers of his factories make on average 4,000 to 5,000 RMB per year, and Chairman Zhao may make as much as 20,000 RMB per year. Mr Zhao's contract with the province was signed in 1987 for three years and was up for renewal at the end of 1990.

Director Zhao's approach to redundant workers (in the sixty-five factories that he has taken over and consolidated into Gold Cup Automotive) is to transfer the workers to another task or to move them to another workshop.

To summarize Director Zhao's views on reform, continued effort is needed to create a good outside environment (presumably in the marketplace for the trucks), to tie worker productivity to wages, to free managers from micro-management by government, and to allow increased manager freedom to make investments in technological improvement. Gold Cup Automotive workers, during our inspection of the factory, seemed to be doing very little work. They said that this was due to decreased demand, although projected production figures would not bear that conclusion out. It is more likely that there were simply a number of redundant workers in this provincially-owned enterprise, despite the efforts of Director Zhao to improve efficiency.

Northeast General Pharmaceutical Factory

I interviewed Mr Yan Chengmin, the Vice President. The factory was built in 1936, under the Japanese, and produced mostly synthetic drugs. It is the largest such factory in north China, and is under national rather than provincial control. It has its own research institute, staff hospital, schools, nurseries, housing, and all the other attributes characteristic of the "iron rice-bowl" form of company town that is built as part of a Chinese medium and large enterprise.

Northeast General Pharmaceutical mainly produces antibiotics and vitamins of about sixty varieties, including steroid hormones, dextromonohydrate, and vitamins A, C and E. Products are generally up to world standards and are exported to fifty-five countries and regions. The company has a factory in the newly constructed Shenyang Export Processing District that produces sulfadiazine and sulfaactophine.

In terms of the contract system in the factory internally, there is no fixed model for the internal contracts with the workers of various workshops. The most important goals of internal contracts at Northeast Pharmaceutical are to control quality and to build enthusiasm and worker initiative. The contracts also contain targets for production. Each subunit of the factory is independently responsible for quality. They have fired only ten workers over the last two years, out of 10,000, but even that action has helped to increase productivity and quality. In terms of worker productivity, the factory has increased by 200 workers over the last four years, while increasing 20 percent in value over the last four years, therefore increasing productivity 5 percent per year.

Mr Yang wants certain additional reforms: he wants to be able to attract good workers from other factories (a freer labor market); he wants to be able to train workers in his factory; he wants to stop the system of parents giving their jobs to their children and to make employment opportunities fair for all; and he wants a higher minimum level of education for employment (i.e., primary through middle school, eight or nine years, plus two years of classes and one year of practice before becoming a worker), and the passing of an exam in the factory. Currently, workers are simply assigned to him.

He also would like a 30 RMB training wage, then a 50 RMB plus bonus and subsidies package, equaling 80 RMB. He feels that among new workers now, only about 20 percent are excellent. Wages currently for new workers are 60 RMB plus bonuses and subsidies of 40 RMB for a total of 100 RMB. Workshop managers get a bonus of 0.2 times the average total wage, for a total wage of about 120 RMB.

Production is currently 80 percent within the plan, and profit of the plant is about 5 to 10 million RMB on a total sales per year of 500 million RMB domestically, and US$30 million exported. The Northeast General Pharmaceutical Factory has currently established a joint venture with a Hong Kong firm where Northeast General has contributed three-fourths, or US$4.5 million, and the Hong Kong firm has contributed one-fourth, or US$1.5 million.

In summary, Mr Yang wants more control over hiring and training of workers, and is eager to establish more joint ventures.

Shenyang Non-Ferrous Metal-Rolling Factory

I interviewed Mr Tang Jiyue, factory director and "economist." The US Consulate said that this factory, owned by the city and producing mostly copper products such as pipes and radiators, was in financial trouble and looking for a foreign business partner. Director Tang was anxious to get foreign technology, such as is found only in factories in Loyang and Beijing. He said that the products of his factory are popular, but the technological level is low, and in order to satisfy a large market, the factory needs more advanced technology.

The market that he is aiming at is the automotive market of China at 500,000 units per year, in five centers decided by the State Council. The factory is the only radiator factory in northeast China, and one of the biggest in all of China, selling, for example, to China First Auto in Changchun.

Director Tang has three assistant managers – one for production, one for technical matters, and one for management (personnel). He has been director for four years, and was chosen in 1987 by the city Metallurgy Bureau and Finance Bureau. He has six areas of responsibility laid out in his *chengbao* (contract): total production, quantity, quality, asset increasing, profit and taxes, and the management system that oversees the workers (personnel). Director Tang would like changes in the *chengbao* in terms of profits and taxes, and permission to increase assets through investment. State regulations currently determine these matters, though they were to have been reviewed by October 1990. In the new contract, he would like to have increased his profits from 10 to 15 percent, or from 3.7 million RMB (out of an income of 40 million RMB). Profit and taxes total 5.75 million RMB, providing 3.5 million RMB to the state plan and 1.5 million RMB for the factory. Of that 1.5 million RMB, 55 percent goes to the factory development fund, 35 percent to welfare, and 10 percent for worker bonuses.

To summarize his management concerns, he wants more funds to be retained by the enterprise as part of the contract and less in profit and taxes to be paid to the state.

Shenyang Steel-Rolling General Mill

Director Gao Songshan of this city-owned factory was the most interesting and assertive of the directors I interviewed. He dressed like an army colonel; when he talked during the interview, his office staff stood almost at attention. At the same time, he was aware of the power of the workers and of the Communist Party. He pointed to a pennant that he had been given by the workers; and when asked who decided whether he could continue as a manager, he turned almost automatically and looked at the pennant. The factory was originally set up by the Japanese in 1933 by the Sanyo Corporation, which also built the Anshan steel mill. Then it became the Jungshan Steel Institute, and then in 1949 it became the Shenyang Steel Plant.

Director Gao started off by stating that after liberation, one can't forget Mao, and after 1978, one can't forget Deng Xiaoping. He pointed out that since 1984, enterprises have changed extensively; over the last five years the indexes at his factory that have doubled under his management include: fixed assets, per-capita income of workers, and the housing of workers. Factory size has expanded as smaller enterprises have merged with his factory until it has become one of the largest in steel-rolling in the northeast. My translator, a Chinese economics professor who had interviewed him before the June tragedy, said that previously Mr Gao had talked more about wanting to merge with other smaller enterprises than he did in this interview. She also said that Mr Gao and other managers were now mostly unable to raise their salaries beyond 400 RMB without encountering strong worker criticisms.

The production output value of the enterprise expanded from 800 million RMB in 1984 to 1.2 billion RMB in 1989, a 50 percent growth. Profits and taxes went up even faster, from 18 million RMB in 1984 to 37 million RMB in 1989. The workforce more than doubled from 2,013 in 1984 to 4,314 workers in 1989.

Per-capita worker income per year in 1989 was 3,050 RMB, with wages at 60 percent, or 1,830 RMB per year, and bonuses at 40 percent, or 1,220 RMB per year. Workers also received a yearly apartment subsidy of 2,500 RMB, 400 RMB for medical care, 306 RMB for other subsidies and 200 RMB for retirement. There are additional worker compensations. There are subsidies for workers with large families whose wages are low. There is a seven- to ten-day factory holiday. Salaries do vary by as much as three times; but overall, workers' expenses are low and subsidies have improved the life of the workers and have increased the attractiveness of the factory to the workers.

In Mr Gao's view, the core of reform is developing a close connection between the workers' livelihood and productivity. Over the last five years, the following two reform goals have been pursued in enterprise–state relations: (1) an increased distributive relationship between the state and the enterprise, so that although the enterprise is state-owned and its fixed assets belong to the state, more of the income is put under the control of the manager; and (2) increased efforts to make the enterprise more independent from the state, though not changing the actual ownership system, and also to make enterprises more active and flexible. Before 1980, there were no rights for the enterprises, but now there are great changes.

A third area of reform has been only partially achieved. There is increased but still only partial separation of enterprise economic activity from the control of the state and of the rights of management from the powers of state ownership. Currently, for example, while the factory can find and employ workers using want-ads, tests, and interviews, and has the right to refuse a worker and to not hire more workers, it can still be told the upper limit of how many workers to hire and the range of their wages.

The Steel-Rolling Mill has the right to sell products within the state price range and to sell overseas. One major difference between Mr Gao's factory and others I visited was that it retained a high rate of its profits. Last year the factory received 15 million RMB out of 37 million RMB total profit and taxes. Of that 15 million RMB, 10 million RMB went for welfare, bonuses, and so on, and 5 million RMB went for depreciation. That level of depreciation was based on a 6.5 percent depreciation rate on 80 million RMB fixed assets and equaled 0.2 percent of total sales of 240 million RMB. Management rights include the right to increase worker wages. Increases are based on the following formula: for every 1 percent increase in taxes and profits, a 0.75 percent increase in wages is permitted. The wage increase is given to workshop managers to distribute, based on a list submitted to Director Gao. The current reform-driven structure is "two systems (contract and management responsibility) and one authority (the manager)." Recently, wages have been increasing 4 percent and bonuses 10 percent so that wages are now 147 RMB and bonuses are about 250 RMB.

Director Gao has pursued five areas of reform.

(1) The leadership system has been reorganized. The general manager is appointed by the government, and he can hire his own assistant managers – though some enterprises said that they had lost this right. Director Gao reduced the previous six assistant managers to one, following the American model, he said. All of the previous six assistant managers have gone back to being heads of departments whereas the present assistant manager was a workshop leader only three years ago. "I found him and hired him and have through him raised efficiency."

(2) The plant organization structure has been streamlined. In the past there were thirty divisions and sections, and now there are just nineteen.

(3) The "iron rice-bowl" for administrators has been broken by reducing the number of cadres from 430 to 324, by cutting the clerks from 105 to thirty-five, and by reducing the division leaders from 105 to seventy. General Manager Gao also promoted seventy-eight workers to leadership, for a total of 148, but then reduced division leaders by forty-eight, for a total of 100 division leaders.

(4) Personnel policies have been changed. In the past, in state-owned enterprises such as this one, all of the workers were permanent employees. Now all of the workers are contract workers. Mr Gao said:

China has many redundant workers, and in this factory we give redundant workers other jobs. So far, 508 redundant workers have been moved to some new division. Each workshop has an index of workers needed. If there are workers beyond that index, they are asked to transfer. If they refuse, they get 70 percent of wages for one half-year, then 50 percent for as long as they continue to refuse transfer. So far, all of the redundant workers have accepted transfers.

As of April 1990, more than 508 employees had been transferred to small factories, including a clothing factory, a hotel, a restaurant, and a barbershop, all services for the factory. The transferred workers appear to be functioning well in their new settings.

Firing can happen only with serious violation of regulations and then the worker must go back to his or her former district. Fired workers may retain their living quarters at a cost of 5 RMB per month and they still get a government subsidy, according to state regulations, of 20 RMB per month. They do not, however, receive medical insurance.

(5) The distribution system has been reformed. Workers are paid according to what they contribute, and there are two connections with work. First, there is pay according to the group contribution, based on each worker showing increased work proficiency. The usual bonus was 14 RMB per month, with the highest being 28 RMB per month. Wages were 100 RMB for assistant general manager, based on post and responsibility, 60 for assistant managers, 60 for division leaders, 100 for workshop leaders, 30 for clerks, and 80 to 120 for workers. Director Gao commented that he has been such a successful manager that he was offered HK$30–50,000 per month to work in a foreign–Chinese joint venture, although he now makes only 400 RMB per month. He stated that, as a manager, he believes he has to have a pleasant side and a strict side.

Since 1989, there has been only one change: the loss of the right of Director Gao to hire the assistant manager. His goals include increasing the power of the manager to make enterprises more like those in the US:

> If they would give me the right, I would reduce clerks by two-thirds, and reduce workers by 40 percent. I have already sent ninety workers to Libya, and have seen no decrease in productivity. . . . I also look for ten years or more of engineering experience for workshop leaders.

Mr Gao wants to continue the open-door policy and to set up joint ventures that will permit increasing foreign investment. He also would propose decreased submission of profits to the state, from 80 percent return to 60 percent, and in terms of foreign exchange, from 75 percent down to 55 percent.

In summary, Director Gao stated that he wants increased control, increased profit retention, increased foreign investment, and increased ability to fire or transfer clerks, cadres, and workers to more productive positions or supplemental enterprises. He seems to have achieved a much higher level of reforms than other Shenyang factories. For example, he has all workers on contract rather than as permanent "iron rice-bowl" workers, and seems to tie bonuses closely to productivity.

Shenyang Hardware Casting Factory

Director Zhou Guiying describes herself as an economist. Director Zhou agreed with the statement that 80 percent of factories in Shenyang were having trouble, but said that she was not. She said that she was little affected because she has good sales as the result of having excellent light consumer products. Since 1980, this has been a collective enterprise producing electronic parts for air-conditioners and for televisions. The main product currently is a voltage-surge protector.

The average wage of workers is 100 RMB, of which 70 RMB are wages and 20 to 30 RMB are bonuses. There are 120 workers, and 180 retirees, for a total of 300 to support. There are two clerks and seven section leaders. The clerks make 200 RMB. Director Zhou wants to increase wages more than 10 percent but needs permission, and 90 percent of profits currently go back into production.

She contracts for production and profit with the Shenyang Municipal Bureau of Light Industry. She is appointed by the bureau, and has been manager for seven years. She could be voted out by workers. She has fired two workers. She has rights over income, distribution, personnel management, new product development, sales, and production. As a manager, she wants to make people happy. In order to recruit, she goes to the labor bureau, but workers still have to pass three months' probation, then take a test.

In summary, she has gained much control, lost none, and seems to be deeply involved in marketing, particularly since 1980.

Shenyang Water-Pump Factory

Mr Ming Guoqing, Deputy Director and Chief Engineer, said the nationally-owned factory was founded in 1932, by the Japanese, and since then it has become a large water-pump factory, producing products for the country's chemical plants, power stations, oil pumps, and so on. Of the output, 60 percent goes to power stations, 30 percent to petrochemical uses, and 10 percent, other. The factory has China's largest research institute on pumps.

Since 1979, the pump factory has worked with foreign companies as part of the open-door policy, has imported foreign technology and software, and has sent people abroad for training and for technology transfer. Foreign technology imports have improved management and quality control. About 10 percent of production is exported, mostly to developing countries, with the right to export gained in 1988. This is a key enterprise and therefore it enjoys the *shuangbao* (double guarantee system). As part of the reforms, there is a contract system that sets out the powers of management in taxes, technical forms, welfare policy, and rights to control salary. Three interests are represented in the reforms: the state, with highest priority; the enterprises, with middle priority; and the workers, with the least priority.

Production has gradually increased, with increases also in quality. From 1985 to 1989, workers increased from 4,900 to 5,620, while production increased from 60 million to 100 million RMB, and profits increased from 6–7 million to 10 million RMB, though still about 10 percent. Profits over the contracted amount can be kept, but must be used according to rules. Yearly wages total 2,400 RMB, including 15 to 20 percent bonuses. There seems to be little reform, and little increase in profits, though some increasing productivity.

As for change, it is hard to tell, but none was evident except for adoption of the *shuang-bao*. This is an example of a factory that is not seeking primarily to increase productivity, but rather is trying to increase quality through importation of foreign technology. It is also a factory where reforms did not appear to be an issue, although this impression may have had to do with my not being able to actually interview the factory director.

Shenyang Pneumatic Tools Plant

Mr Zhao Suiyuan, the production director, described the factory as being middle-sized for Shenyang but nevertheless the largest such tool plant in China. It was one of the 156 major factories set up by the Russians in 1949. After forty years it has 4,000 workers in ten workshops, with 400 technical people and engineers, and five machine shops. Of the total production, 10 percent is for export, and the factory produces 60 to 65 percent of the pneumatic tools for all of China.

The plant has one director and four deputies: a technology

director, a director of research, a director in charge of inspection, and a production director. In addition, there is an overall chief engineer, and a chief engineer in charge of quality. Mr Zhao, the production director, is also a senior engineer. The business director (a position that did not exist until five years ago) is in charge of import and export development, planning development, supply marketing, publicity, exports, marketing, and planning. There are 3,000 workers, with personnel and welfare department sections and a chief accountant.

Before reforms, the enterprise was rather large, but all things were determined by the plan, and all products were sold to the domestic Chinese market. The enterprise therefore did not need to buy materials by itself or to sell by itself, and there was no competition between factories and other enterprises. Since reform, the factory has changed from a production company to a business and production company that is trying to sell within a market-oriented economy. The enterprise now has the right to export and to set up new departments. Average profit has remained at 10 percent of production, while production has increased greatly with a decrease in workers.

Now there are no inputs from the plan, and no products planned. The enterprise still has relations with the suppliers, but now has to purchase materials. There are many factories short of power, money, and materials, but the situation is different in different factories.

Mr Zhao is currently borrowing from the bank to make payrolls, while the state is trying to solve the problems (caused by unpaid bills) through an influx of funds. Currently the enterprise has one-third excess workers, although some have become *getihus* (individual business people). Mr Zhao pays a 55 percent tax-rate of income in the *chengbao*. The factory has to give 30 percent of profits, but would like to give only 10 percent.

Mr Zhao would like to revise his contract because last year and this year the enterprise is making little or no profit. The national authorities are currently trying to resolve the financial problems of enterprises such as his by using a five-year average of income for calculating taxes, and also by having a new contract that has different ratios for different situations. For example, there should be one rate for an enterprise when there is no profit, but the existing management is continued. The enterprise pays no taxes, and the state will use the last five years as a basis to calculate the level of tax and profit. Mr Zhao, whose enterprise is probably among the two-thirds in Liaoning currently losing money, would like changes in the state demands for taxes during hard times.

CONCLUSIONS

There is much variation in the amount of power that managers have gotten as a result of the reforms. The largest enterprises seem to be most comfortable with the stability of the *shuangbao* (double guarantee) arrangement. Most of the provincial and city factory managers had reforms that they still wanted to be approved or implemented, whereas managers of the large nationally-owned factories seemed to have fewer pressing concerns. The most flexible factories appeared to be the city-administered cooperatives and the middle-sized city-owned factories. Even among factories in that category, there was great variation in the power and the structure of the factory – although still within the context of government control over wages, profits, and investment levels. All managers had been appointed by the city or province, and there has been relatively little turnover.

Possibilities for continued enterprise management reform

The extent to which many of the managers still seem to want continued enterprise reform is striking. This observation coincides with the comments of both former Consul General Gene Dorris and Economic and Political Officer Steve Fox. They reported that perhaps one-third of the area managers were considering not even signing extensions of the contract system unless more reforms were included. Although the Chinese authorities finally finessed the issue in July 1990 by basically renewing the *chengbaos* without renegotiating them, the desire for reform still remains, and was clearly articulated in almost every case where I had the opportunity to meet with an actual factory director.

My impression, therefore, is that there is substantial pressure for continued reforms in Liaoning Province, a pressure that was articulated quite clearly even to an unknown foreigner on a first meeting despite the potential political problems that such expressions might create. A major pressure for continued reforms from above will probably come because of a need for additional income and the increased enterprise efficiency that that implies. A major pressure from the enterprises for continued reforms comes from the fact that enterprises are increasingly being directed by professional and efficiency-oriented managers. Most of the managers I interviewed either had or wanted to have foreign technology. Most seemed aware of the high level of redundant workers. Most wanted to manage more, rather than simply carry out centralized policies.

Despite pressures from many levels, continued reforms will have to await resolution of the differences in top leadership opinions on the issue of management reforms. But to the degree that managers and indeed top leaders come increasingly from the ranks of educated classes and engineers rather than simply from the Party, there will probably be continued and over time inevitable pressure for various reforms.

Implications for foreign business people

The continued open-door policy will be especially important in keeping the pressure for reforms alive. Competition from the world market will demand increasing levels of technology, of quality, and of efficiency, all necessary for China to maintain a comparative advantage in inexpensive yet capable labor. There will therefore be continuing demands by Chinese managers for foreign technological and marketing expertise. Because Liaoning enterprises will probably continue to retain little foreign exchange, most foreign participation will have to come as part of joint-venture arrangements, such as have been generally successful over the long-term in Liaoning Province (see Thomas, *CBR*, 1990).

In sum, 1990 brought increased Liaoning enterprise dependency on the state for funds to ride out the business contraction. Since the enterprises examined were all state enterprises (with one exception), they were given loans and assured some level of materials input for production. In the nationally-owned enterprises, this was codified in the newly instituted *shuangbao* (double guarantee policy), which promised both assured supply and assured demand. In return, however, these nationally-owned enterprises were not encouraged to venture out very far into exports (no more than 10 percent), or in trying to produce outside the plan or call for more management powers. Smaller enterprises not a part of the *shuangbao* system and city-owned enterprises seemed more willing to call for continued management reforms.

Increases in efficiency seemed to be inversely correlated with size and level of central government patronage. The larger and the more important to the economy, the less the increase in efficiency. But overall, even managers who had achieved fewer efficiencies over the last five years were still interested in continuing reform, and most wanted more power to try to increase worker productivity. This observation, though it may not be generalizable, seems to be consistent with a paradox about Liaoning Province. Even though

Liaoning Province might seem to be less interested in reforms, by virtue of most of its heavy industrial state enterprises being beneficiaries of the old planned economy system, Liaoning has been in the forefront in China in the area of enterprise reforms. That trend will no doubt continue to the degree that my findings are accurate and my sample of enterprises is representative of Liaoning's managers.

Management reforms in Liaoning cannot be said to have suffered any substantial damage in the post-Tiananmen environment, at least up until June 1990. The major changes so far have been that some enterprise managers are not able to continue to take over poorly-run companies or to continue various personnel reforms (e.g. tying wages to individual productivity, firing redundant workers, and hiring workers on contract).

Perhaps the current period of retrenchment will in the future be seen as a needed breathing space before the next round of fundamental reforms. At the same time, there is little indication that there will be a total breaking of the iron rice-bowl by managers, even with a major turnaround in the economy or a change of political leadership. Reforms in Liaoning Province will probably continue to take place within the context of broader social and economic policies that have been developed over the last forty years in the People's Republic of China.

NOTE

1 I want to acknowledge the kind assistance of my Liaoning Province host unit, the International Economics Department of Liaoning University, as well as the generous cooperation of the Liaoning Province Foreign Affairs Office. Financial support for my research visit came from a University Affiliations Program grant from the United States Information Agency.

REFERENCES

Thomas, Stephen C. (1990) "Catching up: Liaoning Province has something to offer foreign investors," *China Business Review*, Vol. 17, no. 6, November–December, pp. 6–11.
Warner, Malcolm (1987) *Management Reforms in China*, New York: St Martin's Press.

4 The role of the legal environment in doing business in the People's Republic of China

Ronald C. Brown

INTRODUCTION

China, historically and in modern times, is a land and people of contrasts; and so it is with China's approach to law and the regulation of international business. Like a mistreated lover, it cautiously reaches out to once again embrace the Westerners in whose hands they have suffered before. China seeks to entice foreign trade and investment with its sweet siren songs of economic benefits, while at the same time somewhat petulantly seeking to regulate the contact and the degree of influence. It is a country where some of the banks' employees will work with an abacus while others will work with a computer. It is a country which has its political differences with Western-style capitalism and yet, in late 1990, introduces a national computerized securities trading system that allows brokers in six major Chinese cities to trade state bonds. It is a country which in 1979 inaugurated economic reforms with market-oriented elements while at the same time having a relatively undeveloped system of foreign trade and investment legislation and supporting legal infrastructure.

With the 1979 economic reforms and China's "open-door policy," many foreign traders and investors found reasons to develop closer relationships with China and to do business in and with the People's Republic of China (PRC). Along with the economic reforms came the legal reforms that sought to provide security to the foreign business trader or investor while at the same time providing control of these activities by the PRC government through a spate of laws and regulations, and a number of international business offices with various layers of bureaucracy.

To fully appreciate the obstacles and opportunities in successfully doing business in and with China and to have a window into seeing and understanding what needs to be done and how, *before* business judgments are made – an introduction to the role of China's legal environment in that process is indispensable and is provided by this chapter of the materials. China's legal system, and its regulation of foreign business, while often looking quite familiar is also a collection of kaleidoscopic contrasts – ever changing, creating and removing mosaic windows of business opportunity – and opening and closing doors of invitation or warning about potential costly mistakes. The best business strategy by far is to be prepared before undertaking the international project, to understand the role and importance of the law, the existence and application of the law, and how the law is best used in reaching business judgments.

This introduction to the role of the legal environment in doing business in China is organized into three parts; first, a brief summary of the legal structures and the role of law, courts, and lawyers. It is essential to business planning to understand how the laws and regulations are used, particularly in a socialist country. And, it is necessary to know what government pronouncements are treated as law (regulations, orders, decrees), which apply (central, local, special economic zones), what role the Communist Party has, and whether the laws are enforceable. Laws with ambiguity and which do not afford the expected security rights are meaningless indeed.

The second part deals with the laws and regulations which control foreign trade and investment. These laws and their economic incentives are ever changing and can provide the advantage of knowing what type of legal arrangement to establish; what business activity or location provides the greatest benefits, tax relief, or easiest profit repatriation.

The third part of this introduction discusses practical aspects of using the law for business advantage. Considerations of culture, customs, and negotiation differences, as well as paths to utilize the law in making business judgments are presented. Its strategy is to provide a useable approach of combining legal considerations with practical business judgments that have a reasonable possibility for success in China.

LEGAL STRUCTURES AND THE ROLE OF LAW, COURTS, AND LAWYERS

Overview: Chinese legal tradition

Chinese legal tradition is embodied in a much larger and very long social history dating over centuries to at least the third century BC.

Historically, two major philosophical traditions underpin and explain the current jurisprudence and are based on Confucianist (*li* – model behavior) and Legalist (*fa* – written law) thought. Confucian ideas stress virtue, relationships, and societal harmony; and law, therefore, by use of mediation, education, and reform should be flexible to accommodate the circumstances. By contrast the Legalist tradition uses written law as a standard to impose order through strict enforcement and as a deterrent to inappropriate conduct through the use of severe punishment.

Historically, these two philosophies have blended over the centuries with different emphases during various periods of history. Traditionally *li* has dominated over *fa* and continues to be an integral part of the Chinese legal system, especially in the area of dispute resolution. Largely for this reason and the fact that law was typically applied *to* the people rather than applied *by* the people, the Chinese people have come to regard the law as a matter to be avoided, since to be involved in the process is thought to reflect on them disharmony and absence of virtue.

Twentieth-century Nationalist China continued the earlier nineteenth-century emphasis on written laws and utilized European Codes. In 1949, after Mao won the Civil War and the People's Republic of China was established, there was movement away from Western influences including the use of Western written legal codes. However, during the first decade of the young republic, new laws were reestablished which, although Chinese laws, were often patterned on the Soviet-style socialist model. Although these laws were in effect for some ten years, the law never really made its influence known before the 1966–76 Cultural Revolution occurred in China which distrusted and displaced written laws or other non-communist or non-Mao doctrine, as interpreted by the Red Guard.

Not until the death of Mao in 1976, and the rise of Deng Xiaoping did reforms take place which opened the way for economic and legal development. Deng's proclamation in the late 1970s of the Four Modernizations for agriculture, industry, national defense, and science and technology, which were later embodied in China's 1982 Constitution, placed China back on the track not only of economic development, but also of legal development. In order to achieve necessary economic growth, there needed to be rebuilt a legal infrastructure and a commitment to the new "rule of law" rather than the former "rule of men" system which would permit public and especially foreign confidence and security in new economic development. There would be a fueling of that development by foreign investment and the much needed foreign currency. Thus, there developed a political strategy for a twin-purposed, intertwined approach to rebuild China by economic and legal reforms.

Legal reforms took the shape of a plethora of new laws, initially aimed at providing security to foreign investors, such as the Joint Venture Law, but gradually the laws were also developed for the domestic needs of China. Along with these developments came the rebuilding of a legal infrastructure to make the new laws work, the law-making organizations were reactivated, courts were rejuvenated, and lawyers were again educated. New emphases were given to education of the personnel (court and legal workers) needed to make the laws and courts work to achieve the goals of the Four Modernizations.

The new legal developments reflected the continuity of the Chinese culture and its *li* and *fa* approaches while at the same time borrowing some Western approaches, both for their content and so that their form would be recognized and welcomed by the cautious foreign investor. Inasmuch as the People's Republic of China is politically dominated by the Chinese Communist Party (CCP), some attention should be noted that in this type of system, the Western notion of the Rule of Law is often subordinated to the will of the Party. While periodically, the central power announces an intent to recede from direct involvement in the legal processes, its real and potential participation and influence in law-making, operation of the courts, and in law enforcement, often are distinguishable from comparable Western processes. This fact is not necessarily detrimental to the foreign investor who has available a number of alternative methods of protection, and who can enforce interests not only with the court system, but also in international arbitration, and other forums of mutual negotiation and accommodation.

In sum, today's Chinese legal tradition is a collection and reflection of ideas, Confucian and Legalist theories, Western and Soviet legal approaches, and CCP influences, all blended into what must correctly be called "Chinese" law. It was the goal of China's executive body, the State Council, to establish a fairly comprehensive system of laws and regulations by 1990, the end of the Seventh Five-Year Plan. By all measures it has made much progress on that goal.

Law: Sources and administration

Some introduction should be provided as to what is "law" in the People's Republic of China, what are its sources, and how is it administered? Since 1979 there have been more than 300 laws promulgated by the National People's Congress (NPC), almost all dealing with economic matters, and the State Council has issued in excess of 400 regulations. To understand the significance and priorities of these "laws," including regulations, administrative decisions, etc., one must know the sources of Chinese law-making which is established in the Chinese constitution.

Though only very roughly analogous (in form only) to Western parliaments, the PRC has its unicameral National People's Congress, a single-chamber Parliament, which is its highest organ of state power. The PRC Constitution provides that the NPC enacts basic laws (*falu*); and its Standing Committee also can issue laws in the form of decrees (*faling*), orders (*mingling*), decisions (*jueyi*) and instructions (*zhishi*) under prescribed and proscribed circumstances.

The State Council (Council of Ministers), which is designed as an executive branch of government, is empowered by the Constitution to enact administrative rules and regulations (*guiding*) and orders (*mingling*) that are in accordance with existing laws. In 1985 the NPC empowered the State Council to enact provisional rules and regulations regarding economic reforms and dealings with foreign investment.

Ministries or Commissions of the State Council likewise issue directives and regulations. All of these central government laws and regulations, including those from the NPC and State Council, have the force of law and are applicable throughout China.

Further "local" law emanates from provinces, autonomous regions, municipalities of Beijing, Shanghai, and Tianjin, and from special economic zones. These laws and regulations come from local governmental bodies, similar to those described above, and apply to their regions in ways that may supplement or fill voids, but not supplant, central government laws. And finally, all laws in theory are limited by the Constitution, and are reviewable by the Standing Committee of the NPC to see if they contravene statutes or the Constitution (only this body has the right of constitutional review).

The administration of law is normally performed through the governmental bodies (central, regional, or local) responsible for their application, and alternatives exist for resolving legal issues, such as the use of mediation, conciliation, arbitration, as well as the ultimate enforcement through the use of the courts.

Again, it must be noted that there may not be clear governmental independence of decision-making, administration, or issuance of the laws, in that the CCP has influence at every level of government. As stated, there are periodic attempts by the CCP to distance itself from other than policy influences on these matters.

Finally, another possible source of law may arise from its administration in the court system. Unlike the familiar system of the US that uses the British common-law approach of court decisions providing a source of law, China relies more on the continental Roman-based civil law approach where courts use and interpret legal codes rather than relying on prior case law interpretation. Thus, there is no body of precedents similar to that in the common-law jurisdictions. To be sure, the Chinese system is uniquely Chinese, but there are occasionally recognizable elements or functions of the common-law system. For example, the Supreme Court regularly offers directives and general explanatory clarifications (though not deciding individual cases) that provide "guidance" to the lower courts.

In sum, the laws originate from a number of governmental sources and are administered in a variety of ways. Familiarity with the Chinese legal system overcomes obstacles that may arise in negotiations regarding the attempted use of restricted (*neibu*) laws and regulations or from misunderstandings that can arise in the absence of general knowledge of the laws and their significance.

Courts and the judicial system

In 1979, the Organic Law of the People's Courts established a judicial system to decide civil and criminal cases and to apply the law independently and equally to all persons (including foreigners).

The court system is centrally organized into four levels; at the top is the Supreme People's Court; at each provincial level (including the municipalities of Beijing, Tianjin, and Shanghai which are under the central government, and autonomous regions) is the High People's Court; at the regional level (with the same political subdivisions) is the Intermediate People's Court; and at the local level is the Basic People's Court. There are also specialty courts dealing with the military, with railroads, and shipping, etc. The courts are further divided into four divisions: civil, criminal, economic, and administrative, with foreigners' interests normally falling under the economic courts which deal with trade and investment, maritime, insurance and related contract and commercial disputes. Interestingly, this court also presides over cases involving economic crimes including worker safety, bribes, tax evasion, and trademark infringement.

The jurisdiction of the courts varies, with each capable of having primary jurisdiction over certain cases, and all but the Basic Courts having appeal authority. Also there is a "one-appeal" rule from whichever court has taken original jurisdiction. Intermediate Courts normally have original jurisdiction over claims by foreigners and claims of patent infringement.

The operation of the court is that the higher court supervises the lower courts and each court has a so-called "adjudication committee" which reviews cases or bodies of decisions to help formulate internal guidance to the courts. Normally, cases are decided by a "collegial panel" of judges, sometimes consisting of one judge and two laymen, "assessors," who generally defer to the judge. The trials are typically open to the public.

In working to implement the Four Modernizations, the Supreme People's Court under the leadership of its President, Ren Jianxin, has instituted large-scale training centers to increase the professional abilities of the judges and decrease the need and use of laymen assessors. In China, judges are appointed by the relevant People's Congress or their Standing Committees, and their terms are limited.

Under the 1982 Constitution (Article 123) the Court is the judicial organ of the State and Article 135 affirms it is to be responsible for its own work without improper influence by others, including the law enforcement organs (procuracy and public security) or the Chinese Communist Party (CCP). As most judges are members of the CCP and CCP has its internal law committee organization available at every court, clear lines of demarcation between inside decisions and "outside" influence are not always easily discernible.

As stated earlier, the legal system and its judicial system follow the civil-law rather than common-law approach and therefore the judges usually play a much more active role in the trials than do American judges. However the system is described, it appears to be working and litigation continues to grow at an explosive pace; where, in recent years literally millions of cases have been decided in a country where only a relatively few years ago people resisted involvement with the law or the courts. At the same time that courts are being used, the Chinese citizens also widely use local mediation and conciliation procedures to resolve every manner of case, including neighborhood arguments. And in commercial disputes, arbitration is a common form of resolution, as subsequently discussed.

Lawyers in China

In most of China's history there have been few lawyers. When they did appear, as they did particularly in the early 1900s under the

Nationalist Government, their role usually was to apply the law *to* the people on behalf of the government or the powerful sectors of the economy. Thus, neither law nor lawyers were well thought of by the general population.

In 1949 after China's Civil War, the new government of the PRC eliminated private lawyers from the national scene and prohibited private law firms. During the 1950s there were fewer than 3,000 lawyers in China (supervised by the Chinese Ministry of Justice) who generally worked in the government's legal advisors's offices around the country, in a manner similar in approach to that in the USSR.

In the middle 1960s during the Cultural Revolution, law and lawyers were again completely swept away and even the Ministry of Justice was rendered inoperative. Not until the late 1970s after the reemergence of the use of law in the trial of the Gang of Four (accused of fomenting the Cultural Revolution) did law and lawyers reappear in China. As part of the Four Modernizations, Deng's plans called for both economic and legal reforms. These reforms called for increased legal education and laws.

Regulations on lawyers were promulgated in 1980, effective in 1982, which reestablished lawyers and set forth their duties and responsibilities; and in 1986 a new lawyers' examination was put into place. Obviously, with China's history and a population of one billion people, there was a shortage of lawyers, which law schools in China have been working to meet since the early 1980s.

Presently, there are law service offices throughout China, with their lawyers active in the litigation explosion described earlier. Some lawyers are part-time and others are full-time. Most of these lawyers are paid civil servants, though there is increasing experimentation with negotiated fee participation and "private law firms." In fact to meet the needs of foreign business traders and investors, new law firms (not necessarily private) have been created, specializing in foreign economic law. These firms hope to represent foreigners in their business dealings in China. (These law firms tend to charge fees at the international rates, not the cheaper "local rates.")

Although foreign lawyers are not authorized to "practice law" in China or to appear in courts (at least with the same rights as Chinese lawyers), they have established offices in some of the major cities in China and represent the business interests of the foreigners.

The role of the Chinese lawyers is to advise, negotiate, file and appear in court, and make appeals. Some Westerners view them as distinguishable from American lawyers in their approach, the scope of their responsibility (usually limited by explicit documents similar to a power of attorney), and in their independence. As Chinese lawyers they are required to work closely with and on behalf of their government, which obligation concerns some foreigners who worry about their confidential business matters. In sum, this legal environment is the backdrop for foreign trade and investment in China. The legal environment and the rules, though at times looking similar, are different; and one must cleverly negotiate through paths of cultural and business approach differences as well as seek to protect and provide legal security to those transactions. Understanding the legal environment and its limitations and using it to one's business advantage enhances the likelihood of success in the US–Sino transaction.

REGULATION OF INTERNATIONAL BUSINESS ENVIRONMENT

Economic and legal reforms and regulation of international business

China's history is filled with mixed experiences involving foreigners doing business in and with China and that has led to policies over the years past that, while permitting some trade, basically limited commercial contacts with foreigners and instead sought to protect Chinese autonomy by promoting self-reliance. It was not until 1978 with China's program of the Four Modernizations that China decided to carry out an open-door policy which would bring in needed foreign capital and access to high technology and management skills. Foreigners in turn would be attracted by inexpensive labor costs, hopes of a market share of China's huge domestic market, and the availability of raw materials. The government's twin strategy to achieve these aims of modernization were both economic and legal reforms.

China proceeded on the path to these reforms by decentralizing control, permitting more profits and incentives, and increasing managerial autonomy. These reforms often distinguished between *foreign* business involvement and *domestic* activities, with reforms usually coming first to the foreign business dealings, commonly in the form of "provisional" regulations. These reforms were to induce foreign investment by providing familiar security devices such as laws and recognizable private settlement techniques such as international arbitration. Reforms brought both, with the 1979 Chinese Foreign Equity Joint Venture law and the system of international arbitration put into place by the China Council for the Promotion of International

Trade (CCPIT). It should be noted that China has some aspects of a "dual" legal system in that certain laws apply to foreign business involvement and some apply to purely domestic activities. An example in contract law (economic contract law is domestic; and the foreign economic contract law is for foreign activities) and tax law. However, some laws apply to both foreign and domestic affairs, such as the patent law and the trademark law.

These legal developments paralleled economic reforms, and thus China's open-door policy was put into place which would eventually help implement China's constitutional mandate to permit foreigners and foreign enterprises to invest in China and to enter into other activities of economic cooperation with Chinese economic organizations.

The leading institution which initially supervised the foreign trade and investment was the Ministry of Foreign Trade (MFT) which implemented policies established by the government's State Planning Commission and the State Economic Commission. In 1979 additional institutions were formed to assist the MFT and to guide the modernizations and further the open-door policy. These included two Commissions, one on Foreign Investment Control and the other dealing with Import–Export; and a third institution was the State General Administration for Exchange Control. Major new institutions were created such as the China International Trust and Investment Corporation (CITIC), a state-owned corporation to facilitate finding and negotiating international transactions.

In 1982, the Ministry of Foreign Trade, the Ministry of Foreign Economic Relations, the Foreign Investment Control Commission and the State Import–Export Commission were all joined to become the Ministry of Foreign Economic Relations and Trade (MOFERT). MOFERT supervises foreign trade and foreign investment, interprets laws, handles licenses, technology transfers, service exports, and negotiates and approves international trade and investment agreements.

Other organizations involved in international transactions include the "non-governmental" China Council for the Promotion of International Trade (CCPIT), in existence since 1952, which organizes trade exhibits, technical exchanges, and supervises the work of its international arbitration organizations. Finally, there are government-authorized foreign trade corporations (FTCs) which are numerous and are authorized to conduct foreign business, particularly for those enterprises not otherwise authorized to engage in international trade.

Economic policies which further helped implement the open-door policy, included establishment in 1980 of four special economic zones (SEZs) which were authorized to provide special regulations and preferential incentives to attract foreign business. These are located in or near Shenzhen (near Hong Kong), Xiamen (in Fujian Province), Zhuhai (near Macao), and Shantou (in Guandong Province). To a great extent these SEZs have accomplished much of their purpose and also have incidentally resulted in a higher standard of living for those residing in these geographical areas. In 1983, Hainan Island was added and given a status similar to an SEZ; and in 1984 fourteen coastal cities were designated as export-oriented coastal open cities; and since 1985, many large cities like Beijing, Shanghai, and Tianjin are allowed to establish economic (and technology) development zones (EDZs). These coastal cities and EDZs were also authorized to provide incentives and regulations to attract foreign business.

At the same time these reforms were succeeding in increasing foreign business activity in China and making a ready supply of foreign currency available, this same currency increasingly was used to purchase needed foreign imports which in turn caused a trade deficit during the mid-1980s. China's response was to tighten foreign exchange controls and increase restrictions on imports which predictably caused a reduction in foreign trade and investment. China's approach to balance this withdrawal of foreign capital was the issuance of legal/economic regulations in 1986 that created incentives for foreign investors who dealt with selected areas of the economy, namely export-oriented or high-technology products. These were called Provisions for the Encouragement of Foreign Investment – also known as the "22 Articles."

Tax incentive benefits and retention of a greater percentage of profits also were added to keep the foreign businesses interested in China. But, by late 1988, the Chinese economy was "overheating" and economic conservatism reasserted itself with implementation of austerity programs, increased central control, and a forced pull-back and reduction of Chinese enterprises involved in foreign dealings. Then came the events of June 1989 at Tiananmen Square which further fueled foreigners' insecurity about China's future and at least temporarily dampened foreign business activities.

To accomplish the economic reforms designed to implement the modernization of China, laws were put into place to facilitate foreign trade and investment. The principal laws and regulations, by now quite numerous, dealt with several categories: forms of Sino–foreign cooperation (e.g., joint-venture law); technology transfer and protection of industrial property (e.g., patent law); rules of foreign economic law (e.g., foreign economic contract law); authority of special economic zones; foreign trade (e.g., licensing and customs); and specialized areas covering taxes, foreign exchange, labor, and economic disputes. There are a variety of laws, regulations and other guiding directives under each subject area with which the foreign investor would benefit from some familiarity before commencing business in or with China.

In sum, the Chinese economic and legal reforms and regulation of international business were all designed to implement the Four Modernizations through the open-door policy. This policy under economic and legal guidance and control was to induce foreign trade and investment with resulting benefits to China's economic development. The gain of foreign capital and technology transfer was to be China's primary benefit while the lure of China's huge market and inexpensive labor costs was to be the draw for the foreigners. In the process, China also has received the benefit of a new legal structure and economic policies which combine as the "legal and business environment" for the foreign investor.

Foreign trade regulation

In 1979 a US–Sino Agreement on Trade Relations was signed which ended decades of US restrictions on trade through the use of export controls on shipments from the US to China and high tariffs on Chinese imports to the US. The new Agreement granted China the "most-favored-nation" trade status and the US removed most of its export controls. Special agreements on textiles were negotiated and some export restrictions remained on strategic products. This treaty, freeing-up trade, worked as planned, as only ten years later US–China trade had reached about US$17 billion, ranking the US as third trading partner, after Japan and Hong Kong.

Further implementing the purpose of the Agreement and to facilitate investment, the governments of China and the US signed a tax treaty in 1986 (effective in 1987) to avoid double taxation and also agreed to use and abide by the requirements of the Overseas Private Investment Corporation (OPIC) which provides insurance and guarantees to overseas investors, permits payouts to US private investors and substitutes OPIC as claimant for amounts due from China. These guarantees protect private investors and traders on many of their qualifying insurable risks.

As mentioned, the major Chinese institutions working to facilitate this trade are CCPIT, promoting international business and exchanges; CITIC, which as an international investment and trust corporation organizes business deals and invests in China and overseas; and MOFERT, which plans, oversees, and approves international trade projects. CITIC has coordinated investment of hundreds of millions of US dollars in various ventures in China and abroad. While CITIC is at the pinnacle of Chinese investment companies, there are many other specialized corporations facilitating trade in various industries such as shipbuilding, metals, and oil. Additionally, foreign-trade corporations (under the supervision of MOFERT), often tied in with "consultancy" activities, busily engage in billions of dollars of trade per year, primarily with China's chief trading partners Japan, Hong Kong, USA, the EC, Canada, and Australia.

Lastly, in addition to certain large state enterprises authorized to directly trade with international parties, there also are trade-related agencies such as the China National Foreign Transportation Corporation, organized under MOFERT, which deals with the transport of China's imports and exports; the Bank of China, which along with the State Administration for Exchange Control, deals with trade financing and foreign exchange; and the People's Insurance Company of China.

One of the more important laws or regulations at the national level regulating international trade with China is the Foreign Economic Contract Law of 1985 (FECL) which was further importantly clarified in 1987 by an interpretive guidance notice from the Supreme People's Court. This law provides coverage in many areas of the contractual relationship, especially where the parties do not make provisions, and deals with such important matters as canceled contracts and damages.

Some legal issues, such as dispute resolution, can be dealt with in a variety of ways, through mediation, judicial processes, or by commercial arbitration. In the event the parties do not or are not able to reach agreement on certain items, laws now exist which can fill the gaps. For example, in trade disputes, questions arise as to so-called "choice of law" clauses – whose law will apply? Since 1988, the US and PRC have acceded to the UN Convention on the International Sales of Goods (CISG), which will govern most trade contracts and disputes between Chinese and US parties. And China has begun to join other multilateral conventions including the 1958 New York Convention on the Recognition and Enforcement of Foreign Arbitral Awards; and the Paris Convention for the Protection of Industrial Property Rights.

Many other laws and regulations may apply to particular trade transactions, depending on what is being traded, who is trading it, and where it is traded. Central and provincial agencies, as well as SEZs, coastal open cities, and EDZs, often try to take the lead in having "controlling" regulations and foreign traders must first learn where the real authority lies. Contradictions between preferential regulations of SEZs and more restrictive non-SEZ laws can sometimes arise which require an understanding of the priorities of authority under PRC law as well as the general layout of the legal environment.

Foreign investment regulation

Foreign direct investment in China since 1978 has grown from nothing to over US$33 billion by 1990; and during that same period MOFERT had approved over 21,000 contracts involving equity joint ventures, contractual joint ventures, wholly foreign-owned enterprises, and contracts for cooperative development of mineral resources and offshore oil. Also included under investment are certain types of compensation trade where there is capital investment and/or technology provided by the foreigner and other needs such as land, labor, etc., provided by the Chinese.

Where the investments are placed most often reflect the economic benefits and preferences provided by the laws and regulations of the government. Early investments emphasized the service sector (e.g., hotels, restaurants, etc.), but this later changed in 1986 when legal regulations were promulgated ("22 Articles") encouraging investment in the ventures which were export-oriented or involved in the importation of certain high technology. A majority of the foreign investment comes from Hong Kong, the US, Macao, and Japan, and is invested in "favored" areas such as the coastal cities, EDZs, and SEZs where preferential regulations tend to maximize the investment potential.

The chief methods of legal regulation of foreign investment, at least initially, were rigidly and centrally controlled by China's State Planning Commissions and coordinated with the five-year economic plan promulgated by the State Council. Strict bureaucratic approval was necessary at successively higher levels of authority; this was intended to ensure "compliance" with the economic goals of the government. It became apparent that this cumbersome method did not facilitate foreign investment; and therefore programs of decentralization of authority (often within *renminbi* (RMB) discretionary ranges) were granted to specialized agencies, provinces, SEZs and EDZs. The combination of central, regional, autonomous, and specialized agency approvals can still present formidable legal and practical obstacles to the uninitiated, but for the most part, except during political changes, many of the major decisions can be resolved at the decentralized levels.

In 1979, China promoted foreign investment through equity joint ventures by issuing a law authorizing them and later promulgating implementing regulations. These joint ventures require approval by MOFERT or, depending on the dollar value (e.g., below US$5 million), to a delegated agency (or in the case of oil, by a specialized agency) and involve a sharing of profits and risks according to the proportion of registered capital. The law and regulations specifically delineate requirements in the joint venture contract and operation (covering board of directors, management, labor, etc.). Special provisions guide or control on matters of management autonomy (e.g., hiring, firing), on employee benefits, and on resolving labor disputes and disputes relating to the joint venture contract itself. Likewise, business disputes which arise are usually handled by negotiation; but the legal process of the courts is available or, more likely, commercial arbitration would be used.

In 1988 the State Council, noting that the cause for some recent failures and bankruptcies of joint ventures was undercapitalization, issued new regulations requiring equity contributions mandating full capitalization. Thus, it is clear that the law even in China is always changing; and the investment opportunities may change with the law as risks and benefits are often rebalanced in the process. These equity joint ventures give the Chinese the most control over the operations and are highly favored by the Chinese. Presently there are over 12,000 such joint ventures throughout China.

A second form of investment is the contractual (or "cooperative") joint venture which is similar in appearance to partnership arrangements and which has much less regulation involved than with the equity joint venture, and thus more flexibility is permitted. Additionally, there may be limited liability, no particular division of profits except what is agreed upon, and the venture may be structured so the entity has no tax liability (though the parties are taxed separately). This form of investment seems especially suited for projects limited in duration or scope, such as the construction of a factory or building.

Until 1988, the primary law regulating the contractual relationship was the Foreign Economic Contract Law (FECL). Then, in 1988, the Law on Chinese–Foreign Contractual Joint Ventures was passed which specified what is required to be in the contract. These include terms and duration of the agreement, sharing of risks and losses, management, distribution of earnings or products, and ownership of property upon termination. Certain regulations apply where the contract does not cover the subject, such as disputes; and other regulations affecting taxes, insurance, and foreign currency are also applicable.

A third form of investment is the wholly foreign-owned enterprises where the company is organized in China solely by a foreign company that contributes all the equity, manages the company, and is entitled to the profit. Obviously, this form gives the Chinese the least amount of control over the enterprise, but legal requirements of registration, notification of government agencies of production plans, and approvals for entry into certain markets permit the government an apparently acceptable modicum of control.

The Law on Wholly Foreign Owned Enterprises was passed in 1986 and requires these enterprises to use high technology or be involved in export-oriented products. It also gave the registered enterprises "legal person" status. Most of the some 1,200, wholly foreign-owned enterprises are located in the SEZs, though some are in the major municipalities where, in either location, special economic treatment is more often available through favorable regulations.

Other legal forms of investment include special cooperative development contracts for exploration and exploitation of natural resources (under special 1982 legislation on this subject); and also compensation trading and processing and assembling operations, which typically fit themselves into one of the earlier-mentioned legal forms of organization.

In sum, various forms of legal organization in China are available. Careful assessment must be made, however, as to applicable laws and regulations regarding the type of special preferences given to certain types of business activities, products, or location; and to be sure that items of managerial control, market distribution, taxes, foreign currency controls, and profit are appropriate to the needs of the investor. Again, it would seem that the legal environment controls and guides the foreign business activity to a degree not imagined by the Chinese fewer than two decades earlier.

Areas of concern: Regulations and practical considerations

Another common method of doing business in many parts of the world is through licensing arrangements, either in pure form or as part of a joint venture or other business relationship. Under this arrangement, royalties are paid for the use of the licensed product or process. When done in China, this can raise certain legal and practical considerations. For example, licensing can be done and legal regulatory requirements can be met; however, questions must be addressed as to how royalties can be paid and whether patents, copyrights, trademarks, and trade secrets are protected by enforceable laws.

Inasmuch as China is a socialist country, it first must be remembered that the sale or use of certain high technology may be limited by the US government and/or by COCOM (a Paris-based, multinational organization seeking to exclude certain products to communist countries because of potential security risks). Assuming the technology transfer is permitted, there are a number of applicable laws to regulate the transfer. The equity joint venture law and relevant regulations reference such technology transfers and permits them to be included as capital contribution to a limited percentage. The 1985 Technology Import and Export Regulations and the 1988 Implementing Rules for the Regulations form the basic law and govern the transfer (and there are several more which also are pertinent). Practical problems of confidentiality, conflicting or confusing multiple government authorities also can arise as the documentation is put through the various levels and jurisdictions of the approval process. These practical problems of effective protection of trade secrets or know-how, duration of contacts often give licensors concern, since China has no law in torts or trade secrets and the Regulations limit the contract term to ten years, after which licensees are free to use the technology.

This raises related questions whether the technology, their trade names, etc., are protected under Chinese law. In 1984, China enacted a Patent Law, effective 1985, which while providing some protection still left some areas, such as to products and those in the newest areas of technology, either unprotected or in the eyes of the business investors, uncertain. In 1983 the Trademark Law was put into effect (China is now a signatory to the Paris Convention of 1883); and in 1990 China adopted a copyright law which also covers computer software.

These legal protections provide some measure of assurance to foreign investors, but questions often remain regarding the adminis- tration of these laws. Will business interests be protected and will infringements be vigorously pursued by government agencies or through court enforcement where necessary? To some extent, many uncertainties can be made more secure through various negotiated contractual arrangements, though it is important to note that licens- ing agreements are subject to governmental approval. These can also include protections against local partners using or selling licensed enterprise products or technology in an unauthorized way and/or through non-enterprise outlets.

Other practical problems continue notwithstanding a plethora of regulations. Besides the dilemma, already discussed of overlapping authorities and regulations (central, provincial, SEZ, etc.), there is the recurring problem of foreign exchange and its non-convertibility into Western currencies. Many regulations suggest alternatives and exceptions to the rule; these regulations include the general foreign exchange controls, the Foreign Exchange Balancing Provisions of 1986, the 22 Articles, 1987 and 1989 offsetting provisions relating to import substitution alternatives. In sum, it is a problem and the Chinese know it and the foreign business investors presently must seek legal and practical ways of dealing with it.

The list of practical concerns and considerations goes on depending on the nature and industry of the foreign business investment. Costs of land-use fees, labor, and taxation are all governed by multiple layers and geographically dispersed laws and regulations. The extent of available managerial autonomy over these areas often depends on the nature of the enterprise (joint venture or wholly foreign-owned?), or its location (SEZ?) or possibly its product (export-oriented or high-tech?). Again, the point is that meaningful business decisions cannot (or at least should not) be made without some understanding of the legal environment.

DOING BUSINESS IN AND WITH CHINA: PATHS OF LAW AND PRACTICALITIES

Business practices and law: Considering culture, customs and negotiation differences

The Chinese civilization has a long history and experience teaches that the way to get things done in China and with the Chinese is to do it the Chinese way. This is especially true in the process of business negotiations and the administration of the agreed-upon contract. The foreigner must first understand that while self-interest may be foremost in both parties, the Chinese negotiator's self-interest is often less individualistically-oriented than that of the foreigner, particularly the American. And success may not be measured in profits, but in other concerns, such as accessing technology and/or management skills not just for the benefit of the Chinese enterprise, but for the country as a whole.

It has become axiomatic that the Chinese place great importance on personal relationships; and, where trust between "old friends" prevails, much flexibility may be possible on obtaining contracts and, to the foreigners' surprise, on "renegotiating" them when conditions may change. Favors and benefits are often given on the basis of these friendships (through *guanxi*) rather than on merit or "regulations"; and obstacles of laws, delivery problems, or the availability of needed resources are made much easier by using these channels or connections, based on relationship.

This emphasis on relationship also explains the historic approach of the Chinese to negotiate contracts shorter than what Westerners might expect. Details often have been left to future resolution based on "mutual understandings and friendship." While this ambiguity could benefit either party, it should be noted that under various legal forms, such as joint ventures, these decisions often are made by boards of directors that may have a larger Chinese voice.

Other generalizations about cultural differences reflecting in negotiation styles are that Americans tend to be impatient, want immediate responses, approvals, and deals, ultimately memorialized in specific written detail. Time delays of course cost money, but perhaps more importantly, impatience can often cost mistakes in deals that are bad, premature, or lost. It must be recognized that today in China there are real differences in the technology of negotiations, the authority to negotiate, the treatment of people, the use of language, and the list goes on and on. Axiomatic though it may be, one of the chief obstacles facing Americans is the lack of patience and the ability to consider and work into the deal the best mutual benefit for the "business relationship."

Times are changing of course, and particular Chinese businesses may have faxes, statistical data about markets and production capacities; and some negotiators may be adopting more Western approaches to informality, shorter negotiations, and longer contracts; but don't count on it. And even when such trends appear, the needs of negotiation may cause real or feigned delays in gaining necessary approvals of authorities, making translations of documents, or securing necessary approvals. Experienced negotiators consider that these negotiations may involve representatives who are relatively inexperienced, may have misunderstandings about regulations, product, authority, etc., and who may have different perspectives on the business transaction due to differences of culture, language, and economic/political system. Or they may not; but either way, therein lies the challenge of international business.

Legal reforms have produced many new laws and regulations though, to date, relatively few lawyers. Therefore, Chinese businessmen may have little knowledge of the law and certainly have a traditional disdain for it. Though compliance with the law is often a necessity in most areas (e.g., corporate form, compliance with taxes, etc.), it must be kept in mind that in China the law is one of many considerations evaluated by the business enterprises. That is, it may not have the force or weight or urgency that the Westerner might place on it; and, on the other hand, it might be introduced into the negotiations as a matter that might be negotiable or might "limit the flexibility" of the Chinese partner (and perhaps this also is part of the negotiation).

The presence of the law is an important consideration for the Western business investor, but of most particular interest is whether the law *means* what it *says* and will be enforceable to provide security to the business transaction. Therefore, the credibility of commercial arbitration and/or the Chinese courts are of high importance to Westerners, since that often is an important part of the system with which they are familiar which protects their business contracts and investment. The Chinese, on the other hand, see that there is now so much law, and much of it unclear to them, that they might ask the question whether the law really *says* what it *means*. Their reflexive approach, therefore, might be to enter into negotiations with the aim of working out mutually beneficial arrangements, with "due consideration" of the law.

In determining the proper place of the law in international business transactions with Chinese enterprises, it must be remembered that before 1979 there was a long period of history where politics, not law, was important; and the "clever" man would use political connections and avoid the law. Therefore, when it was announced by the government that the "Rule of Law" would now prevail, a legitimate question to ask particularly in a socialist country, is whether law was also above politics, particularly that of the Chinese Communist Party (CCP). This issue was discussed earlier as it related to the autonomy of the legal system; but there is also another aspect worth considering.

The power and presence of the CCP is real and even after policies seeking to withdraw much of its influence in business and in legal judgments, its importance in relationships and the corresponding ability to cut through bureaucratic obstacles has been the subject of some commentary. It is in this context that an added dimension may be understood to include the axiom that friendship may be as important as a legal position. A corollary point, true in most societies, but especially in China, is that it is always helpful to have the express support of governmental departments and particularly officials in a position to help remove obstacles to the project.

Finally, the foreign negotiator should not overlook the fact that Chinese enterprises which can successfully conclude international agreements for trade and investment, under applicable legal regulations and incentives, can and do fare better than other Chinese enterprises. Opportunity for increased autonomy as to management, access to materials, enhanced contacts with government officials, and personal opportunities for higher wages, skill training, travel, and advancement all blend to create keen incentives to enter into successful negotiations with the foreign business investor. Given the country's history, its use of law, and the benefits involved, it behooves the foreign investor to have a basic understanding of the legal environment of China (from his or her own sources), before commencing negotiations with representatives of Chinese enterprises.

Law and business judgments: Using the law in practical ways

Law can be viewed as a basic primer helping business investors understand the transactions that are legally possible; and, as a window, to peer into an immense and complex country with practical problems, to see and help identify the kinds of issues, practical and legal, that will need to be dealt with by the international trader or investor. Once developing a "checklist" of sorts, business practices can be combined with legal possibilities that will assist in the formulation of the business plan that has the best chance for success.

Use law as an approach to business judgment

A general approach to an overseas business judgment and commitment in China might proceed as follows.

Plan the project comprehensively

Proper research is a necessity. Market research and overseas production capabilities, industry patterns, standards, potential partners all
must be combined with eventual on-site visits and evaluations of
whether the project is politically, economically, and legally acceptable to China and also profitable and capable of being financed. Does
it fit within the country's economic goals? Does it qualify for special
treatment, e.g., export-oriented or high technology? What is the best
location, a municipality, an SEZ or an EDZ, and can a justification
for that selection be made?

Decide the form of the business and the Chinese entities best
equipped to assist

Whether the project involves trade and/or investment or a combination, such as investment and countertrade, decisions must be made
whether to be a wholly foreign-owned or a joint venture company.
How much control is required; how much local expertise is needed?
What Chinese institutions and/or enterprises are best equipped
to supply information useful to the business judgment above,
and to provide assistance about industries, markets, partners,
infrastructure, available materials and supplies, and regulations.

Are there sufficient methods available for this project to take out
profits notwithstanding the foreign currency problem?

While the investor may go to China for the "long term," normally
some reasonable expectation of profitability is involved in US for-
profit corporations. Exploration of "compensation" or "countertrade"
as means of capturing and exporting investment profits must be
made. Alternatively, some projects are legally permitted to repatriate foreign currency and/or escape some tax liabilities under different
schemes; or certain projects may have waivers, exemptions, or a
moratorium for specified periods for specified reasons, in various
geographical locations (e.g., SEZ).

How much security and protection can be provided for this project?

The law, contractual provisions, financing arrangements, and treaty
protections can all provide some measure of security if they are
understood and utilized properly. Whether the Chinese law, the

negotiated contract, or the commercial arbitration clause provide this protection depends very much on whether its limits are understood and adequately compensated for either through insurance, financing, contract, or negotiated contribution or risk-sharing by Chinese partners. The secret is in knowing what is needed and how much.

What should be apparent in reviewing this four-step analysis in exercising business judgments, is the need to know and understand the law, the legal environment, and how it relates to a particular project. For example, under the first step of planning the project, what legal preferences might be available under what economic regulations, in what locations, and by what authority; in the second, what legal forms for the enterprise are available and most advantageous for the needs of the investor; in the third, what legal means are available and most effective in capturing and repatriating profits; and fourth, what protection to the project investment do laws provide and what must be supplemented by other means such as insurance, financing, or finally by contract; and, it should be noted, these provisions in each case must be legally enforceable.

Lastly, of course, whatever business judgment is reached on the above issues must then be considered in light of US laws, especially tax laws.

Channels of legal regulation

By identifying the legal issues that may arise, some useful organization can be obtained which will facilitate the legal analysis and the resulting business judgments that must be made. Forearmed with knowledge of the kinds of issues that need to be addressed, some certainty can be gained through this organization by steering them into "channels of legal regulation" for analysis. As a result, a description of the legal environment in which the project will be placed is presented, as illustrated below.

Projects may require "project financing" where the project itself may be looked to as the primary source of revenue to fund debt service and meet operating and other project costs. There are first a number of particularized issues to be resolved as to the form of financing (equity, shareholder loans, export credits, RMB loans, countertrade, leases, bonding, etc.), the approvals required, the documentation necessary, how disputes will be resolved, and the usual tax, labor, insurance, etc., considerations. There are laws and regulations dealing with all of these areas; but there is a larger context, or "channel," if you please, to examine the question of project financing. This channel, or body of related law, deals with *banking and finance*. To gain full advantage of the business opportunities and risks of project financing, an examination must be made and a basic understanding gained of the legal environment of the related areas of China's banking and credit system, foreign banking policies, and the legal requirements of lending in China by domestic and foreign banks. Bodies of Chinese laws and regulations already exist to control the transaction and determine many of the choices of the ultimate business judgment.

If countertrade or technology transfer is also involved in the project, then the channels of law regarding business ventures in and with China must be examined, such as the body of specific laws on these activities, as well as related areas of licensing and even bankruptcy.

Depending on the needs of the project, other specialized channels of law might need attention, such as the laws and regulations regarding taxation, labor, and dispute resolution. Certain bodies of law are almost always necessarily involved, including contract law and questions of priorities of competing laws. Immersing the identified issues into the channels of regulation presents a somewhat comprehensive legal landscape of the proposed project which will then facilitate the business judgments on that project.

As may be seen, since the "Open-Door Policy" of 1979, legal reforms have resulted in a plethora of laws and regulations designed to induce foreign investment and provide added security for those investments. While the sheer amount of these laws may seem massive, foreign criticism suggests still further legislation and legal reforms are necessary to fully accomplish the goals of the Four Modernizations at least in the minds of the foreign traders or investors. Understanding the laws and how they are used is the full-time job of an international US–China law specialist. Understanding the *legal environment* and its importance in business judgments is much easier.

CONCLUSION

It is hoped this brief introduction to China's legal system, its regulation of the international business environment, and the practical suggestions of how to use that law in formulating and reaching business decisions, will provide a sufficient description of the legal landscape so as to alert business investors to be cautious and to be informed, but most of all to be prepared.

BIBLIOGRAPHY

Barale (1990) "Wholly foreign owned enterprises," *China Bus. Rev.* (January–February), p. 30.

Casey (1987) "The 1986 provisions to encourage foreign investment in China: further evolution in Chinese investment laws, *2 Am. U.J. Intl L. and Policy*, 579.

China Laws for Foreign Business: Business Regulation (1989), Commerce Clearinghouse Australia Limited (CCH) Sydney, Australia.

Folsom, R. and J. Minan (eds) (1989), *Law in the People's Republic of China*, Martinus Nijhoff Publishers.

Gross (1988) "China's special economic zones," *IV China L. Rptr.* 23.

Huang (1987) "The present situation and development trend of Chinese legislation concerning foreign economic affairs," *IV China L. Rptr.* 119.

Lieberthal and Oksenberg (1986) "Understanding China's bureaucracy," *China Bus. Rev.* (November–December), p. 24.

Ren (1987) "Mediation, conciliation, arbitration and litigation in the People's Republic of China," *15 Int'l Bus. Lawyer*, 395.

Simon (1990) "Beyond Tiananmen: the future of foreign business in China," *The Fletcher Forum* (Winter), 40.

Streng, W. and A. Wilcox, (eds) (1990) *Doing Business in China*, Matthew Bender.

Wang (1988) "China, exchange control and regulations relating to foreign capital investment," *16 Int'l Bus. Lawyer*, 78.

Wang (1987) "The investment environment in China, IV China L. Rptr., 141.

Weil (1990) "China's exports: on the edge," *China Bus. Rev.* (January–February), p. 36.

5 The foreign-exchange balancing rule in the People's Republic of China

Sylvain R. Plasschaert

INTRODUCTION

This paper analyzes the rule, whereby foreign direct investors, usually operating through joint ventures (JVs) with Chinese partners, are expected to be self-sufficient in foreign exchange (for short, "forex"). In other words, their outlays in hard currencies for the importation of machinery, components, raw materials, and other inputs, for the payment of interest or licensing fees, the remittance of dividends or the repatriation of capital, must be offset by forex receipts out of their venture.

The core, the third section of this paper, describes the operation of the foreign exchange balancing rule, and a number of measures that were introduced to relax that prescription, without succeeding in basically solving the problem. Previously, the typically closed character of centrally-managed economies (CMEs) and the foreign direct investment (FDI) dimension of the opening of China's economy since 1979, are sketched in the first and second sections respectively. The fourth section discusses the emergence of essentially free, parallel forex markets, in which foreign investors and others can buy and sell forex at a premium over the official rate.[1] The last section looks at the inhibiting effects which the balancing rule exerts on inward FDI and examines whether alternative approaches could alleviate or remove that negative impact.

It should be noted that, in such a vast subject-matter, one easily becomes enmeshed in excessive detail about legal arrangements. Accordingly, some of the less relevant finer points are left out. The treatment here is basically that of an economist, not of a legal expert.

A similar forex-balancing rule applies to JV in Russia. While a comparison between China and the CIS is tempting – the more that the Chinese rule appears to have greatly inspired the Russian stance –

no such attempt will be made here, although the implications are analogous.

CHARACTERISTICS OF INTERNATIONAL ECONOMIC RELATIONS IN ORTHODOX CENTRALLY-MANAGED ECONOMIES

Orthodox CMEs – i.e., those patterned on the Stalinist model – are characterized by strong autarchic tendencies. The reasons for this "trade aversion" are not only ideological, but are essentially systemic (for an excellent analysis see Winiecki 1988).

Production is essentially predicated on physical planning, which relies on "material balances" between the anticipated outputs and the inputs needed in the production process. Some inputs (mainly machinery, semi-finished commodities, possibly food) must be imported.

CMEs conduct trade amongst each other, and with other countries (especially with a number of developing countries) in a bilateral fashion, which balances the value of the trade in both directions. Countertrade, in various forms, is also widely practised.

Imports from countries with hard, convertible currencies obviously require forex resources, which must be earned through exports. As orthodox Marxism does not recognize the theorem of comparative advantage in inter-country trade, no real effort is made to maximize export earnings. CMEs become involved in export only to the extent the latter allow to secure the imports that are needed to fulfill the plans. Import and, accordingly, export targets are part of the overall production plan.

The logic of central planning also implies that decisions about imports and exports be centralized. A limited number of foreign trade corporations (FTCs) conduct all negotiations; thus, the producing (state) enterprise itself does not enter into direct contact with the foreign firms at the importing end. Apart from reaching the assigned export target, the exporting enterprise basically does not have to care about the monetary export proceeds. Anyhow, the prices of exports are significantly divorced from those prevailing on international markets. Furthermore, the exchange rates applied to exporters are highly differentiated among, and even within, economic sectors. Trading losses or profits are not fundamentally relevant to the producer firm or to the FTC, as losses are subsidized out of the "common bowl" of the state budget and as profits and even (the typically low) depreciation allowances accrue to the budget.

The currencies of CMEs are not convertible into other currencies. This is the case even for payments between CMEs. The so-called transferable rouble within COMECON is basically only a unit of account; anyhow, it appears nowadays to be doomed, together with COMECON itself. As Holzman (1979) pointed out, various factors, such as the neglect of the quality of civilian output, the reluctance to downward adjustment of overvalued national currencies, and the taut planning targets, result in a chronic lack of forex in CMEs.[2]

For the above reasons, the structure of foreign trade in CMEs resembles more that of a typical developing country than of a more developed capitalist country. As *The Economist* once quipped, exports from CMEs are those of "newly undeveloping countries" (NUCs) and not comparable to those of the NICs, the high achievers in exports of manufactures. Exports to world markets consist mainly of raw materials (excluding oil, and diamonds or gold in the CIS) and possibly of agricultural primary commodities (of which food exports from the Romania of Ceaucescu are a celebrated but saddening example). This is a paradox, as, contrary to most free-market developing economies, CMEs typically have exerted a tremendous drive towards a fully-fledged industrial structure.

In orthodox CMEs, until recently, there was no room for genuine ("equity") foreign investments, whereby foreign multinationals would acquire full or partial ownership rights in production units within the CMEs. This is precluded by the very communist ideology; the latter does not recognize domestic private ownership of the means of production either. Apart from machinery and possibly raw materials (excluding lumber from Finland to Russia), imports consist also of key-turn projects, whereas over the years in Eastern Europe there have been a number of "cooperative ventures" with foreign firms, which do not involve equity participations.

INWARD DIRECT INVESTMENTS IN THE PEOPLE'S REPUBLIC OF CHINA

The general thrust of the "opening" of the Chinese economy after 1979

During the Maoist period (1949–76) the huge Chinese mainland was largely isolated from the outside world. This was particularly the case after relations with Russia were abruptly broken in 1960. The Western world, and particularly the United States, also largely held China in quarantine, until Nixon's visit to Beijing in 1971. The autarchic bias of Communist regimes was reinforced by Mao's credo, forged in the Yanan guerrilla period of "relying on one's own forces only" and by the fact that large countries typically display a lesser degree of openness in their international economic relations.

The (economic) "opening of China" to the outside world has been one of the major policy planks of the Dengists, once they had secured control over the top echelons in the party and the government. Since 1979, imports and exports have grown impressively. Imports were needed to sustain the rapid growth of the economy, which was especially noticeable in the rural sector.

Exports have also grown rapidly, the more that they benefited from various but often economically not well-founded incentives (particularly subsidies). They consist of about 30 per cent of crude oil. Light manufactures, especially textile products, also represent a substantial share of export earnings. The latter are apparently closely related to foreign-funded investments in labor-intensive investments in the southern coastal areas – as will be discussed below.

The monopoly of the FTC has also been abandoned, although, in this respect, the course of events since 1979 has been sinuous. A major reason of such roller-coaster evolution was that in China two strands of decentralization have been introduced, which should be clearly distinguished. Reinforcing the devolution that already occurred in the early 1970s, the Dengists have accorded more decision-making powers to provinces and autonomous cities, and through the latter to lower-level administrative units; most relevant was the transfer of control over enterprises which, whether they remit their profits or (after 1984) pay taxes, are the main source of revenue for the various levels of government. These moves towards "administrative" decentralization were "hurriedly instituted, excessive in certain respects, and in the end were modified and substantially weakened if not rescinded outright" (World Bank 1988a, p. 381).

The other variety of decentralization, which we might term the "managerial" one, is more critical for systemic reform, as in principle it vests managers of state enterprises with discretionary powers about such economic variables as the composition and level of output, the acquisition of inputs, the appointment of workers, and marketing outlets which are the preserve of managers in market economies. In China this "urban reform," which was officially launched at the end of 1984, has been only partially implemented, with the notable exception of the pricing area.

One typical feature of the reform consisted of the institution of various types of "responsibility systems," whereby managers or managing teams (sometimes appointed after an open "bidding" procedure from interested individuals or small teams), enter into a contract with their appropriate public authority and commit themselves to reach an agreed-upon level of profits, or of public revenue. The basic differences with the previous orthodox CMEs are that the physical output targets are replaced by financial ones and that the target-setting derives from a negotiating process, which results in contractual arrangements instead of being imperatively imposed by the planning bureau.

This brief excursion into the main axes of systemic reform should contribute to a better understanding of the changes in the organization of foreign trade and how they might affect joint ventures in China. Here also, the moves have been far from straightforward. In 1985 a number of large enterprises were granted the power to initiate foreign-trade deals, instead of passing through the appropriate FTC (the latter were controlled by the Ministry of Foreign Economic Relations and Trade. (MOFERT)). After much rather confused experimentation, early in 1988 this important reform was given a more coherent shape. The local branches of the FTC now had to report to the local authorities; they were henceforth held responsible for their profits and losses; in other words, export targets were agreed upon between that enterprise and the local governments – or, for those remaining under central control, with the central government. The role of the FTC was also being modified in principle; they would now act no longer as principal, but as agents on a commission basis. They will put their experience at the disposal of the firms which can act autonomously in the field of international trade. The rather extensive gamut of import duties and licenses and of export licenses,[3] however, apply equally to the enterprises to which autonomy in the foreign trade field was granted. In turn, local governments had to enter into a contractual arrangement with the central government in order to undertake the fulfillment of a given level of export performance.

Inward foreign investment

In 1979, the Chinese government announced that it would welcome foreign investment channeled through JVs with Chinese partners. A set of legal rules and regulations have since been enacted.

In China, six categories of foreign direct investments from abroad are now being distinguished (World Bank 1988b). They are, respectively, as follows.

Wholly foreign-owned ventures

At the end of June 1988, only 2 percent of all foreign-funded units were of this type (IMF 1989). China was the first Communist country to allow, in 1986, such 100 percent-held affiliates of foreign companies.

Equity joint ventures

These corporate entities, jointly founded, owned and operated by a foreign and a Chinese partner, come closest to what is usually understood by a JV in Western parlance. Their legal format was first molded in a rather general Law on Joint Ventures, of August 7, 1979, but has since been complemented and detailed by many other legal prescriptions in various forms. The foreign partner should contribute at least 25 percent of the equity.

Contractual joint ventures

This category displays a high degree of flexibility as, in principle, the contracting parties agree upon such items as their respective contributions to the venture (often partially in kind). There may be but there is no need to set-up a joint subsidiary. Hence, there has been wide recourse to this category by investors in ventures which, from all indications, are quite similar to an equity joint venture but enjoy more flexibility. This has been facilitated by the fact that until the Law of April 13, 1988 about "Chinese Foreign Cooperative Joint Ventures," there was no legal statute for such variegated ventures; in the meantime, the provisions of the Equity Joint Venture Law were applied, *mutatis mutandis*. The new law maintains a high degree of flexibility according to the wishes of the contracting parties. In legal terms, they can be likened to quasi-partnerships, whereas the equity JVs represent corporations with legal personality (for a discussion, see Easson 1989).

Joint development

This form of international collaboration is used in the natural resources area, more particularly as regards offshore oil exploration and production. They are subject to separate legal provisions, "production sharing," whereby each party is entitled to part of the output – with the foreign partner committed to selling the crude oil in world markets – a typical feature of such contracts.

Compensation trade and processing and assembling

The last two categories are also considered as FDI by the Chinese authorities and statistics, to the extent that they involve the importation of technology. Yet they do not involve any sharing of enterprise risks. Compensation trade in its various guises basically amounts to barter trade, with the foreign partner being remunerated by goods produced out of the common venture or from other sources. Processing and assembling refers to a sort of subcontracting whereby the materials needed (and sometimes machinery and technical know-how) are contributed by the foreign partner, whereas the Chinese side provides labor inputs. The apparel sector and other labor-intensive productions provide obvious examples.

Differentiated incentives

In order to attract foreign investors, China accords various tax and non-tax incentives. Several differentiated incentive regimes have been instituted over the years. In 1980, four areas in Guandong and Fujien provinces have been designated as "special economic zones" amongst which Shenzhen is the most important one. In 1984, fourteen coastal cities – amongst them the megalopolises of Shanghai and Tientsin – and Hainan Island (later established as a separate province, apart from Guandong) were requested to open development zones. As another step in the open-door policy, three delta areas – respectively those of the Yangtse (Blue River), Zhujiang (Pearl River), and the southern Fujien – were also identified for preferential treatment. A number of major cities have obtained provincial status, thus enjoying more autonomy in the management of their economy. Accordingly, the regulatory framework in China has become quite differentiated amongst regions, the more that each of these entities appears empowered to enact its own, complementary regulations.

Those regimes are largely similar; to detail the differences between them falls outside the purview of this chapter. However, the motivations of the Chinese authorities are worth recalling. The introduction of high technology was a major consideration, whereas the success which several countries (such as Malaysia and Taiwan) have scored in attracting the production of labor-intensive products and processes, had also inspired the authorities. Facts have vindicated the selection of the second objective in the original four economic zones, especially that a great number of generally small entrepreneurs from Hong

Kong, and in a later stage (although in a more covert way) from Taiwan,[4] and well acquainted with Chinese mentalities, have relocated their labor-intensive production processes to Szenshen or other special zones; this has probably prompted the Chinese government to "open" the fourteen coastal towns for preferential foreign investment, as in those cities both the existing physical infrastructure and the skills endowment were more conducive to the absorption of higher-technology production. More generally, the option to first develop the better located coastal area has been repeatedly stated, in the hope that the rapid increase in productive capacity and wellbeing – which has indeed occurred in many of those areas – would subsequently trickle down to the inland areas. Even before the Tiananmen Square tragedy of June 3–4, 1989, however, the preferential treatment given to the designated coastal areas has in some respects been scaled down; this was causing envy in other provinces.

THE FOREIGN EXCHANGE BALANCING RULE

The rule

Joint ventures must undertake in principle that the forex needed for investment (such as for imported machinery) and current operations (such as inputs that cannot be procured locally at comparable conditions of quality and price, and the remuneration of the equity provided, i.e. dividend remittances or royalties) must be equaled by the forex the JV generates. While the original Law on Sino-foreign JVs of July 8, 1979 does not explicitly state the prescription, the balancing rule has been stated in subsequent Implementing Regulations of September 20, 1983 and especially in the "Provisions of the State Council on the Question of the balancing of Foreign Exchange Receipts and Expenditures of Chinese–Foreign Joint Ventures" of January 15, 1986. (For a discussion, see Gelatt 1986 and Frisbie 1988.) That document, in Article 2, states the general principle as follows:

> The products produced by Chinese–foreign joint ventures should be exported to a great extent, to generate more foreign exchange and to achieve a balance of foreign exchange receipts and expenditures.

Often the Chinese side has obtained the contractual commitment from the foreign partner to export a given percentage of the JV output. Although such obligation is not posited by the legal prescription, it is instrumental in securing tax gratifications for the venture. This is obviously a tall order. JVs with a high local cost content, both at the construction stage and in the course of operations, and ample revenues from outside customers, normally do not have any problem in meeting this condition. First-class hotels, catering to a foreign clientele, are the obvious example, provided they reach adequate occupancy levels. Labor-intensive investments often amounting to a mere relocation of such processes from Hong Kong into economic zones across the border into Guandong or Fujien, can also readily cope with the prescription as the price of the exported end-product should exceed that of the imported inputs by at least the value added, corresponding to the wage sum and the profits. Oil production is also capable of fulfilling the prescription, although the results of offshore oil exploration have remained far below expectations by the Chinese government and by the petroleum companies themselves.

The going is much rougher for most other industrial sectors: Chinese goods most often are not yet of adequate quality to reach international quality norms; the design of exportable consumer goods so far lacks inventiveness. The overheated Chinese economy until recently implied that raw materials and other inputs were often difficult to obtain domestically, so that JVs were often led to import such inputs.

Relaxations

Over the years a number of measures have been taken aimed at facilitating the achievement of the forex balance. All in all, while useful in some circumstances they have not been able to fundamentally solve the problem for a great many foreign investors. As will be seen, in this realm central and local officials retain substantial discretionary powers. Hence, foreign investors must be able to exercise negotiating skills and to build up a trustworthy relationship with the appropriate authorities.

Such relaxations are briefly discussed here without adhering to a chronological order.

Ad-hoc exemptions

The 1983 implementing regulations of the JV contained Article 75 which "in a highly ambiguous way, indicated that provincial or central authorities would 'resolve' the foreign exchange imbalance of ventures that were approved to sell goods on the domestic market" (Gelatt 1986, p. 1). This article allows discretionary deviations from the general rule. The same author mentions that "if such provisions were difficult to negotiate in 1984, they were virtually impossible to secure in 1985," when the Chinese authorities, in order to stave off a serious balance-of-payments crisis, adopted a more restrictive stance – as is again the case since mid-1988 after the more liberal allotments of forex in 1987.

This facility has been successfully invoked by some firms, such as Volkswagen, Hewlett-Packard, and American. But often the consent of the Chinese authorities to obtain forex was prompted by their desire to avoid the failure of a highly-visible venture.

Qualification for import substitution status

Introduced in 1983, this measure was intended to allot forex to the foreign partner in such cases when the production by the JV and the subsequent sale of output within China would entail the substitution of imports, and thus allow the country to economize on forex. This clause was reinstated in 1986. Procedural rules remained quite vague, but have been specified in additional regulations in October 1987; the latter, however, have restricted the scope for such an exception to the basic balancing rule.

It should be stressed that this exception does not mean that JVs, having sold in the domestic market, can automatically convert their renminbi (RMB) profits into hard currencies. It only allows them to charge forex for such domestic sales; this implies that one must find a Chinese firm that is willing to purchase the products from the JV and to pay in, say, US dollars. This is not an easy proposition, as few Chinese enterprises possess excess forex, and as they may prefer to utilize such funds for directly importing foreign-made goods. The authorities, however, may step in and order Chinese firms to acquire the goods against payment in forex. In fact, the 1986 provisions explicitly state that the appropriate authorities "shall actively support Chinese end-users in concluding [such] purchase and sales contracts" (Article 5). This provision clearly reflects the fact that in China, in the present stage of economic reforms, allocations and commands by the planning authorities are still fairly much in use.

Other conditions restrain the scope for obtaining import-substitution status. Obviously, import-substitution status must be granted by the apposite authority. Besides, the regulations impose various conditions related to domestic demand, price, quality, specifications, performance, delivery times, technical services, and training (Linn and Cheng 1988). On occasion, some of those prerequisites with respect to the price can apparently be negotiated away. And the 1987 instructions have stated that the import-substitution facility can only be accorded as a short-term solution to the balancing rule.

Reinvestment of RMB profits in a Chinese enterprise

The 1986 regulations, Article 10, allowed the foreign investor with a deficit balance to request the use of forex for the purpose of remitting profits, which, if he reinvests his RMB profits in a Chinese enterprise, in turn is capable of generating forex. This route appears to have had some success, the more that the tax gratifications granted to reinvested profits, in general, also extend to the case mentioned here. However, it assumes that a Chinese counterpart can be found who is willing to exchange forex for what is, in fact, an RMB loan. Only in circumstances in which the Chinese firm generates ample forex and/or has an interest in securing the cooperation of the foreign partner to facilitate, for example, penetration into foreign markets, is the Chinese firm – likely to consider entering into the scheme just analyzed.

Purchasing Chinese commodities for subsequent exporting

Another provision, enacted in 1986 and reconfirmed in 1987, entitles the foreign partner to forex if he purchases Chinese goods from Chinese enterprises for subsequent exporting. This idea may appeal to foreign investors with a forex deficit in their manufacturing activities, say, and who, when branching out into pure trading activities, are intent upon diversifying their export portfolio of exportable products. It took some time before the Chinese authorities were willing to adopt such mitigation of the basic rule, as they were not looking favorably upon foreign enterprises engaging in pure export trade. There are, however, rather stringent restrictions to this facility: the approval given is valid for only one year; only temporary shortfalls of forex are meant to be alleviated: the gamut of exportable commodities that qualify for this relaxation is limited and apparently mainly covers a number of goods for which an export market has not yet emerged (Frisbie 1988).

Yet this provision can be particularly helpful when a foreign partner could factor the goods thus purchased into his own production chain abroad, or fit it into its marketing channels, Thus, Pepsi-Cola is known to have bought mushrooms, various herbs, and other commodities from Chinese enterprises. Again, the difficulty consists in finding a Chinese counterpart who is willing to renounce the forex he could earn by exporting himself. The retention schemes for forex, to be discussed below in the fourth section and the premium which the possession of scarce forex affords, further reduce the eagerness of potential Chinese counterparts to accommodate the foreign partner.

Globalizing the forex earnings from multiple ventures

The 1986 Regulations allow foreign investors with multiple projects to balance the forex shortfall in one venture with an excess in another. This device was initially applied to some extent in so-called "umbrella companies," which were in fact JVs of the holding-company type that are capping several operational units; later, foreign multinationals involved in more than one joint venture benefited from this measure. This provision could also induce a firm to complement a project that suffers from a forex shortfall (say, an industrial project) with activities in which the net forex earnings can easily be generated, such as hotels. However, since September 1989 such an approach is no longer feasible and JVs must now supply their excess forex to the Foreign Exchange Adjustment Centers, to be discussed below. The drastic curtailment of the permission to build hotels is related to this measure.

THE ALLOCATION OF FOREIGN EXCHANGE AND RETENTION SCHEMES

The Dengist reforms have entailed some major changes in the mode of allocating forex to the enterprises in need of it. This aspect while related must be clearly distinguished from the forex balancing rule.

In an orthodox CME setting, all forex revenues must be remitted (by the FIC) to the appropriate financial institution, which resells them against RMB to the departments and, in the end, to the enterprises that have been designated by the planning bureaus as recipients of forex in accordance with the overall import plan.

Since reforms have been shaping up in China there have been two important modifications to the centralized allocation system (even if largely effectuated at the level of provincial or lower authority, in line with the territorial decentralization already mentioned). First, exporting Chinese firms and local authorities have been entitled to retain some forex. Besides, a free forex market of sorts, parallel to the official one (or "swap" market, as it is officially called) has emerged, in which holders of excess forex sell to parties lacking forex at a market clearing price (or "swap").

Foreign partners in JVs are not directly concerned by the retention rule as they are naturally empowered to retain all the forex they generate, otherwise the forex-balancing rule would be senseless. Yet it is worthwhile briefly explaining how the retention scheme evolved for Chinese enterprises, were it only because the latter are participants in the swap centers, to which JVs have been admitted in 1986. (For more details, see Yowell 1988.)

Forex retention rights

Already in 1979 the decision had been taken to grant the right to retain a certain percentage of forex earnings to central or provincial authorities, and to a number of large state enterprises. This could not at all be equated with a market mechanism; the allottees were not permitted to sell forex but only quotas, whereby they could buy forex against RMB subject to approval by the State Administration of Exchange Control (SAEC). Nor were there any interbank transactions in forex. The 1979 decision was essentially a move towards decentralizing forex management; by attaching the right to retain a portion of the earnings, even if the SAEC could still refuse permission, the beneficiary entities would also be encouraged to maximize their export performance.

This system was modified and substantially expanded in 1985 and 1988. It contains a great many differentiations in the retention rates, according to the sectors or the regions; they vary also in line with the degree of processing within China.

The system, in force in early 1989, can be summarized as follows:

> Typically, domestic enterprises are allowed to retain 25% of their foreign exchange earnings up to a target amount for such earnings, established for each enterprise in negotiations with the central government; the remainder is remitted to the central government. In turn, a portion of the foreign exchange retained by the enterprises has to be shared with local governments. This portion is usually 12.5%, but it can vary depending on agreements between the local authorities and individual enterprises. Enterprises are generally allowed to retain a major share of foreign exchange earnings in excess of targeted amounts
>
> (IMF 1989, p. 57)

In other words, the responsibility system, with its negotiated financial targets which are so pervasive in China's present stage of reforms, also applies to forex; the higher, above-target, retention rates are meant as an incentive to promote export endeavors.

The Foreign Exchange Adjustment Centers (FEACs)

As explained earlier, thanks to the rapid growth of the Chinese economy and the serious obstacles impeding exports, a large number of Chinese enterprises or entities are in need of forex – even if they would limit themselves to purchase only equipment and materials needed for their production processes, without indulging in speculative imports in durable consumer goods, for which there is a pent-up demand – and which have entailed some well-publicized scandals. Many Chinese–foreign JVs are unable to meet the balancing target. As against this, there are enterprises or entities which happen to have an excess of forex. Hence, naturally, the idea is to create a mechanism in which the two sides of the market could meet, thus improving the allocation of a scarce resource in the economy.

Such transactions have apparently emerged spontaneously between excess and deficit enterprises. The authorities, while allowing them, soon took control of such transactions. The conversion of RMB into, say, US or Hong Kong dollars, occurred at the official exchange rate, which soon implied a substantial overvaluation of the RMB.

A real breakthrough came in 1986, when a "Foreign Exchange Adjustment Center (FEAC)" was set up in the special economic zone of Szenshen. Since then, the number of FEACs has grown: by October 1988, there were eighty FEACs. They are still largely segregated from each other and have different trading procedures; thus in Shanghai forex is auctioned off. Steps are envisaged to link the centers nation-wide so that this forex market would gain depth and breadth.

Originally, only JV enterprises (in the broad Chinese definition discussed earlier) participated in this so-called swap market. Early in 1988 all Chinese enterprises, enjoying forex retention rights, could join. This factor may largely explain the substantial growth in the amount of market transactions, from a mere US$30 million in the first quarter of 1987, to US$1,860 million in the second quarter of 1988 (IMF 1989).

The exchange rate which soon emerged displayed a serious depreciation of the RMB against the US dollar and other currencies. The accelerating inflation rate in 1988 obviously eroded the purchasing power of the RMB, besides, as enterprises enjoying forex retention quotes, will not put all of it in the FEAC market (Nianlu Wu 1988). The Chinese government until recently has kept to the official exchange rate of 3.72 RMB to US$1, lest the rise in import prices would further fuel the socially-disruptive domestic price rise. Accordingly, the forex prices that have been noticed on the parallel FEAC, despite the latter's small scale, give a more reliable indication of the real value of the RMB.[5]

It might also be viewed as a first step towards convertibility for the RMB – an objective which is nowadays frantically pursued by all reforming CMEs in Eastern Europe, including the CIS – as they realize that the present official forex rates are ludicrously unrealistic so that, contrary to Gresham's law, good money (dollars or DM) drives out bad money (zlotys or roubles) and that only eventual convertibility with its reliable price signals will allow their economies to become part of the international trading arena.

One should add that the rate on the FEAC also depends on factors other than the demand and supply of forex within China. Thus, the gyrations of the US dollar against other major convertible currencies influence the latter. Besides, early in 1989 the dollar price declined somewhat as, faced with a dearth of RMB resources as a result of the severe credit squeeze, a number of enterprises have taken the return route and converted available forex for RMB.

ASSESSMENT

The record of incoming foreign direct investment

From 1979 to the end of September 1989 the Chinese authorities approved 20,278 foreign-funded enterprises, involving an anticipated investment of US$32.17 billion, of which US$14 billion has actually been inputted. There were 11,286 equity joint ventures, 7,713 cooperative ventures, and 1,230 solely foreign-owned enterprises (*China Economic News*, February 12, 1990). It is worth noting that most of the 100 percent-held foreign projects have been approved during 1989: the difficult balance-of-payments situation and the desire to counteract the reluctance of foreign firms to become more immersed in China has apparently led the Chinese authorities to broaden the possibility for solely-owned ventures from abroad.

These are, in themselves, rather impressive figures and in a very short while China has become a major member of the league of host countries to the FDI; although some other CMEs in Europe, before the dramatic turn of events in the fall of 1989, had already taken steps to allow foreign investment through the JV channel (such as Romania and, long ago, Yugoslavia, a maverick in the Communist camp), the opening of China to inward direct investment has been truly rapid, the more that it signalled a significant change in policies and attitudes. It has involved the promulgation of approximately 100 laws and regulations over the 1982–7 period (UNCTC 1988, p. 276) – a noticeable event in a country which had forsaken legal procedures during the cultural revolution and in which the discretionary powers of the Party secretary or the Emperor's mandarin traditionally tended to prevail over enforceable laws that protect the citizens.

Relative shortfall against expectations

Yet the number of JVs in their various forms and the amounts invested so far must be related to the huge size of China, and the vast potentialities anticipated by foreign companies when the "opening policy" was first announced.

It is fair to say that expectations of Chinese leaders, when inviting foreign enterprises to join with Chinese firms, have not been fully borne out – even when accounting for the time required for finalizing negotiations on large projects, and although the Chinese government has displayed a high degree of flexibility and allowed foreign enterprises to voice their frustrations and complaints, as happened for example at a seminar convened by the United Nations Centre for Transnational Corporations (1985).

From the statements of some leaders one gauges that they were somewhat disappointed not only by the inadequate quantity of investments but also by its concentration on the service sector (hotels) and comparatively low technology sectors.

A great many foreign investors have also become disillusioned after the initial burst of enthusiasm. Various irritations, such as the tendency on the Chinese side to reopen an issue, or the persistence of interference by bureaus, despite legal prescriptions to the contrary, and more generally the differences in cultural values and attitudes, have rendered the task of foreign investors much more difficult and less profitable than had been hoped for. This is not to deny that a number of large foreign firms appear, on balance, to be satisfied with their operations, were it only because it is not conceivable not to be present in a country with more than one billion inhabitants.

The disillusions on both sides are in fact basically rooted in divergent basic objectives and perceptions. China is interested primarily in securing more up-to-date technology and know-how, not in sharing the potentially immense Chinese market with foreign firms. The insistence on forex balance is also viewed by the Chinese authorities as an inducement for foreign partners to engage in the production of components; and even of capital equipment within China (UNCTC 1987). This then is the Chinese version of the "domestic content rule," which a number of developing countries impose on foreign direct investors with the objective of deepening their industrial structure. On the other hand, foreign investors are intent upon conquering a share of that promising market.

The forex balancing constraint

The balance between favorable and adverse parameters of the "investment climate" in China was probably not inferior to that of a great many developing countries: the Tiananmen Square tragedy in June 1989 and the lingering uncertainties about China's future political course, despite the claims of the present leadership that the country is again stable, have substantially reduced the propensity of foreign investors to install production within China. The drastic deflationary measures that were taken in China[6] have also harmed the prospects for foreign investors, although the present leadership has confirmed its intention to maintain the open-door policy, and has taken some measures to improve, in some respects, the regulatory framework for inward FDI.[7] The depressed demand in China, no doubt, negatively affects their short-term prospects for sales within China.

The forex balancing prescription, however, is widely and generally indicted as a major constraint on operations in the PRC; it has restrained many would-be investors from entering the Chinese scene, and has led others to restrict their involvement to small investments of the "bridgehead" type.

Developing countries – and even industrial ones in some instances (witness Canada and Japan) until recently – attempt to maximize the net benefits from inward FDI, although it is very difficult to estimate the benefits and costs. They typically wave both the "carrot" (incentives) and the "stick" (various restraining measures).

Amongst the latter, out of a large spectrum, one may mention the "domestic content rule," which imposes upon investors the obligation to source an often high percentage of value added locally, i.e., to secure inputs from suppliers in the host country. Other countries, especially in Latin America, have limited the repatriation of profits to a specified percentage of the equity invested, thus encouraging the plough-back of profits within the subsidiary. A few countries disallow the payment of fees by the local subsidiaries to the foreign parent company. The gamut of restrictions applicable in developing countries is a variegated one, indeed, as is the spectrum of incentives.

In all fairness, one should add that most developing countries are faced with an intractable balance-of-payments problem. Unable to earn adequate forex for their potentially immense import needs, they are led to operate a battery of restrictions on import trade and on external payments; this is even more the case when they are burdened with substantial debts in hard currencies.

The forex-balancing obligation, on the other hand, is a rare occurrence. "There are only two others that allow FDI but impose a balancing requirement for foreign exchange [Egypt and Yugoslavia]. The requirement has worked very badly in both countries, having been abandoned in Egypt and frequently modified, without success, in Yugoslavia" (World Bank 1988a, p. 272). As already mentioned, a similar rule today governs JVs in the CIS.

The basic reason for this negative assessment has already been discussed: the balancing rule discourages would-be investors, who see little possibility of generating sufficient net foreign exchange out of the venture contemplated, unless they would commit large amounts of their home or other convertible currencies to it.

Foreign firms understandably attach major importance to the possibility of repatriating a substantial portion of their earnings in the host-country currencies and converting them in their home-country currency, even if during the initial years they are willing to reinvest a major portion of their profits in the subsidiary. This insistence on the unhampered repatriation of profits is voiced even when the two currencies involved are convertible ones; as a matter of fact, in a highly-multinationalized company, the foreign subsidiaries must contribute towards the overall pool of earnings, which serves to remunerate the shareholders of the parent company and to allocate investment funds for the projects that hold the promise of maximum returns (Plasschaert 1985).

The repatriation of profits is even more vital when the affiliates are operating in countries with an inconvertible currency – as is the case for the RMB. Such currencies are worthless outside the country itself; often, their official parity grossly overvalues the domestic currency, as suggested both by purchasing parity indicators and by prices on black (illegal), gray (tolerated), or officially-permitted parallel forex markets (as in the swap markets in China). Hence, the possibility to repatriate return from foreign ventures (profit proper interests on advances by the parent company and fees for the use of know-how) is a major ingredient in the perception by foreign investors as regards the investment climate in a host country. Even in a potentially large market, such as Brazil, India, or China, the prospect of having to reinvest the local currency returns is at best a second-best option.

Alternatives to the foreign balancing rule?

The forex balancing rule, even with its string of relaxations, discussed above, does seem to inhibit inward investments into JVs in China, especially as regards sectors that embody advanced technology and in which the prospects of exportable output are dim.

One alternative approach, widely used in a great many developing countries (see IMF 1985), consists in allowing approved foreign investors to repatriate their profits without restrictions, or in a given proportion (except as a percentage of the equity). Such commitment is often enshrined in bilateral treaties with countries in which the parent company is headquartered. The outflow of such remunerations on the investments should be weighed by the host government against the incoming flow of new direct investment capital, and the other advantages in terms of technology transfer and the strengthening of the industrial structure which FDI most often allows, even if foreign investors (whether operating through JVs or their 100 percent subsidiaries) are in a position to conquer a solid niche in the local market. Experience has shown that such positioning is often a bridgehead to approach, at a later stage, foreign export markets.

The World Bank (1988a), and its affiliate the IFC, favor for China the further expansion and strengthening of the "swap" markets. One major drawback of the present dual system is that the foreign investors bring forex for use in China, which has to be converted at the official exchange rate, whereas the investor can only acquire additional forex through the swap market at a premium. The World Bank rightly sees the institution of a swapmarket, hopefully to be expanded to an all-China perimeter, as a first but essential step towards eventual full convertibility for the RMB.

It is doubtful, however, that China is in position to move quickly towards full convertibility, although there are obvious merits with the latter. As events in Eastern Europe have shown, the move to convertibility is one of the vectors of the fundamental and difficult changeover from a CME to a market-economy setting. Other prerequisites must therefore be fulfilled, more particularly the reform of the highly skewed system of relative prices. The country itself must preferably enjoy a rather easy balance-of-payments position. Unless, as in Poland, the decision is taken to plunge overnight – and in one jump – into the market economy; or unless, as in East Germany, there is no other option than to achieve a monetary and economic union with the natural partner in West Germany. In China and despite the recent devaluation of the RMB (by 21.2 percent on December 12, 1989), conditions – and not the least the political prerequisite of the abandonment of the power position of the party and the planning bureaus – are not yet ripe for the advent of an advanced degree of convertibility.[8]

NOTES

1 "Currently, China maintains a managed floating exchange system, whereby the exchange rate for the renminbi (RMB) is based on developments in the balance of payments and movements in costs and exchange rates in China's major trading partners. The US dollar is the intervention currency. In practice, adjustments in the rate for the renminbi *vis-à-vis* the US dollar tend to be made infrequently . . ." (World Bank 1988a).

2 Holzman's findings must be qualified on two counts: first, recently East European countries, caught in the maelstrom of systemic reform, no longer hesitate to devalue their currency (neither did China). Besides, central planning in the PRC was notably never as taut as in Soviet Russia.

3 These restrictions on exports are linked both to the scarcity of raw materials – when, until recently, the Chinese economy was growing rapidly – and to the traditionally low domestic prices on such commodities, as fixed by the planning bureaus, so that producers prefer to look for export outlets.

4 A great many producers of shoes have recently relocated from Taiwan to mainland sites.

5 Local and provincial governments, in the present state of forex scarcity, are reluctant to bring excess funds to the FEACs; this is another instance of the widely noticed provincial protectionism.

6 Even if the reformist camp had prevailed against the present hardliners, the unsustainable rapid growth would have to be restrained. The instruments used thereto, however, would have been less bureaucratic than today, although mechanisms of indirect macro-control are still notoriously inadequate.

7 Amongst such recent measures, figures the pledge not to nationalize foreign ventures. This article was written in 1990.

8 Since 1991, and definitely since the beginning of 1992, inward investments have been booming. The endorsement of the open door policy by the paramount leader Deng Xiao Peng, during his visit to Shenzen, and other parts in the South, has played a major signalling function.

REFERENCES AND BIBLIOGRAPHY

Easson, A.J. (1989) "Contractual, co-operative and equity joint ventures in the People's Republic of China," *Review of International Business Law*, pp. 145–72.

Frisbie, J. (1988) "Balancing foreign exchange," *China Business Review* (March–April), pp. 24–8.

Gelatt, A. (1986) "The foreign exchange quandary," *China Business Review* (May–June), pp. 28–30.

Holzman, F. (1979) "Some systemic factors contributing to the convertible currency shortages of centrally planned economies," *American Economic Review* (May), pp. 76–80.

International Finance Corporation (1988) "Foreign direct investment. Foreign exchange balance and joint venture balance," mimeo.

International Monetary Fund (1985) "Foreign private investment in developing countries," occasional paper 33, January.

International Monetary Fund (1989) "People's Republic of China – recent economic developments," mimeo, January.

Plasschaert, S. (1985) "Transfer pricing problems in developing countries," in A. Rugman and L. Eden (eds), *Multinationals and Transfer Pricing*, Beckenham: Croom Helm.

United Nations Centre on Transnational Corporations (1987) "Report on the round-table on foreign direct investment," Beijing, mimeo.

United Nations Centre on Transnational Corporations (1988) "Transnational corporations in world development. Trends and prospects."

World Bank (1988a) "China: Finance and development."

World Bank (1988b) "China: External trade and capital."

Winiecki, J. (1988) "Central planning and export orientation in manufactures. Theoretical considerations on the impact of system-specific features *on* specialization," *Notes Monte dei Paschi di Siena*, pp. 133–53.

Wu, Nianlu (1988) "Evolution of China's forex market," *Intertrade*, April, pp. 75–7.

Yowell, D. (1988) "Swap center system to expand," *China Business Review* (September–October), pp. 10–12.

Zafar, Shah Khan (1981) "Patterns of direct foreign investment in China," World Bank Discussion papers.

6 Economic reform and foreign direct investment in China before and after the Tiananmen Square tragedy

K.K. Seo

Since initiating new economic policies in the late 1970s. China has pursued the twin objectives of economic reform and expansion of international economic ties through their "open-door policy." Since then, China's economic achievements have been phenomenal.

As shown on Exhibit 6.1, China's annual GNP growth rate averaged 9.1 percent during the decade 1980–90. This remarkable growth took place at a time when US growth was standing still and the growth rates of most other countries were declining. According to a recent study by the Rand Corporation, the Chinese economy is predicted to continue growing at a rate of about 4.5 percent annually through the coming decade 1991–2000.[1] This is a high rate of growth, although not quite so high as expected by the newly industrialized economies of Hong Kong, Korea, Singapore, and Taiwan, referred to hereafter as the NIEs, or by countries in the Association of South East Asian Nations, specifically, Indonesia, Malaysia, the Philippines, and Thailand, referred to hereafter as ASEAN-4.

Exhibit 6.1. GNP growth rates in various nations, 1970–2000 (percent/year)

Area	1970–80	1980–90	1990–2000
United States	2.8	2.8	2.6
Japan	4.7	3.9	3.0
Asian NIEs and ASEAN-4	7.9	6.2	5.3
China	5.5	9.1	4.6
West Germany	2.7	1.8	2.1
France	3.6	1.7	2.8

Source: Adapted from Yeh, Sze, and Levin, "The changing Asian economic environment and US–Japan trade relations," Santa Monica: Rand Corporation, R-3986-CUSCJR, September 1990, p. 7. The 1980–90 growth rates are based on historical data from 1980–8 and projections for 1989–1990.

Much of China's success in stimulating economic growth over the past decade can be attributed to the expansion of foreign loans and foreign direct investment (FDI), the concomitant transfer of technology to China. China's development, however, has not been without problems. These include overheating of the economy because aggregate demand exceeded aggregate supply, structural problems, lack of adequate infrastructure, imbalances in key economic resources such as energy, and a large government deficit. All these problems contributed to severe problems with inflation, beginning in the latter part of 1987.

In the latter part of 1988, the government adopted a policy of retrenchment designed to combat inflation. Unfortunately, the Tiananmen Square incident of June 1989 caused the suspension of many foreign loans and disrupted the flow of foreign direct investment in China. At present, the government is trying to blend elements of central planning with some form of market system into an economic structure that may support stable, coordinated growth while avoiding the dramatic boom/bust cycles of the past decade, mainly by means of monetary and credit constraints.

In order to attract investments of foreign capital and to accelerate technology transfer, China has reaffirmed their open-door policy by including it in the five-year and ten-year plans adopted at the National People's Congress in March 1991.

To analyze a number of questions about the Chinese economy's ability to sustain the high growth rates attained in the past decade, this chapter tries to provide an overview of China's economic progress and problems during their economic reform that started in 1979. It examines the stimulating and restraining factors that may govern the Chinese economy's growth or lack thereof, with particular emphasis on some of the problems China has been having in attracting foreign investment. The paper is divided into discussions of four major topics:

- China's open-door policy and foreign trade;
- retrenchment policy: causes and consequences;
- economic effects of the Tiananmen Square tragedy;
- China's difficulties in attracting foreign direct investment.

CHINA'S OPEN-DOOR POLICY AND FOREIGN TRADE

At the third plenum of the Eleventh Party Congress, which was held in December 1978, Deng Ziaoping convinced the other Party leaders that economic reform was necessary and persuaded them to adopt an open-door policy designed to propel China into the front rank of industrialized countries. Deng claimed that China must actively cultivate mutual and equitable relationships with the rest of the world. He said that China must make every effort to advanced technology while still maintaining the long-held socialist principle of self-reliance. Such action would not contradict the principle of self-reliance, Deng said, because in the long run it would enable China to become more self-reliant.[2]

One of the reasons China had remained backward for so many years, said Deng, was their lack of contact with the rest of the world. Their door must be opened in order to acquire foreign capital and technology.[3]

Under the Deng doctrine, the Chinese officials view foreign trade as an "instituted process" in which international exchanges are government controlled and manipulated to achieve specific objectives. Their foreign-trade policy is one of "import-led" growth, which may be contrasted with the "export-led" growth of other nations in which the international marketplace shapes their futures. In the Chinese system of foreign trade, the government controls both imports and exports. They restrict imports to those items that will further the socialist goal of self-sufficiency while also promoting modernization of the nation. After determining the cost of the desired imports, the government directs the production of goods for export sufficient to pay for the imports.

Foreign trade before reform

The leaders of pre-reform China had been strongly impressed by the apparent success of the Soviet Union in industrializing a primarily agricultural economy over the relatively short period of forty years, without any significant outside assistance. Therefore the Chinese leaders adopted an inward-looking development strategy modeled after the Soviet Union. Foreign trade had a passive role in China's development strategy. It was an integral part of their ten-year plans, but only to the extent that it served to make up shortfalls in China's own production. The level of imports was determined by projected shortages, and the planned level of exports was just sufficient to provide the foreign currency necessary to finance the planned level of imports. Thus China ignored the fundamental economic principle of the comparative advantage of foreign trade.

China's development strategy placed primary emphasis on development of heavy industry rather than production of consumer goods.

By pursuing this strategy of heavy industrialization, China has succeeded in building a well-diversified industrial structure. In comparison to many, if not most, of the developing countries, China produces a far greater variety of industrial goods and depends far less on imported equipment and other capital goods. China's technical and scientific capabilities are evident in a range of ventures from putting satellites in orbit to design, construction, and operation of nuclear power plants.

On the down side, however, is the fact that these achievements have been attained at very high cost, and China is not industrially competitive in either cost or quality of its products. Moreover, most of the public sector industries have yielded little or no return on the resources invested in them. Since they have been shielded from competition, the managers of the protected capital goods industries have not had the opportunity to accumulate the dynamic learning experience that is necessary to bring about significant technological improvements in either their processes or their products.

Foreign trade after reform

Although both imports and exports have increased, not much has changed in China's basic attitude toward foreign trade. It is still import driven; that is to say, the Chinese government determines what shall be imported and how much, and then directs sufficient exports to provide foreign currency to pay for the authorized imports. China's foreign trade thus has three major objectives:[4]

1 The primary objective is to acquire advanced technology and capital equipment for modernization of their industries. There is a widely-held belief among Chinese economists and political leaders that China's deficiency in economic development is primarily due to its outmoded production technology. They believe that the use of foreign technology is a short-cut to technological modernization of their industries. Consequently, the first priority in foreign trade is the importation of advanced technology and capital equipment.

2 The second objective is to ensure that the nation has adequate supplies of food, especially food grains, raw materials, and certain intermediate goods that are inadequately supplied by domestic production.

3 The third objective is to increase the country's ability to earn foreign exchange.

In pursuit of these objectives, the Chinese government controls imports so that only capital goods and "necessary" consumer goods are brought into the country. To obtain the foreign exchange for payment for these imports, the government directs selected government-run enterprises to expand their exports and encourages provincially-run and collective enterprises to obtain export licenses to compete in the global market.

Thus we see that even under reform, their underlying philosophy is to maintain the long-held socialist principle of self-reliance. This means that their "open door" is not really open–it is only cracked a little way. This is what sets China apart from the other developing nations of Asia, and will undoubtedly hinder their economic progress in years to come.

Implementation of reform strategies

China's modernization program began in 1978 with the importation of large-scale plants from foreign countries. China soon realized, however, that the country lacked export industries to earn the foreign exchange needed to pay for the imported plants, and further lacked a stable supply of energy necessary for their operation. Consequently, their development strategy shifted in 1979 from the development of heavy industry to the use of foreign capital and technology for development of light manufacturing and service industries. The new policy recognized that light manufacturing and service industries could make better use of China's abundance of cheap labor while producing exportable goods capable of earning foreign exchange.

The new policy was codified in the Joint Venture Law of 1979. Under this law, China plans to develop six major classes of industry:

1 production of energy, construction materials, and chemicals;
2 manufacture of machinery and offshore oil exploration equipment;
3 manufacture of electronic goods, computers, and telecommunications equipment;
4 manufacture of lighting fixtures and equipment, textiles, food products, and medical equipment;
5 agriculture and animal husbandry;
6 tourism and service.

The Joint Venture Law also prescribes four conditions that joint ventures with foreign investors must satisfy:

1 they must utilize advanced technology and scientific management in ways that enhance product quality with maximum output and minimum use of energy and materials;
2 they must export all or most of their products in order to generate foreign exchange for China;
3 they must contribute to technological improvement, making large returns with a minimum level of investment;
4 they must train Chinese managers and engineers.

The Chinese government's trade and foreign investment policies reflect a basic lack of understanding of what it takes to motivate trading partners and foreign investors. These outsiders are motivated by the fundamental economic principle of comparative advantage and look upon trade as a two-way street. If it costs less to manufacture goods in China than somewhere else, outside investors are quite willing to provide capital resources and know-how to do so, but they are also inclined to want access to China's markets for both industrial and consumer goods. China's policies, however, are clearly designed to provide maximum benefit for China with little or no consideration for trading partners or foreign investors. This has led to rising trade frictions with their principal trading partners, Japan and the United States, particularly after the Tiananmen Square tragedy. That event seemed to be a turning back of reform, and completed the growing disillusionment with the Chinese regime of many foreign investors. This made international loans hard to get. China needs to modify its policies and attitudes toward foreign direct investment, which is becoming increasingly important to the Chinese development plans.

RETRENCHMENT POLICY: CAUSES AND CONSEQUENCES

Between 1984 and 1988, when China's national income rose by 70 percent, there was an increase of 214 percent in the total capital investment in fixed assets, and a 200 percent increase in the cash income of rural and urban residents.[5] In 1988 alone, China's industrial output increased by 17.7 percent over 1987, and the gross national product (GNP) rose by 9.6 percent, a sign of overheating of the economy.[6]

The overheating of the economy caused a shortage of raw materials, electricity, and working capital, and caused many industrial enterprises to cut production. In order to dampen the increasing dissatisfaction of urban workers with their declining real wages resulting from inflation, the government had to increase nominal wages by means of a budget deficit and an increasing money supply, thus quickening the inflationary spiral. The rate of inflation continued to rise in late 1988 and the rise accelerated in the first half of 1989. An official inflation rate of 18.5 percent was reported for 1988. The rise in food prices, however, exceeded 50 percent, and the Chinese people engaged in panic-buying in the spring and summer of 1988.

The retrenchment program adopted by the Chinese government at the third plenary session of the thirteenth Central Committee of the Chinese Communist Party, which was held in September 1988, was supposed to bring inflation below 10 percent in 1989 and 1990 by reducing investment and money supply, and selectively controlling credit. The sudden switch to a tight money policy, the reduction of credit, the increasing interest rates, and the reduction of loan guarantees, threw the economy into chaos.

In the first nine months of 1989, industrial output rose over the same period in 1988, but only by 8.9 percent. In October 1989, output fell sharply and the industrial growth rate was a negative 2.1 percent, the first decline in ten years. Taking alarm at the rapid deterioration of industrial output, the government decided to pump 100 billion yuan (US$22.2 billion) of new credit into the industrial system. But most of the state enterprises used the funds to pay their assigned taxes. This provided very little relief to the credit crunch and exacerbated the liquidity crisis.[7]

In a period of approximately fourteen months from late 1988 to January 1990:

1 output of the machine-tool industry declined 13.8 percent;
2 production of motor vehicles fell 11 percent;
3 production of tractors dropped 8.3 percent;
4 shipbuilding output fell 23 percent;
5 twenty percent of China's textile capacity was idled;
6 output of color television sets dropped 9.6 percent.

In January 1990, total industrial output dropped 6.1 percent from 1989. This was the worst monthly decline since Deng Xiaoping introduced economic reform eleven years before. The slump continued into February 1990, after which a slow recovery began in March and April when the government pumped 25 billion yuan (US$5.3 billion) more in new loans into the industrial system.[8]

China's goal for industrial growth in 1990 was set at only 6 percent, but they were unable to reach even this relatively modest goal. The retrenchment program idled millions of workers and sent several million construction laborers back to the countryside, thus creating serious social problems. This was the cost of cooling-off the over-heated economy and of taming rampant inflation.

Inflation in the Chinese economy: Causes and effects

Other developing countries, such as Taiwan and Korea in the 1960s and 1970s, have learned to live with high rates of inflation that seem to accompany a rapidly developing economy. Why couldn't China learn to live with it for the sake of rapid industrial development? What are the sources of China's inflation and why did China adopt such a drastic retrenchment policy?

The causes of inflation

The high rates of inflation in 1988 and 1989 have emerged from certain inherent defects in the Chinese economy, as well as from flawed government policy and actions. Some of the root causes of inflation are:

1. *Easy money policy.* From mid-1986, credits expanded at growth rate of 20–25 percent per annum, which greatly exceeded the growth rate of industrial production. Thus the aggregate demand greatly exceeded the aggregate supply, thereby driving up prices.

2. *Imbalance of production.* Increases in the supply of goods have not taken place across the board; rather, they have been imbalanced such that shortages have developed in some sectors and have rapidly pushed up prices. A chronic imbalance has developed not only in industrial goods and raw materials, but also in consumer goods and services.

3. *Bottleneck problems.* Chronic shortages of energy, communications services, and transportation services place upward pressure on prices of these basic requirements for industrialization.

4. *Decentralization of the economy.* In 1980, China's economy was decentralized to the local government level. This constituted a major reduction of the central government's revenue base,[9] and the central government turned to their banking system to provide funds for expansion of their infrastructure. The additional bank credit extended to central government projects exacerbated the problem of excess demand.

5. *Problems with agriculture.* Agriculture was the great success story of the early years of economic reform. The growth rate of agricultural output doubled after 1978, culminating in the remarkable bumper crop of 1984. Since then, however, growth in overall

agricultural output has grown very slowly, and grain production has never surpassed the 1984 record. Problems in the agricultural sector have been threefold:

1 Peasants living in the suburban areas of large cities prefer the higher paying jobs in industry to growing food. Consequently, there is actually a shortage of farm labor.
2 Higher incomes have led to greater demand for food and non-staple items. Rapidly growing demand coupled with sluggish growth in supply created rapid price increases. For example, at the beginning of 1988, urban farm market prices were increasing at the rate of 20 percent per annum.
3 Economic reform has failed to put procurement of agricultural products on a market basis. In 1984, a major attempt was made to replace compulsory procurement (i.e., compulsory production) of staples such as grain, edible oils, and cotton with a system of market-based contracts. Growth in production, however, continued to lag behind growth in demand. Under such pressure, the contracts gradually became compulsory, and China's agricultural output is still controlled by government edict rather than the law of supply and demand.

6. *The dual-track pricing system.* Efforts to convert procurement of staples into a market-based system, as described in the preceding paragraph, were accompanied by efforts to transform the entire economy into a market-based system. The Chinese government's vehicle for this reform was the dual-track pricing system which was introduced in 1984. Under this system, items had two prices, one a controlled price established by the state, and the other a free-market price established by the law of supply and demand.

The underlying concept of the two-track system was that when free-market prices were stabilized, controlled prices would be gradually increased until they reached the level of free-market prices. The scheme might have worked except for inflation, which kept pushing up the free-market prices, while controlled prices tended to remain the same.[10]

The main problem with the two-track system is the built-in rigidity of controlled prices over a long period of time. These price rigidities made the problem of curing inflation especially difficult. Inflation can be combated only by policies that modify the relationship between supply and demand in the direction of greater supply and/or smaller demand. In the free-market sector, if either supply or demand is changed, price is directly and quickly affected. If prices are rising because of increasing demand, a sufficient rollback of demand can roll back the increase of free-market prices. In the controlled-price sector, however, prices are set by government decree and are not free to respond to changes in demand. Therefore, if demand decreases, equilibrium of supply and demand at the controlled price can be obtained only by cutting production.

Unfortunately, the existence of two prices for the same commodity constituted a built-in invitation to corruption. Those in a position of power who were able to buy goods at state-controlled prices and then resell them at free-market prices could profit handsomely, and many did so.

The effects of inflation

Inflation has been a significant factor in the Chinese economy since 1985, when the urban cost-of-living index rose by 11.9 percent. Inflation was held to 8 percent in 1986 and 1987. In the latter part of 1987, however, inflation began a rapid climb, and was out of control by mid-1988. In November 1988, the urban cost-of-living index had risen 30 points over the previous year.

Keeping pace with such rapid change was too much for China's unwieldy bureaucratic system. State employee compensation could not be changed fast enough to cope with the rising prices, and profound discontent was the result. In May 1988, General Secretary Zhao Ziyang, with the backing of Deng Ziaoping, proposed decontrolling all prices in order to obtain a market equilibrium. The Chinese people responded by panic-buying and a run on the banks. The government then rescinded the policy and gave economic decision-making power to Prime Minister Li Peng and Yao Yilin, who was until recently the chairman of the State Planning Commission.

Price controls were immediately reimposed on aluminium, copper, steel, and other basic materials. As the policy continued into 1989, restrictions on credit began to sharply reduce growth rates of industrial production. At about the same time, cutbacks in investments began to materialize, particularly investments requiring new construction. This was especially hard on construction workers who lived in the country but worked temporarily on construction projects in the cities. China's official estimates were that ten million such workers would have to return to the country, and that urban unemployment would also climb.[11]

The anti-inflationary policies begun in September, 1988 led to significant economic difficulties in the first quarter of 1989. These difficulties called for effective and highly interventionist policies, but these led to the eruption of a full-scale social crisis in May 1989. After June 4, 1989, central government officials reasserted control over major segments of the Chinese economy, including the creation of credit by the banking system. The deputy director of the State Planning Commission, Fan Weizhong, has announced that the process of retrenchment would include restoration of central planning.[12] Apparently, the new policy includes control of private and rural collective investments that had previously been outside of central planning.

China's retrenchment plan has slowed but not completely broken the inflationary spiral. Urban residents had been suffering declining standards of living for two consecutive years, and this caused the government to raise food subsidies to about 40 billion yuan (US$11 billion) per year. This is the largest item in their budget. The food situation has been eased somewhat by 1990's record grain harvest, but the Chinese economy still faces many severe problems, such as:[13]

1. *Critical and chronic shortage of energy and strategic raw materials.* These shortages constitute an insurmountable bottleneck to industrial growth.

2. *Increasing debt of the central government.* Subsidies to money-losing enterprises (about two-thirds of an estimated 100,000 state enterprises are losers) and to maintain low consumer prices, and increasing military expenditures require deficit financing.

3. *Chronic imbalance between supply and demand.* China's most fundamental economic problem is the chronic and growing imbalance between aggregate supply and aggregate demand. During the five years 1983–8, there was exponential growth in investments, but also in consumption. The net result was a gap between aggregate supply and aggregate demand which widened from 26.5 billion yuan (US$7.3 billion) in 1983 to 224.3 billion yuan (US$61.6 billion) in 1988. This gap was the root of the raging inflation during the same period.[14] Although the gap narrowed somewhat in 1989, it still left the economy with 80 billion yuan (US$22 billion) in domestic debt, US$42 billion in foreign debt, and 700 billion yuan (US$188 billion) of surplus purchasing power held by individuals in savings deposits, cash, and bonds.[15]

ECONOMIC EFFECTS OF THE TIANANMEN SQUARE TRAGEDY

China's economic difficulties were exacerbated by the tragic events in Tiananmen Square in June 1989. The immediate economic consequences of the military crackdown on dissident students and civilians were fivefold:

1 foreign loans were suspended;
2 foreign direct investment commitments were cancelled;
3 revenue from tourism was drastically reduced;
4 there was a sharp rise in China's budget deficit;
5 China's reformist leaders were purged.

Suspension of foreign loans

The first major consequence of the Tiananmen Square tragedy was worldwide economic sanctions. In reaction to the way that military force was used to crush student dissent, Western governments and aid agencies restricted or delayed new loans to China. This was a severe blow to the nation, which is starving for foreign capital and technical know-how to build basic infrastructure. For example, some of China's needs had been met with loans from the World Bank, which in eight years had provided China with US$8.5 billion, of which US$3.44 billion had been loaned interest-free. About one-third of these loans had been used for agricultural and industrial development. On June 27, 1989, the World Bank announced the suspension of US$780 million in new loans. Another example was the Japanese government's decision, in June 1989, to postpone a new seven-year loan of US$5.8 billion.[16]

Cancellation of foreign direct investment

Before the Tiananmen massacre, China had enjoyed a thirty-month boom in foreign direct investment. Starting in January 1987, the number of direct investment contracts signed by June 1989 had increased by 400 percent, and the value of those contracts had grown by 67 percent. The military crackdown, however, signaled that China was reverting to the old system, and the foreign investors' confidence in the economic restructuring of the new China rapidly wasted away.[17]

It is true that most investors decided to stay in China, but very few of them risked the commitment of new funds. For example, Peugeot SA and Pepsi-Cola, Inc. both had planned expansions of their joint-venture factories in southern China, but decided to postpone the additional investment. Five Fortune-500 companies of the United States had planned to invest a total of US$650 million in China, but the deteriorating economic and political outlook caused four of the five companies to cancel their plans. Japanese investors also pulled back to the extent that Japanese companies invested no more than half of the US$200 million invested in 1988.

Reduction of tourism

In 1987–8, before the Tiananmen incident, China's rapidly growing tourist industry was earning about US$2.2 billion per year. About one million Taiwanese and several million Hong Kong residents and other overseas Chinese were visiting their hometowns in China every year, thus providing a crucial source of foreign exchange. China had been expecting one million visitors during the last six months of 1989. Instead they experienced an 81 percent drop in the number of visitors. Their target for 1989 had been an increase in revenues to US$3 billion. Instead, tourism revenues were only US$1.8 billion.[18]

Increase of the budget deficit

For ten years before the Tiananmen incident, an army reduction plan had been in effect whereby in each year the growth rate for military expenditures was less than the growth rate for total government expenditures. Consequently, the defense budget's share of the total budget dropped from 26.1 percent in 1968 to 17.5 percent in 1979, and then to only 8.6 percent in 1986.

The Tiananmen incident demonstrated the government's need to rely upon army support. Military leaders, who had been angered by previous cuts in the military budget, were once again able to demand and get a larger share of the total budget. In 1989, the defense budget rose to 13.9 percent of the total, which was an increase of 11.2 percent over their 1988 budget. The defense budget increased an additional 15.5 percent in 1990. This reversed the ten-year decline in defense funding, but widened the budget deficit. Despite the projected deficit, the 1991 defense budget increased by another 12 percent. These increases are widely perceived as a reward to the army for cracking down in 1989 on the dissident students in Tiananmen Square.

Purge of imaginative leadership

After the Tiananmen incident, most of the leaders who had championed economic reform were purged. Prominent economists and social scientists who understood the necessity for reform were either exiled or forced to rusticate. Thus the country lost the services of its best minds. The current leaders of China seem unable to do more than repeat the failed policies that were implemented in the 1950s and 1960s.

CHINA'S DIFFICULTIES IN ATTRACTING FOREIGN DIRECT INVESTMENT

China's efforts to attract foreign direct investment date back to December 1978, when Deng Ziaoping initiated an open-door policy designed to propel China into the front rank of industrialized nations. Deng's "open door" means open to foreign direct investment and consequent transfer of technology for development of China's industry and economy. Since then, China's eagerness to attract foreign direct investment was indicated by a series of changes that included establishment in 1984 of additional economic zones in the coastal regions and the promulgation by the State Council in October 1986 of the "22 Guidelines" for encouragement of foreign investment.

In a major speech before the National People's Congress held in March 1991, Premier Li Peng reaffirmed China's open-door policy. Apparently, the Chinese rulers still consider that infusion of foreign capital is necessary for accomplishment of their economic goals. Despite all their efforts in this direction, however, foreign capital did not flow in freely. Most notably, China has not been very successful in obtaining commitments from Japanese and American investors, although there has been a continuing increase in investments from Hong Kong and a dramatic increase in investments in Fujian and Xiamen provinces by Taiwanese interests in 1988 and 1989.

The major foreign investors in China

There are four main sources of foreign direct investment in China: Hong Kong, the United States, Japan, and Taiwan. For the years 1979–90, Hong Kong's direct investments in China are estimated to be about US$25 billion. This is a little over 63 percent of the estimated total foreign direct investments of US$39.5 billion. During the same period, the United States was the second largest investor with about 11 percent, Japan was third with about 7.5 percent of the total. Taiwan is an interesting newcomer which began investing in China in 1987. Taiwan's investments amount to a little under 2 percent of the total. As shown on Exhibit 6.2, Japan's share of the

Exhibit 6.2 Cumulative foreign direct investment in China by the United States, Japan, and Taiwan, 1987–90 (In millions of US dollars)

	1987	*1988*	*1989*	*1990*
Total foreign direct investment to China	19,100	26,000	33,000	39,500
Percent of total	(100)	(100)	(100)	(100)
From Hong Kong	14,025	17,491	20,651	25,000
Percent of total	(73.4)	(67.3)	(62.6)	(63.3)
From the United States	2,900	3,400	4,000	4,360
Percent of total	(15.2)	(13.1)	(12.1)	(11.0)
From Japan	1,739	2,035	2,473	not
Percent of total	(9.1)	(7.8)	(7.5)	available
From Taiwan	100	600	1,300	not
Percent of total	(0.5)	(2.3)	(3.9)	available

Sources: Hong Kong data from unpublished document received April 8, 1991 from George Shen, Chief Editor, *Hong Kong Economic Journal*. The 1990 estimates for the total and the US share are based on the *FY 1990 Country Marketing Plan*, US Foreign Commercial Service, US Embassy, Beijing, September 1990. During 1990, foreign firms signed new investment contracts worth US$6.57 billion. Taiwan data extracted from story in *Los Angeles Times*, April 8, 1991. All 1990 data are estimates.

cumulative foreign direct investment in China has declined from 9.1 percent of the total in 1987 to 7.5 percent in 1989. The US share of the total also declined in the same period from 13.6 percent to 10.0 percent. In contrast, Taiwan increased its investments in China from 0.5 percent of the total to 3.9 percent.[19]

Japanese investments in China

The Japanese are the world's largest foreign investors, but as shown on Exhibit 6.3, only a tiny portion of their total investments went into China. The exhibit shows that from 1951–89, Japan made 57,373 individual foreign investments totaling about US$253.4 billion. Japanese investments in China, however, numbered only 694, or 1.2 percent of the total, and the dollar value of those investments was only US$2.474 billion, or 0.98 percent of the total invested over a period of thirty-nine years.

Exhibit 6.4 also points out that practically all of the Japanese investments shown on the exhibit took place during the ten-year period 1979–89, as shown on Exhibit 6.4. Furthermore, over 79 percent of the total investment in China was made during the last three years of the thirty-nine-year period.

Exhibit 6.4 also shows that the number of individual investments in

Exhibit 6.3 Japan's direct foreign investment in Asian countries and in the United States, 1987–9 (in millions of US dollars)

Countries	1987			1988			1989			1951–89		
	No. of cases	Dollar value	% of $ value	No. of cases	Dollar value	% of $ value	No. of cases	Dollar value	% of $ value	No. of cases	Dollar value	% of $ value
Worldwide	4,584	33,364	100.0	6,077	47,022	100.0	6,589	67,540	100.0	57,373	253,396	100.0
China	101	1,226	3.7	171	296	0.6	126	438	0.6	694	2,474	1.0
Hong Kong	261	1,072	3.2	335	1,662	3.5	335	1,898	28.0	3,499	8,086	3.2
Indonesia	67	545	1.6	84	586	1.2	140	631	0.9	1,718	10,435	4.1
Korea	166	647	1.9	153	483	1.0	81	606	0.9	1,793	3,854	1.5
Malaysia	64	163	0.5	108	387	0.8	159	673	1.0	1,340	2,507	1.0
Philippines	18	72	0.2	54	134	0.3	87	202	0.3	792	1,322	0.5
Singapore	182	494	1.5	197	747	1.6	181	1,902	2.8	2,420	5,715	2.3
Taiwan	268	367	1.1	234	372	0.8	165	494	0.7	2,298	2,285	0.9
Thailand	192	250	0.7	382	859	1.8	403	1,276	1.9	2,088	3,268	1.3
United States	1,816	14,704	44.1	2,434	21,701	46.2	2,668	3,250	48.2	20,675	104,400	41.1

Source: *Foreign Investment Research Bulletin*, Export–Import Bank of Japan, November 1990.
Note: Japan's direct foreign investment in China during 1979–89 is 2,473. Japan, therefore, had practically no foreign investment in China before 1979.

Exhibit 6.4 Japan's foreign direct investment in China 1979–89

Year	Cases	Amount invested in millions of US$	Invested amount in thousands of US$
1979	3	14	4,667
1980	6	12	2,000
1981	9	26	2,889
1982	4	18	4,500
1983	5	3	600
1984	66	114	1,727
1985	118	100	847
1986	85	426	2,659
1987	101	1,226	12,139
1988	171	296	1,731
1989	126	438	3,476
Total	694	2,673	3,852

Source: Foreign Investment Research Bulletin, Export–Import Bank of Japan, November 1990.
Note: The amount invested in 1987 includes a US$1.1 billion loan from the Export–Import Bank of Japan.[20]

China by Japan was very small from 1979 through 1983. Then, in 1984, the number of individual investments suddenly increased to sixty-six. In the following year, 118 individual investments were made, which is more than the cumulative total from 1979 through 1984.

In 1987, Japanese investment in China jumped to US$1.226 billion. This investment includes a US$1.1 billion loan from the Export–Import Bank of Japan. The exhibit shows 101 new investment projects undertaken that year. However, since we don't know how the loan money was spent, the investment amount per case as shown on the exhibit may be incorrect.

Japan's investments in China totaled US$2.673 billion during the eleven-year period 1979–89, spread over 694 investment projects, which is an average investment per project of US$3.852 million. This is roughly 1 percent of Japan's worldwide investments.

Hong Kong's investments in China

Manufacturing firms in Hong Kong are oriented to take advantage of cheap labor to produce goods for export. In Hong Kong, however, there is a chronic shortage of cheap labor, so when China announced their open-door policy, the Hong Kong entrepreneurs quickly took advantage of China's low wage rates, which are far lower than in any other Asian country. Their labor-intensive manufacturing technology is particularly well-suited to Chinese workers, and Guangdong province is especially attractive because it shares the same culture and language (Cantonese) as Hong Kong. The provincial capital, Guangchou (Canton), is only a few hours by train from Hong Kong, and many people have predicted that in due time the corridor between Hong Kong and Guangchou will be one vast megalopolis.

From China's viewpoint, investments from Hong Kong are more desirable than from anywhere else because they are in closer harmony with China's economic objectives. The Hong Kong entrepreneurs are already oriented to production of goods solely for export and have little interest in China's domestic market. Hong Kong's technological and managerial know-how and China's cheap and abundant labor are so complementary that some economists predict that most of Hong Kong's manufacturing activities will move to southern China, leaving Hong Kong to function as a center of trade and financial activities.

Taiwan's investments in China

While Hong Kong investors are primarily interested in China as a source of cheap labor, Taiwan investors are looking for places to put accumulated capital to work. With a foreign exchange reserve of US$76 billion (almost the same as Japan's), the Taiwanese are eager to find opportunities for foreign direct investments, particularly in Asia. Exhibit 6.5 shows Taiwan's burgeoning foreign direct investment in other Asian countries.

Unlike the Hong Kong investors who were more apt to approach China with investment proposals, the Taiwanese investors had to be

Exhibit 6.5 Taiwan overseas investment (in millions of US dollars)

Destination	1986	1987	1988	1989
Thailand	6	300	842	871
Malaysia		90	307	785
China		100	600	600
Indonesia	2	1	500	150
Philippines		9	109	149
Total	8	500	2,358	2,555

Source: *Far Eastern Economic Review*, April 19, 1990, p. 84, as reported in Yeh, Sze and Levin, "The changing Asian economic environment and US–Japan trade relations," Santa Monica, California: RAND, R-3986 CUSJR, September 1990.

courted by China and persuaded to invest. China did this by three major steps:

1 The first step was to amend the foreign joint venture law to make foreign investment more attractive. One amendment eliminated the time limit on contracts with foreign investors. Under the former provisions of this law, the joint venture enterprise passed into Chinese hands at the end of thirty years. Now there is no time limit on foreign ownership. Another amendment provides that the nationalization of a joint venture is to be avoided except in extraordinary circumstances, in which case "appropriate compensations shall be made." Another amendment allows foreign partners to become chairmen of joint ventures.

2 The second step was the announcement of a new investment zone in Shanghai which is specifically designed to attract investment from overseas Chinese. The new zone, called Pudong, covers 150 square kilometers with another 50 square kilometers held in reserve. It will concentrate industries into five districts and will include a forty-four-berth harbor on the Yangtze river. The first phase of construction is scheduled to be completed in 1995.

3 The third step was the establishment of Haicang Island near Xiamen as a Taiwan Investment Zone. Negotiations between the Chinese authorities and Y.C. Wang, Chairman of the Formosa Plastics Group conglomerate in Taiwan, for the investment of US$7 billion in a petrochemical complex have been underway since October 1989. To accommodate this ambitious project, the Chinese government is offering to spend about US$5 billion to build railroads and a power station. If this deal materializes, it will be the greatest achievement of the open-door policy.

Apparently the People's Republic of China is prepared to submerge political differences with the Republic of China (Taiwan) in order to obtain the latter's capital and technology. The entrepreneurs of Taiwan are primarily of northern Chinese stock, speaking Mandarin as their native language. Thus investment in northern China has a strong cultural attraction, and this may be reflected in the dramatic increase in Taiwanese investments in 1987, 1988, and 1989, as previously shown by Exhibit 6.5.

There is some speculation that the Taiwanese investments will surpass those of the United States and Japan within a few years. However, other nations are also competing for Taiwanese capital. Unless China's investment climate further improves, Taiwan can be expected to continue pumping capital into Malaysia, Indonesia, and

Exhibit 6.6 Japanese and American joint ventures in China, 1979–86, by industry

Industries	Japan		United States	
	Number	%	Number	%
Agriculture, fisheries	13	4.5	3	1.6
Mining	4	1.4	9	4.7
Construction	9	3.1	4	2.1
Manufacturing				
Food, drink	18	6.2	19	9.9
Textiles	29	10.0	18	9.4
Lumber, furniture	8	2.8	2	1.0
Printing, publishing	4	1.4	7	3.7
Chemicals, plastics	26	9.0	23	12.0
Chinaware	3	1.0	12	6.3
Metals	9	3.1	5	2.6
Machinery	49	16.9	50	26.2
General	5	1.7	16	8.4
Electrical	28	9.7	26	13.6
Transport	4	1.4	4	2.1
Precision	12	4.1	4	2.1
Other manufacturing	8	2.8	11	5.8
Total manufacturing	154	53.1	147	77.0
Non-Manufacturing				
Transport, telecommunications	8	2.8	3	1.6
Wholesale, retail	13	4.5	2	1.0
Finance, insurance	1	0.3	0	0.0
Real estate	15	5.2	2	1.0
Services	73	25.2	21	11.0
Leasing	15	5.2	1	0.5
Hotel	22	7.6	4	2.1
Information	13	4.5	7	3.7
Leisure	12	4.1	0	0.0
Others	11	3.8	9	4.7
Total non-manufacturing	110	37.9	28	14.7
Total joint ventures	290	100.0	191	100.0

Source: Mitsubishi Soga Kenkyujo, Tokyo, Japan (1988).

Thailand in order to alleviate the high wages and high cost of land in Taiwan.

Patterns of Japanese and American direct investments

Exhibit 6.6 shows the investment patterns of Japanese and American joint ventures in Chinese industry during the years 1979–86. The exhibit shows the Japanese preferences for manufacturing (53.1 percent), where they can take advantage of China's cheap labor, and for services (25.2 percent), which are relatively low-risk, high-return projects.

American investors show an even stronger preference for manufacturing enterprises (77 percent), but also prefer service enterprises (11 percent) over other categories outside of manufacturing, presumably for the same reasons. A little over half of Japan's non-manufacturing joint ventures is in leasing and hotels, which are considered to be low-risk, high-return projects. In contrast, the US ventures are heavily concentrated in software development and consulting services. In the manufacturing sector, both the Japanese and American investors have heavy commitments to making electronic and electrical goods and small appliances.[21]

The preponderance in the manufacturing sector of joint ventures for making electronic and electrical goods and small appliances reflects a growing trend among investors from Japan, the US, and other countries toward shifting their least price-competitive manufacturing to lower-wage areas. It might be called "a logical extension of the consumer electronics exports that started pouring into China in the early 1980s" and were subsequently suppressed by the Chinese government.[22]

According to the US Embassy in Beijing, new investment contracts signed by foreign firms in 1990 were worth US$6.57 billion, a 17.3 percent increase over 1989. The number of contracts signed by American firms increased by 26 percent. The dollar value of those contracts, however, decreased by about 54 percent. Japanese investors have exhibited a similar pattern of more numerous but smaller contracts, indicating avoidance of risk.

Investment formats and geographical locations

There are three formats for foreign investment in China: (1) equity joint ventures; (2) contractual joint ventures; and (3) wholly-owned enterprises.

Equity joint ventures are cooperative corporate enterprises into which both Chinese and foreign corporations invest capital in the form of cash, technology, and/or fixed assets. Ownership is determined by the proportion of capital contributions. Contractual joint ventures may be set up as a partnership rather than a corporation, which is a more flexible arrangement.

The Chinese joint venture law, as promulgated in 1979 and revised in April 1990, establishes minimum foreign equity in a joint venture as 25 percent. About 70 percent of Japanese and 66 percent of US joint ventures have maintained equity ownership below 50 percent and as low as 25 percent.[23] These findings seem to indicate caution on the part of foreign investors who prefer lower exposure to risk-to-equity ownership.

Japanese investors have concentrated 92 percent of their joint ventures in the major cities of Beijing, Tianjin, and Shanghai, and in the coastal areas of China. American investors, however, have established joint ventures in China's inland areas as well as in the coastal areas. The geographic pattern suggests that the Japanese investors tend to avoid high-risk projects.

China's investment climate

Prior to 1987, despite China's open door, the newly industrialized countries (NIEs) of South Korea and Taiwan were the favorite receptacles for Japanese and American foreign direct investments. As labor costs began to rise in these countries, they began to lose their comparative cost advantages, so investors started moving into the ASEAN countries of Indonesia, Malaysia, the Philippines, and Thailand. The surge of American and Japanese investments helped to fuel higher levels of economic growth in both the NIEs and ASEAN countries. American and Japanese investments in China, however, have remained disappointingly low. (See exhibit 6.4.)

The reason behind the relatively low level of investment in China seems to be China's inferior investment climate as compared to the NIE and ASEAN countries. As previously noted, in an attempt to bolster foreign direct investment, China's State Council in 1986 issued twenty-two provisions for encouragement of foreign investment, known as the "22 Guidelines." This was followed by Zhao Ziyang's strategy of opening China's coastal cities to foreign investors. The NIE and ASEAN countries also came up with comparable or better incentive programs to actively pursue investments from the US, Japan, Taiwan, and other foreign countries. On balance, the ASEAN incentives are far more attractive than China's.

This may be illustrated by the case of Thailand. In 1990, China was able to obtain new investment contracts totaling UK$6.5 billion. Thailand, a tiny nation when compared to China, attracted investments from Japan, Taiwan, USA, Hong Kong, Singapore, Malaysia, Korea, Australia, Canada, and seven nations of Europe. In that single year, Thailand's Board of Investments approved a total of 617 new ventures involving investments totaling US$13.9027 billion.[24] This is more than twice as much as was obtained by China.

China's incentives versus those in other countries

Some of the incentives offered by China are:

Income tax incentives. Foreign investors are required to pay an income tax of 33 percent. This is on the high end of the range of 16.5 to 40 percent charged by other Asian countries.[25] The Chinese income tax rate in the special economic zones (SEZs) and technological development zones (TDZs) is 15 percent, where other countries charge no taxes in special zones.

Foreign investors in qualified equity joint ventures in China are exempt from income taxes for only two years, whereas the average tax holiday in Asia is around 3–5 years, and Singapore offers a ten-year tax exemption.

Flexible level of equity participation. The legal requirement in China is that foreign participants provide more than 25 percent of equity. In Hong Kong, Singapore, and Taiwan, there are no equity ownership requirements.

Low manufacturing wages. Exhibit 6.7 shows the average wage rates prevailing in 1986 in ten Asian countries: China, the four ASEAN countries of Indonesia, the Philippines, Thailand, and Malaysia, the NIE countries of Taiwan, Singapore, South Korea, and Hong Kong, and Japan.

The wage rates on the exhibit are indexed with the Japanese wage rate = 100. From the index values, it is easily seen that the wage rates of these countries reflect their stages of development. The wage rates of the four ASEAN countries are less than one-eighth those of Japan, and the wage rates of the newly developed countries are one-quarter or less than those of Japan. China's average wage rate is the lowest of all, about one twenty-fifth of the Japanese rate.

Exhibit 6.7 Comparative average monthly wage rates in the manufacturing sectors of ten Asian countries (in US dollars)

Country	Monthly wage	Index
China	51.00	4.1
Indonesia	96.50	7.7
Philippines	101.00	8.0
Thailand	104.00	8.3
Malaysia	150.00	11.9
Taiwan	218.60	17.4
Singapore	275.00	21.9
South Korea	310.00	24.6
Hong Kong	315.00	25.0
Japan	1,258.00	100.0

Source: ILO Yearbook of Labor Statistics, 1986.

Unfortunately for potential investors, the wage rate shown for Chinese manufacturing workers pertains to Chinese firms only. The Chinese government's wage guidelines require foreign companies to pay wages that are at least 120–150 percent above those paid by a state-run company in the same region. In addition, a foreign company must pay to a labor union a "social welfare expense" amounting to 100–150 percent of the workers' wages. When the social welfare expenses and other mandatory fringe benefits are added to the basic wage, it may be that China does not have the lowest wages in Asia.[26]

Obstacles to foreign investment in China

Although the laws passed by Beijing often look good on paper, there is a wide gap between theory and practice. China's relatively unfavorable investment climate stems from a number of factors, of which the following are most onerous:

1 unstable political conditions;
2 ambiguous rules and inadequate legal framework;
3 arbitrary charges and bureaucratic red tape;
4 stiff foreign-exchange balancing requirement and restrictions on profit repatriation;
5 poor infrastructure;
6 excessive documentation requirements;
7 the distressing Chinese tendency to abruptly cancel negotiations;
8 difficulties in recruiting skilled workers;
9 difficulties in procuring parts and raw materials locally;
10 tendency to make abrupt and drastic changes in economic and trade policies.

Some of the most critical problems facing foreign investors are as follows:

1 The problem most often cited by US and Japanese investors is the issue of balancing foreign exchange. The Chinese Ministry of Foreign Economic Relations and Trade has reported that only one-third of the roughly 4,000 foreign enterprises in China are able to maintain a positive balance between foreign exchange revenues and expenditures.

Most foreign investors are lured into China by the Chinese market potential. However, under China's policy of requiring balancing of foreign exchange, most manufacturing enterprises are having difficulties in tapping sources of foreign exchange and have no choice but to export their entire production. They soon learn, then, that it is not easy to make products in China that can compete comfortably in global markets. The foreign investors who manage to balance foreign exchange are either in hotel or service industries or engaged in manufacturing products that are exportable to the investor's home country.

2 Confused legislation is another vexing problem. Because of their failure to generate substantial foreign investment, the Chinese government has been moved to pass a series of remedial measures, but lack of clarity in the new laws has created a large problem. After Zhao Ziyang's economic decentralization move, inconsistent and conflicting regulations at central and local government levels have proliferated. "With the devolution of power from the central government to provincial and local authorities, Peking's policies are implemented – or ignored in some instances – differently in different localities."[27] Too often, interpretation of national guidelines is left up to local authorities. For most foreign investors, China's legal framework is not adequate to protect their investments, and this constitutes a main impediment to their commitment.

3 The aftermath of the Tiananmen Square incident has been a significant new obstacle to foreign investment. The central government's struggle to recentralize its trade and investment policy has compounded the usual bureaucratic problems. Since the central government is trying to redraw the party line on the role of foreign investment in the modernization of China, provincial officials are reluctant to act for fear of stepping over lines of authority that are changing. Observers say that China's retrenchment will last for another year or so. In the meantime, foreign investors are not going to commit substantial new capital to China unless there is substantive support from Chinese leaders at the top.

As long as China remains politically unstable with unpredictable policies and further requires joint-venture manufacturers to export their products in order to balance foreign exchange receipts and expenditures, incentives such as lower land-use fees and tax breaks are of little use to investors.

SUMMARY AND CONCLUSIONS

Under the reforms introduced in 1978, China tried to blend two mutually incompatible elements: central planning and a market system. China's political leadership insisted that China must pursue the socialist objective of self-sufficiency, although they were willing to delegate economic planning to the regional or provincial level. Rapid growth of the Chinese economy introduced a chronic imbalance between aggregate supply and aggregate demand and resulted in severe inflation during 1987 and 1988. To cool the overheated economy and restrain inflation, China adopted a retrenchment program in the latter part of 1988 that idled millions of workers and created serious social unrest. This culminated in the Tiananmen Square incident in June 1989, and the resulting political turmoil set China's economic progress back by several years. It caused the suspension or cancellation of billions of dollars in much needed foreign loans and foreign direct investments, and lost the country substantial amounts of tourism income. The political leadership now is trying to restore central planning from Beijing.

Successful economic reform requires foreign direct investment and foreign loans. Unfortunately for China, the Chinese government's trade and foreign investment policies reflect a basic lack of understanding of what it takes to motivate trading partners and foreign investors. Profitable foreign trade and investment is based upon the fundamental economic principle of comparative advantage, which regards trade as a two-way street. Although it is understandable that China should desire to be self-reliant at this stage of the nation's economic development, self-reliance is not practical in today's global environment. China must steer its course in a more positive direction.

All of the developing nations in Asia are seeking foreign investment and are very competitive in offering incentives to foreign investors. As long as China fails to match or better their inducements, foreign capital will continue to flow into the other nations with only a trickle left for China. China badly needs to remove certain obstacles to foreign investment. Among the most onerous of these obstacles are:

1 the lack of a legal framework capable of protecting foreign investors' interests;
2 the self-centered policy of requiring balancing of foreign exchange;
3 political instability and a bumbling bureaucracy;
4 inadequate infrastructure;
5 low worker productivity which raises labor costs despite low wage rates.

Because they are Chinese, Hong Kong and Taiwan will probably continue to be important sources of capital and know-how. Economic interdependence with China has long been a fact of life for Hong Kong, and is rapidly evolving for Taiwan. Just how large the contributions from Hong Kong and Taiwan may become depends upon China's political stability and a party line that grants a high degree of autonomy to both.

NOTES

1 The new five-year and ten-year economic development plans adopted during the National People's Congress held in March 1991 call for growth of GNP at a rate of 6 percent annually, according to the March 26, 1991 issue of *China Daily*.
2 Taniura, Takao (1989) *"Ajia no kogyoka to chokusetsu toshi,"* (Asian industrialization and direct foreign investment), *Ajia Keizai Kenkyujo*.
3 Larson, Milton (1988) "Exporting private enterprise to developing communist countries: case study on China," *Columbia Journal of World Business* (Spring), pp. 79–87.
4 Fang Kai Bing and Weng Xin Hua (1989) "China's economic reforms and the global economy," *Futures* (December) pp. 528–31.
5 *Beijing Review*, Vol. 33, no. 5 (January 29–February 11, 1990), p. 4.
6 State Statistical Bureau (1989) "Communiqué on 1988 economic development," *People's Daily* (March 1), p. 3.
7 *Far Eastern Economic Review*, April 5, 1990, p. 38.
8 *World Journal* (New York), May 22, 1990, p. 32.
9 Tei Ming Cheung (1991) "Centrifugal forces," *Far Eastern Economic Review* (April 4), p. 26.
10 Barry Naughton (1989) "Inflation and economic reform in China," *Current History*, (September), pp. 270–1.
11 "Three new tendencies in the rural economy," *Renmin Ribao*, March 13, 1989, p. 1.
12 Japan External Trade Organization (1990) *China Newsletter*, No. 84 (January–February), pp. 5–6.
13 Chen Chu-Yuan (1990) "China's economy in retrenchment," *Current History* (September), pp. 254–5.
14 State Statistical Bureau (1989) "Economic structural imbalance, its causes and correctives," *Beijing Review*, (September 4–10), Vol. 32, No. 36 pp. 22–8.
15 Liu Guoguang (1990) "Retrenchment, a boon to reform," *Beijing Review* (January 15–21), Vol. 33, No. 3, p. 19.
16 Simon, Denis Fred (1990) "After Tiananmen: what is the future for foreign business?" *California Management Review* (Winter), pp. 115–18.
17 Chen Chu-Yuan (1990) "China's economy in retrenchment," *Current History* (September), pp. 254–5.
18 Thurston, Anne T. (1989) "Back to square one?" *China Business Review* (September–October), pp. 36–41.
19 This figure is for direct investment in China, but Taiwan has also made investments indirectly through other countries, particularly through Hong Kong and Singapore. If these indirect investments are added, then Taiwan's share is much higher.

20 *Far Eastern Economic Review*, September 8, 1988, p. 177.
21 Zhang Jixun (1988) "*Nihon no taichu chokusetsu toshi no genjo to son mondaiten*" (The current situations and problems of Japanese investment in China), *Keizai Hyoron* (October–November), pp. 24–37, 44–61.
22 Thurwachter, Todd (1990) "Japan in China: the Guangdong example, "*China Business Review* (January–February), pp. 7–17.
23 Inagaki, Kiyoshi (1988) "*Izen to hageshii toshi kankyo*" (China's investment climate stays severe), *Sekai Shuho* (September 20), pp. 46–7.
24 International Division, Board of Investment, Bangkok, Thailand, January 15, 1991.
25 "*Chugoku to shuhen shokoku chiiki to no toshi kankyo hikaku*" (China's investment climate in comparison to those in other Asian countries), *Jetro*, March 1988.
26 Yokota, Takaaki (1989) "*Chugoku no gaishi donyu seisaku to nihon no taichu chokusetsu toshi*" (China's foreign capital inducement policies and Japanese investment in China), *Chuo Daigaku Keizai Kenkyujo Nenpo*, Vol. 19, No. 1, pp. 105–23.
27 *Far Eastern Economic Review*, September 29, 1988, p. 110.

7 Managing countertrade in the PRC

Aspy P. Palia and Oded Shenkar

In the aftermath of Tiananmen, countertrade continues to present foreign firms with both problems and opportunities. This chapter identifies recent trends in Chinese countertrade activity both prior to and following the economic austerity period. First, China's countertrade policies and practices prior to Tiananmen are reviewed. Second post-Tiananmen developments are presented. Third, the need for objective information on Chinese countertrade practices is explained. Fourth, current data on Chinese countertrade activities are analyzed.[1] The data are compiled from *Countertrade Outlook* (weekly) and the *Financial Times* (daily), two major sources of information on global countertrade transactions. Throughout the chapter, cases involving countertrade activity between Chinese and foreign firms are used to illustrate the obstacles to PRC countertrade as well as the opportunities it provides.

COUNTERTRADE IN CHINA PRIOR TO 1989

China's countertrade practices were surveyed in 1988 by the Association pour la Compensation des Echanges Commerciaux (ACECO) of Paris.[2] According to ACECO, Chinese authorities used countertrade at the national level to promote exports, transfer technology, offset protectionist measures in international trade, and acquire training for commercial personnel. At the provincial level, Chinese officials used countertrade to enhance their autonomy, and increase their capital investments without relying on subsidies from Beijing.

PRC countertrade was dominated at the time by compensation agreements. PRC countertrade with organizations based in OECD nations differed from PRC countertrade with developing countries. Suppliers in OECD nations were offered non-traditional goods, especially manufactured goods, whereas suppliers in developing nations were offered cash commodities by the PRC.

Owing to a lack of clear directives regulating the mechanics of a countertrade transaction, foreign suppliers had difficulty in identifying key decision-makers with whom to negotiate the terms of countertrade. Attempts to decentralize the economy compounded this difficulty. The final structure of the countertrade agreement was subject to approval by the Ministry of Foreign Economic Relations and Trade (MOFERT).

The difficulties faced by firms that attempted to engage in countertrade with China are illustrated by the failure of the Hubei Pig Improvement Company. The company, a fifty-fifty equity joint venture of the Pig Improvement Co. of Oxford, England and the Hubei province Bureau of Animal Husbandry, was seeking to generate foreign exchange from the sale of its genetic seed stock in Hong Kong and China. Faced with a continuous shortage of Foreign Exchange Certificates, countertrade emerged as a viable option. Working with the Hubei branch of MOFERT and the state-owned Cereals, Oils and Foodstuffs (COF), the joint-venture company identified a Chinese maker of royal jelly and approached it for a countertrade transaction. In the proposed transaction, the joint venture would exchange its pigs for royal jelly, which would then be sold abroad by the trading arm of the British parent, Dalgerty of London. The deal fell through due to disagreement on the scale of the transaction and on pricing grounds, with the Chinese manufacturer demanding an unrealistically low margin for the seller. Subsequent transactions, involving sugar beet, peanuts, and other agricultural products, were aborted for similar reasons.

COUNTERTRADE IN CHINA DURING 1989

According to a 1989 UNCTAD report[3] entitled "Countertrade regulations in selected developing countries," China did not have a comprehensive set of policies, legal regulations and rules for countertrade. However, through years of practices, China had formulated some policy orientations, promotion measures and guidelines in dealing with countertrade business. The report pointed out that the Chinese had yet to work out or make public a list of countertraded commodities. However, in principle, China stressed that those commodities which were in short domestic supply, easily marketable, or had higher foreign-exchange earning capabilities were not to be countertraded, whereas those in abundant domestic supply or had greater production potentials qualified for countertrade. China particularly encouraged the use of countertrade to promote exports of machinery and electrical engineering products. Chinese regulations and rules for compensation trade and rules and guidelines for counterpurchase are summarized in this chapter. Compensation projects are examined and approved by central or local government depending on the size of the project and the scale of the imported machinery and equipment. The report indicates that as a rule, the provinces, municipalities and autonomous regions approve small- and medium-size undertakings, whereas the central government handles large ones.

In 1989, China experienced a deteriorating trade balance. A policy paper prepared by the State Planning Commission's Institute of Techno-Economics suggested that countertrade be used to improve China's trade balance in industrial sectors that accounted for a large share of the trade deficit. This policy paper suggested that a separate, quasi-governmental institution be established to:

1 formulate and implement strategies and plans for machinery and electrical-products sectors;
2 coordinate imports and exports of these products with industrial ministries and FTOs;
3 directly manage the foreign trade of individual enterprises through "export chambers";
4 establish mechanisms to mediate disputes;
5 set up "transprovincial purchasing corporations" in order to exert leverage on suppliers by centralizing purchases for export production; and
6 establish "information centers" at the national and provincial levels to facilitate countertrade by bringing exporters and importers together and advising them of the potential for expanding exports through linkage with imports.

This policy paper was studied by the countertrade unit of MOFERT, which had not been very successful in promoting reciprocal trade in the (1) mechanical and electric equipment, and (2) iron and steel products sectors.[4]

China's deteriorating 1989 trade balance led to a decline in foreign exchange reserves. Reversing an earlier assessment presented to the US Congress in April 1988, the US Central Intelligence Agency (CIA) concluded that China was likely to increase the use of countertrade in general, and with the USSR and other East European countries in particular. The CIA report entitled "The

Chinese economy in 1988 and 1989: reforms on hold, economic problems mount," submitted to the Congressional Joint Economic Committee, raised the possibility that an increase in countertrade would displace hard-currency transactions with Western suppliers in certain industries.[5]

To help the Chinese sell their products and earn foreign exchange, McDonnell-Douglas conducted direct and indirect offset activities in China related to commercial aircraft sales. These offset transactions were accomplished in China in a difficult operating environment and were used to win future sales. A McDonnell-Douglas countertrade executive indicated that they did not have a "trading-company mentality." They used their extensive network of suppliers and companies in China to bring together interested buyers and sellers. McDonnell-Douglas also assisted American companies through all phases of the transaction. The firm's indirect offsets included exports of commercial safes, industrial batteries used in lift-trucks, aerospace rivets, and high-quality crankshafts used in light commercial aircraft and racing engines. These offset transactions were primarily set to enable McDonnell-Douglas a continuation of coproduction of passenger aircraft, which is an integral part of the firm's strategy. The company considered moving the production lines of the MD-87 and MD-91 to China so as to focus on the manufacture of the MD-11 in California.

At the end of 1989, the Chinese government began a campaign to directly and indirectly inform foreign suppliers that countertrade offers would receive more sympathetic consideration than offers based on conventional financing. The November 1989 issue of the Hong Kong-based *China Market*, whose commentaries on Chinese commercial issues reflect official views in Beijing, featured a commentary entitled "Business opportunities amid a trend of low economic growth." The journal stated:

> As opportunities through ordinary channels decrease, those in barter trade may increase. The opening of the outside world over the last 11 years has taught the Chinese people many lessons, and international economic and technological exchanges and cooperation have brought the country great benefits.
>
> Although imports have to be curbed in the next few years, due to the need to repay debts, and exports will be subject to limits of central Government plans and other factors, barter trade nevertheless will remain a form of trade appreciated by Chinese authorities. Therefore, it is expected that barter trade will

continue to receive support from both the central and local governments.

This report indicated that barter trade – an umbrella term used to denote those forms of countertrade that are not investment related (barter, counter-purchase, and clearing agreements) would continue to receive support from the Chinese authorities. In addition, this report implied that compensation and its variants (classic buyback, coproduction, build-operate-transfer, etc.) would no longer dominate the Chinese countertrade arena. This implied shift in focus from investment-related forms of countertrade such as compensation to non-investment-related forms such as barter, counterpurchase, and clearing agreements, required changes in the countertrade posture of Western business organizations.[6]

Initially, the membership of what was then called the National Council for US–China Trade was primarily concerned with trade. Later, the primary interest of the membership of the US–China Business Council shifted from non-investment-related to investment-related forms of countertrade. Compensation or buyback was used frequently when countertrade financing was required. With the shift in focus toward non-investment-related forms of countertrade, barter transactions with foreign firms based in countries whose governments maintain clearing agreements with China appeared to be on the increase. This resurgence of barter trade posed additional difficulties for Western suppliers in sourcing takebacks and establishing linkage.

This linkage problem was discussed by Jack B. Utley of the McDonnell-Douglas Corporation in his address at the World Countertrade Conference presented by the American Countertrade Association in October 1989 as follows:

The inability to cross ministerial lines represents a serious barrier to foreign companies attempting to accomplish their countertrade obligations. Each FTO or enterprise wants to keep to itself the foreign exchange generated by its exports. Other ministries with products of export quality will be expected to pay a commission to the company that is the beneficiary of the countertrade contract before the export transaction is allowed to be counted against the obligation. These restrictions severely hamper the accomplishment of countertrade obligations with the times stipulated. But, it is expected that the new regulations will recognize these shortcomings and will define a policy that will benefit all.

Following the sale to China of some 420 locomotives in a cash transaction, General Electric (GE) sought to supply additional demand for locomotives in China's coal-haulage regions. Since no foreign reserves were allocated in this instance, a cash transaction was not possible. GE and General Motors were approached by a consortium of the mine-site managers and the Ministry of Railways to countertrade coal for locomotives. Through the sale of coal by their countertrade partners, the Chinese intended to cover their costs and to generate a sufficient margin to cover the cost of procurement of the locomotives. Unfortunately, a decline in the world-market price of coal exerted a cost–price squeeze. In addition, the price the Chinese demanded for the coal far exceeded the market price. Both the above factors undermined the transaction. Company sources emphasized the importance to the Chinese of (1) establishing technology transfer, and (2) cooperating in a long-term coal-manufacturing process. Countertrade was used as a necessary expedient:

If there were other mechanisms later that became a proper tactic, then we would do that too. So that countertrade itself, particularly for a commodity like coal was really the one that was available to us in this transaction. It was only a tactical move, not a strategic move. On the other hand, the long-term process of a coal-manufacturing alliance with the Chinese anticipated that there would be a countertrade of production parts for the products delivered; that parts of locomotives would ultimately be countertraded as part of the overall transaction.

This transaction taught GE that the crossing of ministerial boundaries was a serious obstacle to countertrade. The coal authorities had no incentive to cooperate with GE since they had nothing to do with the sale of the locomotives. GE also learned that it was very difficult to conduct a countertrade transaction based on margin, especially when the margin is slim and the countertraded commodity is subject to world-market price fluctuations. While in this case, GE had Philipp Bros. as a trading partner, the firm's countertrade agreements are usually negotiated directly. Countertrade has been "marginally successful and worthwhile" for the firm's Transportation Division. However, countertrade of GE power-generation equipment has been a success, and the company is positively disposed to future countertrade transactions given a reasonable margin of safety.

With the projected increase in the share of Chinese foreign trade that is financed on a countertrade (barter) basis, firms in the technologically advanced East European countries that maintain clearing agreements with China are likely to capture the market for mid-level technology products. For instance, clearing agreement trade between China and Czechoslovakia is expected to reach a total value of SFr5 billion for the 1986–90 period, a 72 percent increase over the previous five-year period. This substantial increase in China–Czechoslovakia trade is based on exchanges of Czechoslovak machinery and electrical products against Chinese agricultural and light industrial products, and raw materials.

Czechoslovak FTOs use connections established through this trade to negotiate their own countertrade transactions. For instance, FTO Motokov exports heavy-duty trucks, engines and components to China in exchange for auto parts and tires. The Czechoslovak Ministry of Foreign Trade targets specific Chinese production sectors as sources for large-scale purchases, and Czechoslovak traders and trade officials use the resulting leverage to successfully negotiate the necessary linkages. For example, Czechoslovakia imported Chinese color TVs valued at SFr17.8 million in 1988, SFr21.3 million in 1989, and yet another increase was expected in 1990.[7]

CURRENT CHINESE COUNTERTRADE PRACTICES

Chinese trade officials are intensifying their efforts to use countertrade to the maximum extent possible as a substitute for normal credit lines. Previously, Chinese officials were willing to consider a range of reciprocal actions by Western firms beyond export commitments, such as the transfer of sophisticated technology or manufacturing processes not previously undertaken in China, even if the applications were primarily domestic. Currently, Chinese reciprocity demands are focusing on foreign exchange.

This focus on foreign exchange and the resulting emphasis on countertrade was reflected in the announcements of foreign commercial objectives for 1990 by regional and local trade authorities. For instance, Zhang Shi Yong, Chairman of Tianjin City Overseas Economy and Trade Development Committee, stated the municipality's objectives as follows:

The focus of this year's Tianjin business development is on processing with supplied materials, assembling with supplied parts, and compensation trade in such products as clothing, textiles, shoemaking, toys, suitcases, home electrical appliances, light metals, modern construction material, ordinary electronic products, plastic foods, poultry products, medicines, health food, and mechanical and electrical products. We must guide the foreign investors in the correct path and lead them to invest in projects which can increase export exchange and technology.

To maximize foreign exchange earnings, Chinese officials have adopted three principles. First, credit quotas are linked to foreign exchange earned from exports to ensure that the limited funds available are allocated to the major foreign exchange earners. Import authorizations are linked to export performance. Second, the stipulations on both foreign exchange quotas and import and export licenses are strictly implemented. Licenses are issued and quotas are set according to state plans, and the reselling of quotas and licenses are banned. Third, stricter controls are applied to the supply of goods for export so as to achieve greater additionality from countertrade operations. Staple export commodities are handled only by FTOs designated by the government, and FTOs may not act as agents for foreign firms that seek to use renminbi (RMB) to purchase commodities in China for export.[8]

These controls are applied despite the difficulty Sino–foreign joint ventures are facing with countertrade. In a report titled "Business troubles encountered in Shanghai," parts of which were published in December by Wenhuibao, countertrade was ranked by foreign executives as the most difficult problem in the Shanghai business environment. The report stated:

> Although foreign investors have been attracted by the huge Chinese market, the authorities have always demanded that jointly operated businesses export their products as much as possible. This unrealistic proportion of exports (generally 70% of total output) is usually undertaken by the foreign side. International competition and the market situation are commonly ignored.

With regard to technology transfer, another major problem area, the report noted:

> The Chinese side generally demands that the foreign side constantly transfer its sophisticated technology but does not like to pay reasonable transfer fees.

Based on this review of Chinese countertrade practices, it appears that countertrade financing of both foreign trade and investment has become increasingly important in the PRC. Given the importance of countertrade financing and reciprocal trading practices in the PRC, it is desirable to assess the nature and magnitude of recent Chinese countertrade activity.

Existing trade statistics published in the PRC do not provide information on countertrade activity, thus limiting our knowledge of the current countertrade level, major trading partners, and the types of countertrade used by them. Yet, because of the major importance of countertrade in China, such information is vital to any firm considering or conducting countertrade with the Chinese. This study investigates the Chinese countertrade arena and reveals the relative importance of:

1 the major players (nations) involved;
2 the forms of countertrade used;
3 the products imported and exported by China.

These products are classified by (1) final disposition, and (2) degree of processing.

The data for this empirical study were compiled from two prime sources of countertrade information, *Countertrade Outlook* and the *Financial Times*. The study covers the period extending from the beginning of 1988 to the middle of March 1989. Reports on countertrade in China were content-analyzed and classified by country of the trading partner, by form of countertrade used, and by products supplied and countertraded.

RESULTS

The countries involved in countertrade with China together with the number of countertrade transactions are shown in Table 7.1. Eighty countertrade transactions involving nineteen countries were reported during the period covered by the study. The US is the major countertrade partner of the PRC and accounts for twenty-six of the eighty countertrade transactions (32.5 percent). The USSR accounts for nine countertrade transactions (11.25 percent), followed by the UK and France with six countertrade transactions (7.5 percent) each. These nations are followed by Japan with five transactions (6.25 percent). West Germany and Australia each account for four transactions (5 percent).

Table 7.2 presents the types of countertrade used. The most frequently-used form of countertrade is compensation, which accounts for thirty-five of the eighty countertrade transactions (43.75 percent). This result is in agreement with the finding of the ACECO study. Offset agreements account for fifteen countertrade transactions

Table 7.1 The Chinese countertrade arena

Country	Number of countertrade transactions			
	1988	*1989*	*Total*	*% of Total*
1. USA	18	8	26	32.50
2. USSR	8	1	9	11.25
3. UK	6	–	6	7.50
4. France	6	–	6	7.50
5. Japan	4	1	5	6.25
6. West Germany	4	–	4	5.00
7. Australia	4	–	4	5.00
8. Canada	3	–	3	3.75
9. Iran	2	1	3	3.75
10. Netherlands	2	1	3	3.75
11. Colombia	2	–	2	2.50
12. Hong Kong	1	1	2	2.50
13. Argentina	1	–	1	1.25
14. Bangladesh	1	–	1	1.25
15. Chile	1	–	1	1.25
16. Morocco	1	–	1	1.25
17. Sweden	1	–	1	1.25
18. Taiwan	1	–	1	1.25
19. Zimbabwe	1	–	1	1.25
Total	67	13	80	100.00

(18.75 percent), clearing agreements for fourteen transactions (17.5 percent), barter for nine transactions (11.25 percent), and counterpurchase for the remaining seven transactions (8.75 percent).

Compensation agreements are used frequently by the US (seventeen transactions), Japan (five transactions), and the UK and the Netherlands (three transactions each) West Germany, Australia, and Hong Kong accounted for two compensation transactions each, and Sweden for one transaction. These transactions are employed to set up joint-venture production facilities and to facilitate the transfer of technology.

Barter transactions and associated clearing agreements are used frequently by non-market economies such as the USSR. The USSR and Iran resort frequently to clearing agreements to countertrade with China. The USSR accounts for six transactions and Iran accounts for three transactions. Other countries using clearing agreements are Argentina, Bangladesh, Canada, Colombia, and the US.

Offset agreements are used frequently by the US and France (five transactions each). Other nations using offset agreements are West

Table 7.2 Types of countertrade used

Country	Type of countertrade used					
	Barter	Clearing	Compen-sation	Counter-purchase	Offset	Total
1. USA	1	1	17	2	5	26
2. USSR	3	6	–	–	–	9
3. UK	2	–	3	–	1	6
4. France	–	–	–	1	5	6
5. Japan	–	–	5	–	–	5
6. West Germany	–	–	2	–	2	4
7. Australia	–	–	2	1	1	4
8. Canada	–	1	–	1	1	3
9. Iran	–	3	–	–	–	3
10. Netherlands	–	–	3	–	–	3
11. Colombia	–	1	–	1	–	2
12. Hong Kong	–	–	2	–	–	2
13. Argentina	–	1	–	–	–	1
14. Bangladesh	–	1	–	–	–	1
15. Chile	1	–	–	–	–	1
16. Morocco	1	–	–	–	–	1
17. Sweden	–	–	1	–	–	1
18. Taiwan	1	–	–	–	–	1
19. Zimbabwe	–	–	–	1	–	1
Total	9	14	35	7	15	80

Germany (two transactions), and Australia, Canada, and the UK (one transaction each).

Chinese imports of goods and services and exports of counter-traded goods are classified by final disposition in Table 7.3. Goods are classified into three categories: inputs, capital goods, and consumer goods. Capital goods are the primary category of Chinese imports, and are followed by inputs and a few consumer products. In contrast to imports, Chinese exports of countertraded goods and services are primarily consumer goods, followed by capital goods and inputs.

The USA and other developed nations supply mainly capital goods to China. In return, China supplies its major countertrade partners the USA and the USSR with consumer goods, capital goods, and some inputs. The pattern of trade is different with the developing countries listed in the lower half of the table. Here inputs and cash commodities constitute the majority of goods supplied to and by China.

Table 7.4 shows the countertraded goods classified by degree of

Table 7.3 Countertraded goods (classified by final disposition)

Country	Chinese imports			Chinese exports		
	Inputs	Capital goods	Consumer products	Inputs	Capital goods	Consumer products
1. USA	1	26	–	6	9	13
2. USSR	7	6	3	3	7	9
3. UK	–	6	–	1	1	4
4. France	–	5	–	1	4	–
5. Japan	–	5	–	2	–	3
6. West Germany	–	4	–	–	4	–
7. Australia	1	3	–	2	2	1
8. Canada	–	3	–	1	1	1
9. Iran	3	–	–	2	3	–
10. Netherlands	–	3	–	–	–	3
11. Colombia	3	–	–	1	1	2
12. Hong Kong	–	2	–	–	–	2
13. Argentina	–	1	–	–	1	–
14. Bangladesh	1	–	1	1	1	1
15. Chile	1	–	–	1	1	1
16. Morocco	1	–	–	1	–	–
17. Sweden	–	1	–	–	–	1
18. Taiwan	1	–	–	1	–	–
19. Zimbabwe	1	–	–	–	–	1
Total	20	65	4	23	35	42

Note: Some of the 80 transactions involve multiple product categories. Consequently, the total number of product categories imported and exported by the PRC both exceed 80.

processing. In this table Chinese imports and exports are classified into raw materials, components, semi-finished goods, and finished products. Finished products form the majority of both Chinese imports and exports. Other Chinese imports, in order of importance, are raw materials and semi-finished goods. Semi-finished goods and raw materials represent the other major categories of Chinese exports (countertraded commodities).

Comparing Chinese countertraded goods exports to developed OECD nations and developing countries, it is clear that exports to the former are heavily weighted with finished products and semi-finished goods. By contrast Chinese exports to the developing countries listed in the lower half of the table are less heavily weighted in this direction. This supports the finding of the ACECO study that indicated that PRC countertrade with organizations based in OECD nations is different from PRC countertrade with developing countries.

Table 7.4 Countertraded goods (classified by degree of processing)

Country	Chinese imports				Chinese exports			
	Raw matls	Com-ponents	Semi-finish	Finished products	Raw matls	Com-ponents	Semi-finish	Finished products
1. USA	—	1	1	27	3	—	14	12
2. USSR	5	—	7	6	5	—	3	9
3. UK	1	—	—	6	—	—	2	4
4. France	—	—	—	6	—	—	3	2
5. Japan	—	—	—	5	—	—	2	3
6. West Germany	1	—	1	4	—	1	3	1
7. Australia	—	—	—	3	1	—	1	3
8. Canada	—	—	—	3	—	—	3	—
9. Iran	3	—	—	—	—	—	2	3
10. Netherlands	—	—	—	3	—	—	2	—
11. Colombia	2	—	1	—	—	1	1	2
12. Hong Kong	—	—	—	1	—	—	—	1
13. Argentina	—	—	—	1	—	—	1	1
14. Bangladesh	1	—	1	—	1	—	1	1
15. Chile	1	—	—	—	—	—	1	1
16. Morocco	1	—	1	1	—	—	1	—
17. Sweden	—	—	—	1	—	—	1	—
18. Taiwan	—	—	1	—	1	—	—	—
19. Zimbabwe	1	—	—	—	—	—	1	—
Total	16	1	13	66	11	2	41	43

Note: Some of the 80 transactions involve multiple product categories. Consequently, the total number of product categories imported and exported by the PRC both exceed 80.

CURRENT OUTLOOK

A number of US firms interviewed in late 1990 suggested that not much has changed in current Chinese countertrade. While a number of players have left the countertrade arena altogether or have temporarily ceased countertrade activities in China, other experienced firms have seized the opportunity to expand their role in a less crowded field and are actively involved with a number of transactions. Still others continue to seek such transactions with limited success.

Ministerial and provincial boundaries continue to present a major impediment to countertrade transactions. Despite the recent attempts by Beijing to reassert central control, it remains very difficult to conclude transactions across such boundaries. Even within the same province or industrial domain, bringing together the two or more organizations in China to conclude a countertrade continues to be a sometimes insurmountable obstacle. Also many Chinese companies do not have suitable commodities for countertrade or do not control their exports. Those firms that are in a position to export their products prefer to do so directly in order to earn foreign exchange. Some US firms complain that Japanese firms operating through *sogo soshas* have a considerable advantage in the current climate. By relying on the giant-trading houses, Japanese firms gain access to an expanded network of suppliers and product lines which is essential for success. US firms, in contrast, frequently lack the manpower and the international resources required to overcome the obstacles.

In the near future, Western firms will face two additional barriers in structuring countertrade transactions in China. First, while these firms may reemphasize trade at the expense of investment, Chinese officials will continue to prefer compensation transactions. Consequently, Western firms may need to offer additional exports to surmount this barrier. Second, Chinese officials will increasingly require "barter-trade" financing as the range of imported goods accorded foreign exchange priority progressively shrinks. Firms that are well-established in China may be able to handle "barter-trade" requirements in-house.[9] Again, the majority of Western suppliers will do well to use the specialized assistance of intermediaries such as Nissho Iwai and other *sogo sosha*.

NOTES

1 For an explanation of the forms of countertrade analyzed, please see: Palia, Aspy P. and Oded Shenkar, (1991) "Countertrade practices in

China," *Industrial Marketing Management* (February) Vol. 20, No. 1, pp. 57–65.

2 ACECO (1988) *La Compensation en Chine*. Paris: Association pour la Compensation des Echanges Commerciaux.

3 UNCTAD (1989) *Countertrade Regulations in Selected Developing Countries*. Geneva: United Nations Conference on Trade and Development.

4 Countertrade Outlook Staff (1989) "Chinese agency urges aggressive CT unit be created outside MOFERT," *Countertrade Outlook* (May 29) Vol. VII, No. 21, p. 1.

5 Countertrade Outlook Staff (1989) "CIA: increase in Sino/Soviet CT could displace Western sales to PRC," *Countertrade Outlook* (October 2) Vol. VII, No. 38, p. 1.

6 Countertrade Outlook Staff (1989) "Rise in PRC CT foreseen with more 'barter trade', less compensation," *Countertrade Outlook* (December 18) Vol. VII, No. 48, p. 2.

7 Countertrade Outlook Staff (1989) "Rise in PRC CT foreseen with more 'barter trade', less compensation," *Countertrade Outlook* (December 18) Vol. VII, No. 48, p. 3.

8 Countertrade Outlook Staff (1990) "Tight credit in China creates CT problems, opportunities," *Countertrade Outlook* (May 28) Vol. VIII, No. 21, pp. 1–3.

9 Countertrade Outlook Staff (1989) "Rise in PRC CT foreseen with more 'barter trade', less compensation," *Countertrade Outlook* (December 18) Vol. VII, No. 48, p. 3.

8 Foreign direct investment in China

Paul W. Beamish and Lorraine Spiess[1]

INTRODUCTION

This chapter examines the evolution of foreign direct investment (FDI) in the People's Republic of China between 1979 and mid-1990 through consideration of the major alternatives: equity joint ventures, contractual (cooperative) ventures, and wholly foreign-owned enterprises. As part of this review, data is presented relating to 840 equity ventures, the most oft-used form of FDI. Data is provided on the region of investment in China, source of investment, industry in which the investment occurred, total investment, foreign partner equity contribution, foreign equity percentage (by range, in absolute terms, and by country), and the predetermined duration of the joint ventures formed.

The future of FDI in China is considered in the context of recent government recentralization steps, capitalization difficulties, counter-trade potential and the need to successfully implement existing enterprises.

In order to make this data less abstract, appended to this chapter is a case history of one of the largest joint ventures in China, Babcock & Wilcox Beijing Ltd. Written by the president of Babcock & Wilcox International, this case includes managerially-oriented suggestions for joint venture success in China.

A decade of experience

When China first began to experiment with joint ventures in the late-1970s, the country was just emerging from the Cultural Revolution (1966–76). During this period, the concept of using private capital, especially foreign private capital, was a heresy sufficient to land its advocate in jail, if not worse. The subsequent phenomenal growth in foreign enterprises should be seen from this perspective.

During the ten years following the institution of the 1979 Joint Venture Law of the People's Republic of China (PRC), the number of joint venture (JV) agreements signed in China increased almost exponentially. By the middle of 1990, 24,518 foreign enterprises had been registered in China, with total committed capital of US$36 billion and paid-in capital of US$16.6 billion. This excludes the substantial foreign loans to China. Between 1979–88 over US$33 billion of foreign loans had been utilized.

Interest in China evolved from a late 1970s–early 1980s period of caution, to the mid-1980s' explosion of involvement, what Pye (1986) called the Westchester County Syndrome. This syndrome resulted in US *and* other Western CEOs rushing to China to "score points at their country clubs or among business associates." Their interest in China had been as much a rational interest in a newly opening large market as it had been an almost irrational undertaking in which many executives seemed to view themselves as modern-day Marco Polos.

By the late 1980s the expanded regulatory environment, the responsiveness of Chinese authorities to investor concerns, and the strengthening of the market reforms in China all contributed to rapid growth in foreign investment. For example, in 1988 alone there were 5,945 foreign-funded enterprises, a 170 percent increase over 1987, with US$5.3 billion contracted and US$3.2 billion utilized.

Since Tiananmen, the number of new joint-venture agreements signed has decreased in absolute terms. Most observers agree that the first part of the 1990s will be characterized by a more sober view of what the stakes are for doing business in China.

The principal structures

There are three principal structures for foreign investment in China: equity joint venture, also simply called joint venture; contract joint venture, also called cooperative venture; and 100 percent subsidiary corporation, also called wholly foreign-owned enterprise.

The equity joint venture is the oldest form of foreign investment in China, and the law dates to 1979. In an equity joint venture, the distribution of dividends is fixed in accordance with each share-holder's capital contribution, and the joint venture is a limited liability corporation.

In a cooperative venture, the distribution of dividends is not subject to the percentage of equity contribution: repayment of the foreign partner's investment may receive priority, for example, and a sliding scale over time for dividend distribution is common. In other respects, the cooperative venture is also more flexible: there is no minimum 25 percent participation by the foreign party, as with an equity joint venture, and the lifetime of the project can extend beyond the fifty-year limit established for equity joint ventures. The cooperative venture structure avoids the issue of valuation of foreign technology and equipment which has derailed many equity joint-venture negotiations. Depending upon contract terms, the cooperative venture may or may not be considered an independent legal person. The structure has been used for most of the large natural resource and offshore oil projects in order to keep distinct each partner's separate obligations.

In a wholly foreign-owned enterprise, all capital is provided by the foreign company. This structure has been adopted by companies for a variety of reasons. As Stevenson-Yang (1990) notes, these include flexibility, lack of working capital from potential partners, to protect trade secrets, management control, and, in some instances, the need to create a new market. Nevertheless, a Chinese partner must be found to assist with sourcing labour and raw materials, although this partner is not entitled to board or management participation.

The number of equity and cooperative joint ventures is approximately even, with a much smaller number of wholly foreign-owned enterprises. As Table 8.1 notes, the 15,955 foreign enterprises

Table 8.1 Foreign investment in China, 1979–90

	Number of contracts signed	Contracted amount (US$ billion)	Utilized amount (US$ billion)
Direct investment (1979–88)	15,955	28.20	11.52
of which:			
Joint ventures	8,532	9.89	4.81
Cooperative enterprises	6,829	16.79	6.42
Wholly foreign-owned enterprises	594	1.52	0.29
Direct investment (1988)	5,945	5.30	3.19
Direct investment (1989)	5,779	5.60	3.92
Direct investment (1990–6 mos)*	2,784	2.40	1.20
Total direct investment (1979–mid-1990)	24,518	36.20	16.64

Sources: Canada China Trade Council Newsletters, April 1989, September 1990.
*Country Report – China, *The Economist Intelligence Unit*, No. 3, 1990.

registered by the end of 1988 included: 8,532 equity joint ventures; 6,829 cooperative ventures; and 594 wholly foreign-funded enterprises. Western countries have until recently preferred the equity joint-venture structure because the final laws governing cooperative ventures were not passed until April 1988. Some investors, particularly those from Hong Kong, were not deterred by the absence of a legal framework. In fact over 5,200 cooperative ventures had already been approved and many implemented before the legislation finally appeared.

This is typical of China's approach to regulations governing foreign investment. As with its economic reforms, China prefers to first experiment with actual implementation on a case-by-case basis, allowing the problems to be worked out, before promulgating new laws. China has been open to criticism of its new laws, and in response to the concerns of foreign investors the State Council issued "22 provisions for the encouragement of foreign investment" in October 1986.

The joint-venture experience

Although there has been a steady supply of anecdotal information on China, many of the "insights" offered by observers have been based on very small samples. Furthermore, as Walls (1986) notes, "they tell more about the observer than about the observed, since most observers tend to see what they expect to see, need to see, or want to see." One implication of having larger-sample history regarding JVs in China is that it permits foreign visitors to make a more informed decision about investing in that country.

Until recently, most of the information on JVs in China was of three types. The first type as mentioned, was anecdotal and was from the perspective of the foreign firms. The second type – from the Chinese perspective first but foreign perspective subsequently – was technical (i.e., the 118 articles of the 1983 "Regulations for the implementation of the law of the People's Republic of China on joint ventures using Chinese and foreign investment"). The body of technical information has grown rapidly, and during the ten years following the institution of the 1979 Joint Venture Law, over 400 laws relating to foreign investment were implemented. This in turn spawned a large amount of legal and accounting interpretation within each of the foreign countries which was contemplating investment in China. (Not surprisingly, due to on-going changes in the legal and accounting areas in China, much of the published foreign country interpretation was out of date before it was even published.) The third type of information – from the Chinese perspective – was promotional. As China's modernization program evolved and gained momentum, China showed no reluctance to advertise the number of JVs signed, the billions of investment dollars committed, the regulatory changes designed to improve conditions, and so forth. This promotional material, because it was typically presented in aggregate form, contributed to the 1980s bandwagon for investment in China. During this period, China was not above using the attraction of its domestic market to gain concessions from MNEs, a point raised by Gomes-Casseres (1990). Encarnation and Vachani (1985) had observed this pattern in India.

While the Westchester County Syndrome was instrumental in attracting people to the market earlier on, by the end of the decade investor confidence and experience was growing, and the track record from the early 1980s was perceived to be fairly positive. Not surprisingly, subsequent to the summer 1989 events of Tiananmen Square, this promotional material has placed much greater emphasis on damage-control.

Analysis

With the experience of a decade to draw upon, it is no longer necessary to rely merely on anecdotal, technical or promotional surveys of foreign investment in China. In this section we have taken the descriptions of 840 joint ventures from the China Investment Guide (1985, 1986), compiled and analyzed them, and present them in summary form. For more detail see Beamish and Wang (1989). This hard data on China – which has been lacking – was then combined in the analysis with the authors' personal experience in doing business in China.

When foreign companies are thinking about where to invest in China, they are typically pointed in the direction of Beijing, the fourteen coastal cities (especially Shanghai, Guangzhou or Tianjin), the special economic zones (SEZs) or, most recently, Hainan Island or Pudong. Most investment has taken place in these areas.

While focus on these areas does dramatically reduce the search time for where to locate investment, frustration still remains with respect to deciding between locations. Due to lack of coordination between regions, for most projects it is still necessary to approach officials in *each* province, major municipality, coastal city, or SEZ to determine if demand for the foreign firms' technology or product exists.

The implication of this lack of coordination should not be lost on firms considering investment in China. Particularly in regards to smaller investments – for which a higher degree of decentralized decision-making power exists in China – foreign firms must recognize that there may be literally dozens of regions/groups that can be approached.

One strategy successfully employed by foreign firms wondering if there is a need in China for the technology they possess has been to write/telex/fax *each* group several months before visiting the country. This may seem unnecessarily redundant. However, China, like most developing countries, does not possess sufficiently coordinated information systems. For example, it has nothing like the system of the Hong Kong Trade Development Council's trade enquiry databank, which contains information on more than 18,000 local manufacturers, exporters, and importers, and a file on more than 80,000 overseas importers (*South China Morning Post* 1985).

Approaching local authorities individually is usually needed for smaller manufacturing plants, especially by Hong Kong investors. However, for larger projects or more technology-intensive projects, central involvement has often been utilized and can be crucial. While there is no central databank such as Hong Kong has, the central authorities often have very useful information on your product's mix in the overall Chinese economy. By the end of a decade of reform, this information was no longer considered a "state secret" and was often provided by central ministries to help companies in their decision-making process. In fact, many companies have made the mistake of assuming this information is not available, and making decisions in China in a vacuum they would not tolerate anywhere else.

When the aggregate statistics about the thousands of JVs which have been signed are presented, what is not made clear is who the partners typically were, and in which industry the investment has occurred. Up to 1984, over three-quarters of the JVs in China were with partners from Hong Kong, with no other country making up more than 7 percent of the total. Although trade is not as unbalanced as investment, Hong Kong is nonetheless China's major partner for both imports and exports (see Table 8.2).

The heavy emphasis of investment from Hong Kong provides support for Hong Kong's oft-voiced view that it is the 'gateway' to China. The existence of Hong Kong-based firms as either competitor or conduit, has sometimes gone unnoticed by Western firms. In particular, a Hong Kong firm as conduit can be a reasonable approach to the Chinese market. For example, an American firm

Table 8.2 China's main trading partners, 1989

Exports to	% of total	Imports from	% of total
Hong Kong and Macau	42.6	Hong Kong and Macau	21.5
Japan	15.9	Japan	17.8
EC	9.2	EC	15.4
USA	8.4	USA	13.3
USSR	3.5	USSR	3.6
ASEAN	5.8	ASEAN	6.1
Middle East	2.6	Canada	1.8
		Australia	2.5

Source: Economic Information and Consultancy Co., *China's Customs Statistics* as noted in China Country Report of *The Economist Intelligence Unit*, No. 3, 1990.

with a technology which is desirable from China's perspective may wish to enter the Chinese market but lack the particular managerial resources or cultural sensitivities to do so. It can, however, provide the technology to a Hong Kong firm (either through a license or joint venture), which in turn will establish a joint venture in China. The benefits of the third party's (Hong Kong) contribution of management and Chinese market cultural knowledge can exceed the cost of sharing any profits with a third group. Not surprisingly, a number of foreign firms have joined up with Hong Kong-based companies.

However, using a Hong Kong partner can be a double-edged sword. It depends greatly on where your joint venture will be located. For example, a Hong Kong partner will be very useful in southern China, particularly in Shenzhen and in Guangdong Province. However, it can sometimes be counterproductive for a joint venture in the north, where some southerners and particularly Hong Kongers are disliked and distrusted. A significant development in 1990 is the increasing investment from Taiwan. The 1990 investment from Taiwan was second only to that of Hong Kong.

Approximately, 60 percent of the JVs which have been established have been in the manufacturing sector. The second largest area of investment has been in accommodation, in particular, tourism. In this latter sector, by 1990 it was evident that China had overbuilt in certain regions. For example, numerous hotels started in Xian were either incomplete or had no plans to open.

While the mega-projects such as the offshore oil joint ventures and Beijing Jeep assembly have received the headlines, 85 percent of the investments – no matter where the source – involved a *total* investment of less than US$5 million. In fact, in 95 percent of cases the foreign partner's contribution was less than US$5 million. Since decision-making is decentralized for investments under US$5 million, this provides further support for the importance of rigorously investigating across China the various packages which might be offered to any potential foreign joint venturer.

One consideration which has received much attention is the requirement to use a joint venture as opposed to a wholly-owned subsidiary. China has made much of the fact that firms are no longer required to use the joint-venture organization form, but that if they choose to use it, majority foreign ownership is permitted. While this is certainly true, in practice the foreign firm had majority ownership in fewer than 10 percent of the JVs formed, and equal ownership in about 30 percent of cases. This frequent use of a minority-equity position by the foreign partner is consistent with joint ventures in market-economy developing countries as well (Beamish 1988; Contractor 1990).

Use of equal ownership is consistent with the underlying Chinese desire for mutual benefit. Equal ownership does not necessarily require equal control over all decisions within the joint venture. Decision-making may be shared between the partners, or split. For example, in the Fujian–Hitachi Television Ltd joint venture in Fuzhou (CIDA, 1984), the Chinese administer and finance housing, medical, and welfare costs, the Japanese partner oversees the technical and production areas, and they jointly oversee hiring and firing.

A great deal of variability exists between the source of investment and the foreign equity percentage desired. For example, Hong Kong investors seem much more willing to take a minority equity position than investors from Europe, USA, or Japan. Some Chinese officials will privately admit that desire for equal or majority ownership by European, Japanese and American firms contributed – at least in the early years – to their lower levels of investment. Yet as Schaan (1983) has pointed out, in other developing countries, control is possible even with a minority equity position. Some of the control mechanisms available include use of contracts, the ability to set policies and procedures, staffing, and design of the reporting structure.

Fade-out joint ventures

For many Western firms the most unusual element of joint venturing in China has been the use of a fade-out provision. Over half of the JVs formed until 1985 were established in such a way that at the end of ten years, the entire business would become wholly Chinese owned. Such a requirement on China's part was symptomatic of an incomplete embrace of foreign influences. Not surprisingly the fade-out provision made some multinationals nervous since they were forced to make their investment decision based on a finite stream of earnings. They feared that if there were start-up delays or other unforeseen developments, they would be unable to recoup their total investment.

Solutions to this problem have evolved in recent years. Some ten-year contracts have been extended after implementation to increase the likelihood that the foreign partner will be able to recoup its investment and earn a profit. More important, the laws have been changed allowing up to fifty years for equity joint ventures and no predetermined fade-out for cooperative ventures.

These changes were prompted both by foreign criticism, and by the realization on the Chinese side that in order to stay competitive and profitable, foreign enterprises often need continued Western management and access to new market and technological developments provided by the Western partner.

The future

The joint venture process in China is different from that in developed countries and different than with joint ventures in developing countries which have market economies. These differences stem as much from politics as they do from the short time period in which the regulatory infrastructure has been enacted.

Many of the problems with joint ventures in China are external to the joint venture and relate to the interaction of a market organism – the joint venture – to the state-planned economy (raw materials, distribution, transportation). Companies recognizing this problem have counted on a deepening of the reform process in the 1990s with greater reliance on the market mechanism. Political developments in China will determine whether this was a good bet. If in the long-term the Chinese economy reverts to greater reliance on central planning, then these problems will undoubtedly be exacerbated and the investment climate will deteriorate. However, if the early 1990 focus on recentralization and renewed central planning is only temporary, then these types of problems can be addressed more successfully in the future.

Much progress toward a more realistic joint-venture investigation process has been made. The foreign investor contemplating the establishment of a JV in China now has a commercial code as a guide, and has historical data – to clarify what common practice has been.

Yet problems also remain. There have been many more joint venture agreements signed than there are joint ventures in operation. In fact, in mid-1986 *The Economist* noted that less than one-third of the 2,600 joint-venture companies named so far had actually gone into business. As at late 1989, approximately 6,000 foreign investment enterprises were in operation – or about 38 percent of those which had been signed. By mid-1990 only about 46 percent of the contracted investment had been disbursed. This gap between signed and implemented agreements is due to many factors, including inflexibility (from both partners), a short-term orientation; management problems; foreign-exchange difficulties; the time-lag between signing and implementation and full start-up; and the fact that the persons who signed the agreement were seldom the ones who had to implement it. Literally thousands – and no one knows the exact figure – of the contracts signed will *never* be implemented. To date, China has been unwilling to provide an accurate restatement of the true situation.

The differences between committed and paid-in capital also suggest that the aggregate figures for signed enterprises are misleading. While this in part reflects projects which are never implemented, it also reflects the fact that many foreign enterprises use a step-by-step approach to capitalization. In order to prevent undercapitalized joint ventures from failing, China recently issued stringent debt-equity guidelines. For investments of US$3 million or less, debt cannot exceed 30 percent; for investments between US$3 to US$10 million, debt cannot exceed 50 percent; US$10 to US$30 million, 60 percent; over US$30 million, 67 percent. Local currency debt financing has usually been available for approved projects, although it is likely that the new austerity measures will make it more difficult to secure such loans in the future.

To overcome foreign exchange difficulties may require a willingness to consider some form of countertrade, something which many firms consider unwieldy. Certainly the larger firms such as Pepsico's Kentucky Fried Chicken subsidiary have been able to utilize this option as a means of repatriating hard currency. In the usual terminology of China trade, countertrade is a separate form of business from foreign enterprises (it is a strict goods-for-goods trade, with various permutations, e.g. "processing agreement," "barter," etc., and does not involve foreign capital). Rather, foreign enterprises have the requirement "to balance foreign exchange." The evolution of foreign-exchange issues is an important point. It has turned out to be much less of a problem than in the early days, due to possibilities of selling locally and also of joint ventures entering the swap markets, where local renminbi (RMB) currency can be traded for foreign exchange (FEC). Recently, the swap market rates have approached the official exchange rate. Nonetheless, a consideration to be factored in for any investor is the trend toward more frequent currency devaluations in China.

China has – at least during the reform period – been moving in the direction of free convertibility, and large companies especially have been betting on this in the long-term and accumulating RMB locally or reinvesting in plant expansion. Also, joint ventures with foreign exchange surpluses can swap with those needing FEC. As with the "choice of partner" issue, it may be useful to make a distinction between two types of foreign enterprises. Smaller, Hong Kong-financed manufacturing enterprises utilizing cheap labor tend to be export-intensive and generate FEC that way. But Western, technology-intensive enterprises are more interested in selling locally and have found other ways to generate FEC as the investment climate and market forces have increased. The National Council's 1987 study somewhat surprisingly showed the extent to which American joint ventures are selling locally and do not view foreign exchange as their major headache.

Given the explosion of new foreign enterprises in the past three years, a key priority in China right now is not attracting new projects but successfully implementing existing enterprises. This will not be easy due to the lack of skilled managers in China. Many of those who were receiving training outside China in June 1989 exercised the opportunity provided by the various foreign governments to apply for refugee status. Since then, the Chinese government has provided far more restrictions on the ability of high-potential – especially younger – people to visit abroad. Also, because of the recent shortage of RMB local currency (caused by slowing monetary growth to halt inflation) and the retrenchment curtailing new capital investment in downstream industries, there has emerged a surprising preference for wholly foreign-funded enterprises (which were once tolerated primarily to get production facilities using technology that Western companies would not license otherwise). These will probably be the major trends in the early 1990s.

The current political uncertainty has already slowed foreign investment, and until resolved will continue to discourage Western companies. Nonetheless, Hong Kong manufacturing projects using cheap labor will continue, but in lesser numbers. In 1988, the central government of China began actively encouraging Taiwanese investments. Such investment has begun to pick up the slack from other foreign countries whose interests are increasingly turning to the markets of Eastern Europe.

Unless China moves on with its market-and-price reform, the problems presently facing foreign enterprises cannot be solved effectively and this will dampen investor confidence. Any prognosis for the future of foreign-funded enterprises depends upon the political solution in post-Deng China.

In the meantime, long-term flexible approaches will continue to be required. Unfortunately, this is the same requirement that has been present since 1979. For investors in most industries, China remains a market where dabblers and amateurs enter at their peril.

APPENDIX: BABCOCK & WILCOX BEIJING COMPANY[2]

Babcock & Wilcox is a full-line boiler and boiler accessories company that has been in business since 1867. Boilers come in all sizes up to the extremely large ones that generate steam, to power-turbines which make the electricity for most areas of the world. The company also provides a full range of industrial boilers that make steam for many industrial processes. Since 1978, Babcock & Wilcox has been a wholly-owned subsidiary of McDermott & McDermott International Incorporated. McDermott International is in the oil service business and manufactures and services offshore platforms, lays pipelines and provides other services to the offshore oil industry. In China, B&W are 50 percent partners in a joint venture named Babcock & Wilcox Beijing Company. This factory is the largest in B&W's system.

Why an alliance in China?

For utility boilers, those that generate electricity, China is clearly the largest market in the world, much larger than the US market. China has been undergoing an industrial revolution which could dwarf the industrial revolution that went on in the Western world in the first part of this century. We should know within a year or two whether the events of June 1989 will cause only a small hiccup in a continuous trend of progress, or whether progress will essentially grind to a halt in an environment of political unrest, inflation, and economic stagnation. Industry and particularly electricity production was held up in

China due to the cultural revolution and has a great deal of catch-up to do as China progresses toward joining the developed countries of the world. If there is any reasonable economic growth, the very large population guarantees that there will be an increasing demand for electricity, well into the next century. The growth in industrial-steam demand in China in tons per hour per year has been greater than in the United States and should get ever larger. The electricity power output is now one-seventh what it is in the United States and the per-capita consumption of electric power in China is one-thirtieth of the United States. These are the kind of numbers that make a marketer's eyes light up as he projects what happens when China is using as much per-capita electricity as the United States. Labor rates in China are, of course, attractive. They are two-thirds of the rate in India and they are far below the labor rate in Korea, Taiwan, and other countries that we have traditionally been looking to for sources of low-cost labor. We were also encouraged to form the partnership by the government of the PRC who wanted Western technology and particularly wanted Babcock & Wilcox technology. In fact the government helped us a great deal in partner selection. So we formed a fifty-fifty joint venture with an existing boiler company called Beijing Boiler Works. The venture comes under the Beijing city government but we have received a great deal of assistance from the central government as well.

Another major reason is simply that we cannot expect to export manufactured goods to China on an ongoing long-term basis when the country is capable of being self-sufficient. This is the only way we can really participate in the Chinese market in a meaningful and long-term way. Also, in the future, we expect that our Chinese venture will help us compete elsewhere. So far this has not been the case.

Alliance formation

The formation of our alliance took three years (see Table A8.1), about two years from the first approach until both sides were committed and then about another year to get the final contract signed by both sides and to get the business license to commence operation. We planned for and executed a six-month mobilization period during which we had our two key people over there. This was a time for the final audit and for dividing of the people between those who would stay with the Beijing Boiler Works and those who would come with the venture. We started operation in August 1986.

Table A8.1 Events leading to an alliance

1983	Oct.	– First meeting in Beijing
1984	Feb.	– Technical meetings in Beijing
	Sept.	– Chinese visit Babcock & Wilcox
	Nov.	– Evaluate manufacturing facilities in Beijing
1985	Mar.	– Feasibility study negotiations in Beijing
	Apr.	– Babcock & Wilcox Vice President visits Beijing
	May	– President Beijing Machine Building Corp. visits Babcock & Wilcox
	June	– Babcock & Wilcox President visits Beijing
	Aug.	– Negotiations in Beijing
	Oct.	– Vice Minister State Economic Commission visits Babcock & Wilcox
	Oct.	– Alliance contract signed in Beijing
	Nov.	– Contract and feasibility study submitted to government
1986	Jan.	– First Babcock & Wilcox people move to China
	Feb.	– Alliance approved
	June	– Business license issued
	Aug.	– Started operation

We provide a lot of services for all people like housing, medical, child care, transportation, and so forth. Unlike the Western world, large companies in China tend to be responsible for a complete set of services for employees.

The Babcock & Wilcox Beijing Company is ten miles west of Tiananmen Square. Beijing holds many advantages for us. Among these are: (*a*) easy access to the officials of the Chinese government and easy access by them to the joint venture; and (*b*) reasonable living conditions for our expatriates from North America. We took over about two-thirds of the existing land area and about two-thirds of the people of the Beijing Boiler Works. The remaining one-third stayed with the original company. It still operates today and is making smaller Chinese-designed boilers below the size range we are making. The joint-venture company covers seventy acres of land and has 800,000 square feet of production buildings. It includes 2,400 Chinese and nine people from Babcock & Wilcox. We have added three major buildings and some equipment, some of which was purchased new and some was provided by Babcock and Wilcox.

Babcock & Wilcox provides primarily management and technology. The company also provides the vice-chairman, one other non-resident director, a general manager (who answers to a board of directors) and key people to head up the technical departments such as engineering and quality assurance. We have some key people in manufacturing, materials, and project management, and we have a Babcock and Wilcox controller.

We leave to the Chinese the heads of departments such as marketing and sales, since so far our entire output has gone to the Chinese market. There is also a deputy general manager who is from our Chinese partner's firm.

Boards of directors in China are generally very strong. We have eight people on ours, four from each side. Three-fourths of those people have been with the project from the very beginning. Our board of directors' meetings are tough sessions in which we talk about all of the issues that are a concern to either party. And those board meetings are a good forum for the face-to-face discussions that you have to have. One board meeting started at 9:00 one morning and didn't adjourn until 5:00 the next morning.

Our production capacity has been fully used for both utility and industrial boilers for the China market. The venture continues to be profitable. The Babcock & Wilcox boiler design for 200 and 300 MW utility boilers has been well accepted. We delivered seventy boilers of various sizes in 1989 and worked 2.8 million man-hours. We are also beginning to break into the export market.

Successes

When we started we were told, "You must understand that you cannot work more than one shift. Chinese people do not want to work more than one shift." We put in the second shift after five days and the next month we put in the third shift, and the workers responded very well. We are very pleased with the quality of the Chinese workers. They inherently take very good care of the equipment. We have an incentive-pay program in place and they have responded to incentive pay as you would expect people anywhere to respond. In fact, some of our shops have worked an extra shift without pay or without any direction from us in order to meet the shop quota. We are meeting our production and financial goals. We're also pleased with the quality of the experienced Chinese engineers; our only problem is we cannot find enough of them. The technology transfer is proceeding ahead of schedule. As a result of thorough planning and effort, the company has been granted the Asme code stamps "S" and "U." The PRC government considers the venture a success and has frequently held it up as a good example.

Problems

Now, obviously there have been some problems and some of those problems remain to this day. The shortage of foreign exchange has been the worst. We knew it was going to be a problem from the beginning and it still is. So far we have not been able to export enough of our product to earn as much foreign exchange as we need. Both sides understood this from the beginning. We have received support and foreign exchange to keep going but the amount of effort that has been required to get it has been tremendous and a severe shortage currently exists. We also have a shortage of skilled workers. If we had more good ones, we could further increase production. It is difficult to recruit from other factories. There are certainly some unnecessary bureaucratic delays. We spent, for instance, about a year getting a construction permit for apartments for the B&W people and since we were spending one-third of a million dollars a year in hotel costs, that was an expensive delay. The material procurement system is certainly very costly and state-supplied material can only be obtained twice a year. Material purchase outside the planning period is more expensive than material purchases in the planning period and imported material requires foreign exchange so the material area is difficult. Safety standards are poor and we have had more accidents than we would like in the plant during the first couple of years. The housing for Chinese workers is inadequate. We don't have nearly enough for all of our people. That is inhibiting getting more workers, because they won't come from a factory that is now providing them with an apartment if we can't provide them one equally as good. Expatriate costs are high, more than US$150,000 per year per expatriate family. The transportation of the large, heavy components, the kinds of things we make, can be difficult. The transportation system is below par. There continues to be some resentment between the workers that have come with the venture and those that stayed behind with the Beijing Boiler Works. We have several hundred families which decided to hedge their bet. They were not sure the joint venture would work so one member of the family came with us and the other stayed with Beijing Boiler Works. Of course, both members normally do work. So now they go home every night and compare notes, which has caused some resentment. The joint-venture people are making more money. They are also working a lot harder. The high inflation and other economic difficulties have caused many project cancellations which have hurt.

Shipping can be a problem. There is a shortage of railcars and sometimes the material that is ready to be shipped piles up. Because the rail shipments can also be quite rough on some of the more delicate equipment, we make our own shipping boxes. Materials supply and storage is a major problem. Material expense is higher than in North America. We can buy material only twice a year which is a problem and requires high inventory levels so we have material stacked up all over. Just in time material delivery is just not part of the operation. It just doesn't work in China. Because we are dealing in high pressure boilers, each item has to be cataloged and tested as it comes in.

Lessons on getting started in China

Some of the things that it seems to us are necessary to get started in China are called the "nine Ps", since by happenstance each of these principles starts with the letter P. First, **planning**. You have to plan completely and try to foresee every contingency and make your contract absolutely as all-encompassing as possible. A friendly consultation later is not going to be nearly as satisfactory as determining in black and white what each partner is going to do before you become committed. Second, **persistence** on the part of the non-Chinese partner. The bureaucracy makes the decisions slow and hard to come by and you have to be willing to stick to it. Third, you need **partners** who really want a partnership. A Western country cannot sell a joint venture or sell its technology into China. The Chinese have to want it, they have to be pulling from their side. Fourth, you need a **product** that the country badly needs and that the government of the PRC really wants. Fifth, we also think it is important to have a **patron** who is senior enough in the government of China to be able to solve for you the problems which otherwise are unsolvable. Sixth, you need **patience**. Patient negotiation on both sides, and for this we believe you need continuity in the negotiating team. We essentially used our same team throughout the three-year process. Also, the team should be small. We prefer to do our own negotiation; we do not desire to turn it over to any one of the firms who are eager to do it for you.

Seventh, **people** from the non-Chinese partner who are going to go to China to work for the new company have to be carefully selected. They need to be committed; they need to be under a very strong and capable manager; and it needs to be a cohesive team. Of the nine original Babcock & Wilcox people sent to China, most of them had worked together for more than five years before they went overseas.

Eighth, you need a **problem-solving** attitude on the part of both sides and the non-Chinese partner needs to understand that there are certain things from the Chinese side that are not negotiable. There is a need to recognize what those are and not continue to hound the Chinese on something which is just not going to be changed. And finally, **public relations**, certainly always beneficial. We have toured many people from the government and from other factories through our joint-venture plant. The highest-level entourage was headed by Mr Zhao, former general secretary of the communist party and although that kind of a visit doesn't occur every week we have had a lot of visitors.

I could add a tenth P for **patience**. I know this was noted once before, but to be successful in China you now become part of its history and this happens by being patient. One cannot overemphasize this aspect.

Summary

Overall, Babcock & Wilcox is satisfied with our experience in China. Continued success is going to depend on economic and political stability in China and on our ability to control costs and to earn enough foreign exchange. Progress was being made by the government of China in the development of the laws and regulations needed to encourage investment and encourage the continued successful operation of the joint ventures that are already there. What will happen to that favorable trend after the Tiananmen Square incidents remains to be seen. The infrastructure is improving, although slowly. Our bottom line would be that China is not for the fainthearted investor. But if you have a product that they need and that they really want, there are tremendous opportunities.

NOTES

1 The authors wish to acknowledge the financial assistance of the Canadian International Development Agency through the Canada–China Management Program. An earlier version of this paper was presented at the 1990 Academy of International Business Conference in Toronto.

2 This Appendix was originally presented by Mr Paul P. Koenderman, President of Babcock & Wilcox, Canada, at the Strategic Alliances Executive Forum held in London, Canada in September 1989. Edited with the permission of B&W by Associate Professor Paul Beamish, Director of Canada–China Management Program, University of Western Ontario.

REFERENCES AND BIBLIOGRAPHY

"Always open for trade" (1985) *Hong Kong Visitor: South China Morning Post* (July), p. 66.

Baark, Erik, 1987, "Putting domestic technology to work," *China Business Review* (May–June), pp. 53–5.

Beamish, Paul W. (1988) *Multinational Joint Ventures in Developing Countries*, Routledge.

Beamish, Paul W. and H.Y. Wang (1989) "Investing in China via joint ventures," *Management International Review*, Vol. 29, 1, pp. 57–64.

Bovarnick, Murray E. and Jonathan M. Zamet (1986) "Employee relations for multinational companies in China," *Columbia Journal of World Business* (Spring), pp. 13–19.

Campbell, Nigel (1987) "Experiences of Western companies in China," *Euro-Asia Business Review* (July), pp. 35–8.

China International Economic Consultants, Inc. (1985, 1986) *China Investment Guide*, Longmans.

China Trade and Investment, August 15, 1989, pp. 21–3.

"China's budding markets," (1987) *The World Bank Research News* (Winter), Vol. 7, No. 3.

China's Foreign Trade, October–November 1989, p. 8.

Cohen, Jerome Alan and David G. Pierce (1987) "Legal aspects of licensing technology," *China Business Review* (May–June), pp. 44–9.

Conley, Terrance W. and Paul W. Beamish (1986) "Joint ventures in China: legal implications," *Business Quarterly* (November), Vol. 51, No. 3, pp. 39–43.

Consult Asia Inc. (1984) "A guide to technology transfers to the People's Republic of China," *Canadian International Development Agency (CIDA)* (September), pp. 19, 20.

Contractor, Farok J. (1990) "Ownership patterns of US joint ventures abroad and the liberalization of foreign government regulations in the 1980s: evidence from the benchmark surveys," *Journal of International Business Studies* (First Quarter), Vol. 21, No. 1, pp. 55–73.

Daniels, John D., Jeffrey Krug and Douglas Nigh (1985) "US joint ventures in China: motivation and management of political risk," *California Management Review* (Summer).

Davenport, Alice (1987) "Local technology import decisions," *China Business Review* (May–June), pp. 40–3.

Davidson, W.H. (1987), "Creating and managing joint ventures in China," *California Management Review* (Summer), Vol. 29, No. 4, pp. 77–94.

Encarnation, Dennis J. and Sushil Vachani (1985) "Foreign ownership: when hosts change the roles," *Harvard Business Review* (September–October), pp. 152–60.

Goldenberg, Susan (1988) *Hands Across the Ocean: Managing Joint Ventures with a Spotlight on China and Japan*, Harvard Business School Press.

Gomes-Casseres, Benjamin (1990) "Firm ownership preferences and host government restrictions: an integrated approach," *Journal of International Business Studies* (First Quarter), Vol. 21, No. 1, pp. 1–22.

Grow, Roy F., (1986) "Japanese and American firms in China: lessons of a new market," *Columbia Journal of World Business* (Spring), pp. 49–56.

—— (1987) "How factories choose technology," *China Business Review* (May–June), pp. 35–9.

Hendryx, Steven R. (1986a) "Implementation of a technology transfer joint venture in the People's Republic of China: a management perspective," *Columbia Journal of World Business* (Spring), pp. 57–66.

—— (1986b) "The China trade – making the deal work," *Harvard Business Review* (July–August).

Hiemenz, Ulrich, 1987, "PRC: prospects for trade and investments," *Euro-Asia Business Review* (July), pp. 31–4.

Hong Kong 1987, Government Printing Department, Hong Kong.

Hsueh, Tien-tung and Tun-oy Woo (1986) "US direct investment in Hong Kong: the present situation and prospects," *Columbia Journal of World Business* (Spring), pp. 75–85.

"Joint ventures in China: after the honeymoon . . . ," (1986) *The Economist* (August 16), pp. 47–8.

Koenderman, Paul (1990) "Doing business in China," *Business Quarterly* (Spring), Vol. 54, No. 4.

Kraar, Louis (1987) "The China bubble bursts," *Fortune* (July 6), pp. 86–9.

Lockett, Martin (1987) "China's development strategy," *Euro-Asia Business Review* (July), pp. 27–30.

Mann, Jim (1989) *Beijing Jeep*, Simon & Schuster.

National Council for US–China Trade (1987) *US Joint Ventures in China: A Progress Report*, Washington (March).

Noumoff, S.J. (1986) "China: a market of opportunities," *Canadian Business Review* (Winter), pp. 35–9.

O'Reilly, A.J.F. (1988) "Establishing successful joint ventures in developing nations: a CEO's perspective," *Columbia Journal of World Business* (Spring).

Pye, Lucian W. (1986) "The China trade: making the deal," *Harvard Business Review*, July–August.

Schaan, Jean-Louis (1983) "Joint venture control: the case of Mexico," unpublished doctoral dissertation, University of Western Ontario.

Siggins, Maggie (1987) "Mission impossible," *Report on Business Magazine* (Globe and Mail) (September), pp. 72–6.

Stevenson-Yang, Anne (1990) "Why go solo?" *China Business Review* (January–February), p. 31.

Tung, Rosalie L. (1986) "Corporate executives and their families in China: the need for cross-cultural understanding in business," *Columbia Journal of World Business* (Spring), pp. 21–5.

Walls, Jan (1986) "The cultural context of communication in China: cross-cultural business skills," *Issues*, Asia Pacific Foundation of Canada (Spring), pp. 1–7.

Yuann, James K. (1987) "Negotiating a technology license," *China Business Review* (May–June), pp. 50–2.

9 Managing international joint ventures in China

Mee Kau Nyaw

INTRODUCTION

Since the Third Plenum of the Eleventh Central Committee of the Communist Party of China (CCP) held in December 1978, China has adopted the "open-door policy"[1] and gradually opened up its economy to foreign investment. Although the economic reform program has shifted to more central control and less reliance on market mechanism after the Beijing June 4 incident in 1989, the open-door policy basically remains intact.

Five types of foreign investment can be identified in the four special economic zones (SEZs)–Shenzhen, Zhuhai, Shantou, and Xiamen – fourteen coastal cities,[2] Hainan Island, Pearl River Delta, and other areas inside China, namely, processing and assembly, compensation trade, joint ventures, wholly foreign-owned enterprises and cooperative ventures.[3] In official policy, equity joint ventures are assigned a crucial role in achieving the two main objectives of an open-door policy, namely, facilitating the transfer of technology and management techniques, and increasing foreign exchange earnings. Joint ventures are of considerable importance in terms of the number of establishments and value of foreign investment (Henley and Nyaw 1990).

This chapter is concerned with the management system and functioning of joint venture enterprises with special reference to the human resource management. It will focus on the authority and responsibilities of the board of directors, the roles of general managers, interface of management with the enterprise trade union, and labor and wage management of the international joint ventures. Wherever applicable the main differences of the management system of joint ventures will be compared with their counterparts in state-owned enterprises. Common problems of the existing management system will also be discussed.

THE AUTHORITY AND RESPONSIBILITIES OF THE BOARD OF DIRECTORS

Joint ventures in China are now mainly governed by the "Law of the PRC on Chinese–Foreign Joint Ventures" (hereafter Joint Ventures Law) and the "Regulations for the Implementation of the Law of the PRC on Chinese–Foreign Joint Ventures" (hereafter Joint Ventures Implementation Regulations) which were promulgated in 1979 and 1983 respectively. According to the Joint Ventures Law, there is no upper limit to foreign investment in a joint venture, but the law sets a minimum of 25 percent for investment by foreign party or parties (Article 4, Joint Ventures Law, 1979). This would seem to suggest that the pursuit of foreign capital is assigned high priority while the seamless web of the state bureaucracy is assumed to be well able to enmesh any deviant foreign activities.

Ideologically, the establishment of joint ventures in China poses dilemmas for the CCP. First, is the profit-making international joint venture compatible with the ideals of communism and socialism? The views expounded by Xu Dixin, a noted Chinese economist, seemed to be shared by most high-ranking Chinese communist leaders. According to Xu, Chinese joint ventures, cooperative ventures, and compensation trade are all "state capitalist enterprises," and "state capitalism" may exist in a socialist nation. However, activities and operations of a joint venture are subject to the regulation of the state (Xu 1982). As China is now considered to be in the "primary state of socialism," as argued by the Chinese communist leadership, the coexistence of joint ventures and state-owned enterprises is allowed. Furthermore, joint ventures in China are under the control of state regulations that protect worker interests.

Second, in contrast to state-owned enterprises, workers and staff of joint ventures are no longer the "masters of the house." One unionist in Shenzhen even suggested that "there is exploitation because of state capitalism" (*South China Morning Post*, November 13, 1988). However, there is an opposite view that the exploitation of workers by foreign investors is incorrect. Tang argued that employee relations in joint ventures in the PRC are different from those of the capitalist countries (Tang, 1988, p. 244). No conclusion has been arrived at regarding this theoretical issue to date. We will set aside this issue and concentrate on the discussion of how the management system of joint ventures works in China.

The management system of joint ventures in China is characterized by the interlocking relationships among joint venture management, state ministry, trade union and the CCP as shown in Figure 9.1. The

Two Levels:

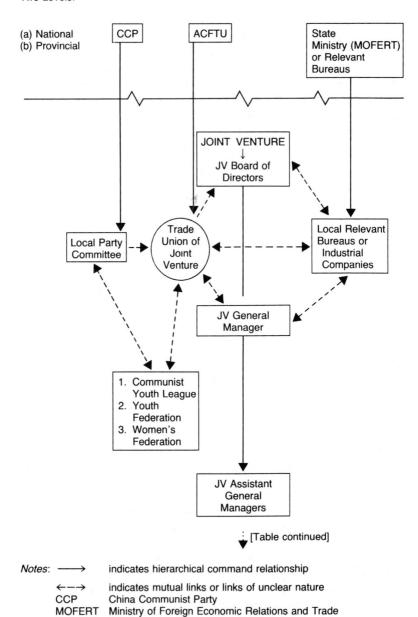

(a) National
(b) Provincial

Notes: ⟶ indicates hierarchical command relationship

    ←→ indicates mutual links or links of unclear nature
CCP   China Communist Party
MOFERT Ministry of Foreign Economic Relations and Trade

Figure 9.1 A simplified diagram of the interlocking relationships among the trade union, joint venture management, state ministry, and the Party.

Joint Ventures Law and Implementation Regulations stipulate that the board of directors shall be the highest organ of authority. Initially, the law required that the chairman of the board be appointed by the Chinese partner, and the vice-chairman (or vice-chairmen) by the foreign partner (Articles 33, 34, Joint Ventures Implementation Regulations). However, on April 4, 1990 a crucial amendment to the Joint Ventures Law was made by the government, i.e. chairmanship of the board of directors will be subject to negotiation by both the Chinese partner and the foreign investor, or by election at the board meeting. Should the chairmanship go to a person from one side, the deputy chairmanship will then be a person from the other partner. This change could be interpreted as a major concession from the PRC. The relaxation of the stipulation of chairmanship of the board of directors is in line with the generally accepted practice of international joint ventures in most countries. However, what is the board's actual authority and responsibilities? What is the appropriate composition of the board of directors in order to function properly? What problems are encountered?

An interview conducted by the author in Shenzhen SEZ in 1990 shows that most joint ventures have articles of association which stipulate the authority and responsibilities of the board (Interview, 1990). As might be expected, the articles are more detailed for larger joint ventures involving European or American partners than for smaller or medium-sized ventures with Hong Kong- or Macau-based partners. In addition, they also vary according to the type and scope of the business. In general, the board of directors of Sino–foreign joint ventures has the following authority and responsibilities.

First, it evaluates and approves annual plans for revenue and expenditure, financial statements such as proposals for the distribution of profit, and plans for the production and operating activities of the venture. Second, it considers the regulations and systems of the venture such as the enterprise rules, financial system and labor contract, pay and welfare system. Third, it decides on the overall organizational structure and key personnel arrangements such as the establishment levels of departments, and the appointment of the general manager, deputy manager(s), the chief engineer, the chief accountant and auditors, their authority and terms of employment. Finally, the board deliberates on the venture's long-term strategic plans for investment, financial restructuring, and cooperation with other firms including mergers.

Respondents commented on two tendencies that work against the smooth working of the board of directors. At one extreme is the tendency for responsibilities to be too specific so that all matters have to be considered by the board, whether or not they are significant. At the other extreme, responsibilities are too vague so that the board is able to ignore or avoid urgent problems which need immediate resolution. However, it was not clear whether these problems arose from the generic features of joint ventures or from the particular situation in Shenzhen SEZ. Certainly the scope for misunderstandings and confusion are considerable when two radically different economic philosophies interface so that it is especially important to establish an appropriate management charter. However, since none of the foreign partners had previous experience of joint venturing with communist regimes it was a case of learning from trial and error with a good deal of forbearance.

Although the composition of the board of directors basically reflects the share of each of the venture's partners, the handling of major issues or problems is supposed to be through consultation between the venture partners rather than through voting. This is emphasized in the Joint Ventures Implementation Regulations. While it was stipulated before the amendment in 1990 that the chairman of the board as the legal representative of the venture should be appointed by the Chinese partner, some cases were encountered in Shenzhen SEZ where the chairman was supplied by the foreign partner. Since constitutionally the chairman of the board is the key figure of the venture, his leadership skills and capabilities ought to play a crucial role in the success of the enterprise.

The respondents complained of a number of problems that arise in relation to the directors appointed by the Chinese authorities which in their view undermined the viability of the board of directors as a decision-making body. First, there are frequent changes in directors as a result of decisions taken elsewhere by government agencies that consequently damage the continuity in top management necessary to maintain effective functioning. Second, many of the chairmen of the boards of directors are the heads of the administrative departments or industrial companies that are responsible for the joint venture. They wear many "hats" and are often too busy to take active responsibility as members of the board of a joint venture. In many instances, they merely serve as figure-heads. Some are retired senior cadres with no business experience. Their new "jobs" are merely rewards for their past service to the state.

There were also complaints about the composition and number of board members nominated from the Chinese side. Very often the "Noah's Ark" principle seemed to operate so that every administrative department with any connection with the joint venture had the right to nominate a director. Because of the large number of interests sometimes involved, the board became a "small government" of China. Perversely, there were also cases of state factories which were true partners of the joint venture and yet could not obtain a seat on the board of the joint venture. In general, there was a belief that those enterprises whose key Chinese directors came from the immediately responsible company or unit performed more effectively.

THE ROLES OF THE GENERAL MANAGERS

According to the Joint Ventures Implementation Regulations, responsibility for day-to-day operations and management rests with the general manager, who "within the scope authorized by the board of directors, . . . represents the joint venture in external matters and, within the venture, appoints and dismisses subordinate personnel, and exercises the other powers conferred upon him by the board of directors" (Article 39, Joint Ventures Implementation Regulations). In other words, the general manager is the chief executive of the joint venture and has full autonomy within the policy guidelines established by the board.

The general manager of a joint venture is assisted by deputy manager(s) and divisional managers (see Figure 9.1). No nationality restriction is imposed on general managers or deputy managers. They can be nominated by either or both partners. A general manager may sometimes be appointed who has no relation with either side.

General managers have close contact with the various administrative bodies or agencies of the government, in particular, the Ministry of Foreign Economic Relations and Trade (MOFERT) through which a general manager must deal (see Figure 9.1). After a venture is approved by the Foreign Investment Commission and is established, MOFERT or its authorized agent is responsible for guiding, assisting or supervising the implementation of the joint venture contract, but is prohibited from issuing directives to the venture. For example, a joint venture may be assisted by government authorities to the extent of being guaranteed priority access to resources, but will be left to work out its own production and operating plans. The author's informants reported that in the past, government departments dealt mainly with the general manager but now deal more with the board of directors. This seemed to be related to the growing maturity of ventures and the gradual extension of the power of the board of directors relative to that of the general manager.

Perhaps wisely, the tasks and responsibilities of a general manager are not stated in the joint venture laws or implementation regulations. While they vary depending on the size and type of business, they nonetheless have some common features. For example, the general manager of a manufacturing joint venture in Shenzhen has the following fairly typical responsibilities:

1 to develop the joint venture's long-, and short-term objectives;
2 to formulate the strategy to achieve the enterprise's objectives;
3 to supervise the implementation of the strategic plan;
4 to assess immediate subordinates' performance;
5 to appoint divisional managers;
6 to readjust the organization structure to meet operational needs;
7 to arbitrate in conflicts between departments or personnel;
8 to plan the major financial plan;
9 to liaise with the government, shareholders, consumers, and financial institutions, in order to promote good relations with them;
10 to deal with urgent and important matters;
11 to monitor the establishment of an effective control system;
12 to plan, implement and control the overall development of the venture

(Interview, 1990)

In the above case, the general manager has to deal with almost all major internal and external issues. However, in some ventures it is stipulated that a general manager has to consult with his deputies on major issues. Moreover, major documents have to be co-signed to take effect. In an attempt to establish what attributes Chinese general managers or deputy managers think distinguish successful joint venture managers from factory directors in state-owned enterprises the author asked his respondents to suggest the vital qualities needed. They agreed on the following qualities:

1 initiative;
2 a strong background in policy and respect for the law;
3 know the relevant industry and have the required modern management skills;
4 commitment to placing good people in appropriate positions and able to work with them as a team.

How to train managers to develop these qualities is clearly one of the critical issues facing joint ventures in China today.

THE ROLE OF TRADE UNIONS

Communist ideology dictates that workers are "masters of the house." In China, this is taken to imply workers' participation in management and, in concrete form, has evolved as the system of workers' congresses.[4] The enterprise trade union committee is another important institution in the decision-making structure of state-owned enterprises operating as the "transmission belt" linking the Party with the industrial workforce (Lenin's doctrine). It is also regarded as a management school for workers in support of the productionist goals of the Party (Littler and Lockett 1983; Nelson and Reeder 1985; Henley and Nyaw 1986).

There is no provision for workers' congresses in joint ventures of China. However, as stipulated in the Constitution of the Trade Unions of the PRC, trade union organizations in joint ventures are an integral part of the All-China Federation of Trade Unions (ACFTU), but "provisions dealing with the special problems of trade unions in such enterprises are stipulated separately by the ACFTU" (Article 35, Constitution of the Trade Unions of the PRC, 1983). Unfortunately, ACFTU to date has no provision dealing specifically with trade unions of joint ventures. Instead, provisions dealing with the joint ventures in China are contained in two separate sources. In the "Provisions for trade unions of special economic zone enterprises in Guangdong Province," it is stipulated that trade unions in such enterprises (including joint ventures) are legal entities and the chairmen of trade unions are their representatives (Article 3). On the other hand, the Joint Ventures Law stipulates that a joint venture is a limited-liability company (Article 4, Joint Ventures Law). Trade unions are therefore not appendages of the joint venture. Trade unions have been formed in most joint ventures in PRC in accordance with the Joint Ventures Law. However, they are not mandatory. Ninety-two percent of foreign or foreign participating firms have their trade unions set up in Shenzhen in 1987 (*Shenzhen SEZ Daily*, April 16, 1987). Although there is no workers' congress in a joint venture, the Joint Ventures Implementation Regulations stipulate that there is a need for the enterprise "to heed the opinions" of staff and workers, particularly on labor-related issues. However, the extent of worker participation in management is far less than in state-owned enterprises.

Unlike its counterpart in the West, the "management" of a joint venture is supposed to "positively support" the work and activities of its trade union (Chen and Li 1987, p. 87). Union representatives have the right to sit in the board of director's meeting to air workers' opinions, although they do not have the right to vote.

China considers that it is the political right of staff and workers to join a trade union in the joint venture. The trade union of a joint venture, like its counterpart of any enterprise in China, is a member of the local union for a particular industry or the local trade union council. Theoretically, the general objectives of the joint ventures are in line with that of the trade unions, i.e., to make the venture a success. A successful joint venture benefits both the foreign investors (in the form of "profit") and the nation (in the form of technology transfer and foreign-exchange earnings). However, it is emphasized that the trade union of a joint venture has a duty to represent the interests of the staff and workers, and "shall have the right to represent them in signing labor contracts with the joint venture and supervising the implementation of such contracts" (Article 96, Joint Ventures Implementation Regulations).

One unique aspect of the trade unions of joint ventures in China is that they deal directly with foreign partners or their representatives with regards to labor disputes or grievance. They are not dealing with the joint ventures *per se* as the latter are owned partly by the state. Unions are a transmission belt between the Party and the masses. They are not supposed to "negotiate" with the Party-controlled state. In dealing with foreign investors, union representatives need considerable skills in negotiation which they tend to lack. The Chinese emphasize "consultation" rather than "confrontation" in dealing with most matters. Should a labor dispute such as a worker's dismissal not be resolved through consultation, one or both parties can request arbitration of the local government, in accordance with the Provision for Labor Management in Chinese–Foreign Joint Ventures (Article 4). However, arbitration seems to be rare in Chinese joint ventures. In contrast to the adversarial roles of many trade unions in Western countries, the Chinese partners emphasize that the trade unions of joint ventures in China are cooperative and conciliatory. Among other things, they organize vocational, scientific, and technical studies, and they educate the workers to observe labor discipline and to fulfill the economic task of the enterprise. Joint ventures have to allot a sum equal to 2 percent of the actual wages of all staff and workers as union funds to finance these activities (Articles 98–99, Implementation Regulations). As a high-ranking official from MOFERT remarked, the role of trade unions of joint ventures in China is different:

A foreign investor needs not worry about the union being unproductive toward the management or the Chinese employees being insubordinate to the foreign managers. Experience proves that, with the guidance of their trade unions, the Chinese staff and workers are highly conscientious, disciplined and industrious employees working for the interest of the ventures.

(Chu 1986, p. 80)

Although the above remarks are promotional in tone, it nonetheless portrays the task of trade unions of the ventures as perceived by the Chinese authority. The trade unions certainly have no intention of disrupting the operations of joint ventures, as the Chinese Communist Party has repeatedly educated workers that it would be in the mutual interests of the state and foreign partners if staff and workers work diligently and efficiently for the joint ventures which employ them (Tang 1988, pp. 244–9).

The management of Chinese state-owned enterprises involve the intricacies of four actors: the enterprise's Party Secretary, the factory director, the workers' congress and the enterprise trade union (Henley and Nyaw 1986). In the joint venture enterprise, the law does not stipulate the role for formation of a Communist Party committee. In one episode cited, the board of directors rejected a request for help to set up a Party organization in a joint venture, and no objection was raised by the Chinese side (Horsley 1984, p. 21). On the other hand, the Chinese leadership seems to favor some form of Party organization to be established in the international joint ventures but does not insist on it (Tang 1988, p. 251). Irrespective of the existence of Party organization, the author's interviews in Shenzhen SEZ in 1990 revealed that party activities do exist and are normally carried out by the trade unions. The influence of CCP is also felt through the State-appointed directors. One of the intricacies of the whole system is that most senior trade unionists and directors are Party members themselves, and they strictly adhere to the Party line and policy. The Party's activities in the joint ventures are mainly to indoctrinate staff and workers to adhere to the Party line and to work in harmony with the investors (Tang 1988, p. 251).

Apart from trade unions, other mass organizations such as the Communist Youth League, Youth Federation, and Women's Federation also exist in the joint ventures just as in many "units," including state-owned enterprises in China. Their activities are channeled through the trade unions of joint ventures (see Figure 9.1). The author's interviews revealed that the secretary of the local Communist

Youth League is usually the vice-president of the joint venture's trade union or a member of its executive committee. As compared to trade unions, the roles played by other mass organizations are far less significant. They organize mainly social support functions.

EMPLOYMENT AND WAGE SYSTEM

We now turn to other issues of labor management such as employment and wage system. As a joint venture in China involves two or more partners from different value structures and socioeconomic systems, its personnel system becomes more complex.

Chinese state-owned enterprises have little control over the employment of the workers and staff. They have to take whoever are assigned to them by the state labor bureau. Workers and staff literally have no mobility once they are attached to a "unit." Although labor management reform has been introduced in the last few years, it is carried out only on a limited scale. The reform so far has achieved little success, as enterprises are very reluctant to release their own workers. Without permission of existing enterprises, other "units" could not take them. In contrast, the workers and staff of joint ventures are hired by the enterprise through the labor service company with approval from the labor bureau. A joint venture may also advertise for workers. Successful candidates may undergo a three-to-six-month probation period, a practice commonly found in a market economy. Theoretically, the joint ventures will have priority to recruit qualified workers and staff previously engaged in other units. However because of the lack of an effective labor market in China, the firms have to "consult" with the units concerned, the success rates of which are known to be low as the latter are usually reluctant to release their workers and staff unless they themselves are partners of the joint ventures.

Staff and workers in the state-owned enterprises are known to have enjoyed "iron rice-bowl" which is a form of lifetime job tenure. Beginning in October 1986, workers in these enterprises are employed on contracted terms on an experimental basis as part of the country's labor management reforms (*Ming Pao*, July 29, 1986; *Wen Wei Pao*, September 5, 1986). According to the new regulations, workers can theoretically be dismissed. However, it is widely known that, only under exceptional cases such as political purges or serious offences, are workers in state-owned enterprises ever dismissed. The "lifetime job tenure system" is still existing, though not necessarily in name. In contrast, the "iron rice-bowl" is not applicable to staff and workers in joint ventures in China. A joint venture has the right to lay-off staff and workers whose employment is considered redundant (Provisions of PRC for Labor Management in Chinese–Foreign Joint Venture, 1986). It can also fire undisciplined workers or those who have committed serious offences. This had in fact taken place. China Hewlett-Packard Ltd has fired nine workers (*Hong Kong Economic Journal*, June 28, 1987), and a successful Hong Kong–Chinese joint venture manufacturer of matchbox toys in Shanghai has dismissed eleven workers since its establishment in 1986 (Koo 1987). None had encountered opposition from the trade unions. On the contrary, they had the latter's support since reasons for dismissals were justified.

Another important aspect of the labor management is the salaries and wages, bonus, welfare benefits, and labor insurance for workers and staff in the joint ventures. According to Article 39 of Joint Ventures Implementation Regulations, a joint venture's salary and wages and bonus system should adhere to the principles of "to each according to his work," and "more pay for more work." The distribution principles are analogous to that of the Chinese state-owned enterprises which subscribe to the "socialist" principle of "from each according to his ability and to each according to his work" after China launched its economic reform program in 1979 (Henley and Nyaw 1987, p. 128). In fact, there is little difference between China and other market economies as far as this particular principle is concerned. What matters is the actual pay practices of the enterprises.

Article 8 of the Provisions for Labor Management in Sino–Foreign Joint Ventures in 1980 stipulates that the wage levels of the local staff and workers "shall be fixed at 120 to 150 percent of the real wages of the staff and workers of state enterprises in the locality in the same line of business." Apparently, the higher wage levels are intended to attract competent staff and workers to work in the joint venture enterprises. However, it does not take efficiency and work intensity into special consideration as the latter are in general higher than 20–50 percent as compared to that of state-owned enterprises. In addition, staff and workers are younger and have brighter ideas as they are generally recruited from the labor market rather than "being assigned." They are also willing to work harder. The *fixing* of wage levels at 20–50 percent higher, therefore, is not entirely justifiable as it lacks flexibility.

The wage fund of a joint venture is derived from its "labor service fees" allotted by the enterprise. Labor service fees paid to local staff and workers include wages, labor insurance, medical welfare, and subsidies of various kinds. According to a survey, wages of staff and workers account for about 70 percent of total labor service fees of joint ventures. It also varies from different localities (Nyaw and Lin 1990). The amounts of these fees are decided at the board level in each year. The foreign partners consider that workers and staff of a joint venture do not enjoy all the fruits of labor services fees paid by the joint ventures. This may have a negative impact on the workers' motivation to work. The Chinese side argues that benefits and various government subsidies currently enjoyed by staff and workers are in fact paid by the government. Therefore, joint venture enterprises have to pay back to the Chinese side for its contribution in accordance with the standards for state enterprises. However, various subsidies are difficult to calculate especially as price in China is an "administered price" which does not reflect scarcity of resources.

There is no single "model" of wage payment to staff and workers of joint ventures in China. Instead there emerges a variety of wage patterns. In general, the wage level can be broken down into the following five components: basic wage, floating wage, position wage, piece-rate wage, and bonus. Basic wage is the wage which guarantees that workers and staff can meet daily basic needs, whereas position wage is a remuneration for holding a certain position. When a position changes, position wage will change accordingly. Floating wage refers to the system that workers' wage may float fully or partially, levels of which depend on the profitability of the enterprise in different periods.

According to a survey of thirty-eight joint ventures conducted in Shenzhen SEZ, there are as many as thirteen combinations of the wage components for firms under survey. It differs from industries, locations, or class of workers (Nyaw and Lin 1990). For production workers, "wage + bonus" model is more common. Bonus is generally linked to workers' efficiency. The different wage patterns are in line with the Provisions for Labor Management which stipulate that the system of wage standards, types of wages, bonuses, etc., are at the discretion of the board of directors (Article 9). A joint venture has autonomy in deciding a wage pattern which suits them best. The survey result in Shenzen shows that workers and staff of joint ventures were generally satisfied with the amount of wages they received. The satisfaction levels were as follows: "extremely satisfactory" (5.3 percent), "satisfactory" (47.4 percent) and "moderately satisfactory" (4.2 percent). Only about 5 percent of workers and staff were not satisfied (Nyaw and Lin 1990). This can be explained by the fact that workers and staff receive higher wages than their counterparts in state-owned enterprises. It can also be justified by the fact that efficiency of joint venture enterprises is higher *vis-à-vis* state-owned enterprises in China. This may also indicate that financial reward is an effective means to elicit greater efforts from staff and workers. The foregoing discussion focuses on compensation for staff and workers from the Chinese side. As far as expatriates are concerned, their remuneration is based on a contract signed between the employees and the joint ventures subject to approval by the board of directors. Expatriates usually hold managerial or supervisory positions or serve as consultants. In general, foreign employees receive a comparable wage which they would otherwise receive in their own countries plus hardship allowances and other benefits. The term "hardship allowance" is not used in China as it is sensitive to the Chinese partners. The general practices are to include them in an "other benefits" item.

SOME EMPIRICAL EXPERIENCE

Henley and Nyaw had undertaken a questionnaire survey of thirty-four firms conducted in Shenzhen SEZ (Henley and Nyaw 1990). Some of the empirical results relevant to this chapter are presented in Table 9.1.

From China's point of view, one of the major objectives of foreign investment is to transfer the Western management knowhow to the country. Participation in management by foreign partners therefore seems to be crucial. Empirical results show that such participation was, however, low and mostly concentrated in upper levels (50 percent). About 40 percent of the sample firms did not have a foreign manager on site reflecting the close proximity of Hong Kong and Macao to Shenzhen as an alternative location. For those foreign managers who were involved on a day-to-day basis in management, they focused mainly on the areas of planning, marketing, financial control, and technology management. Only 20 percent participated in personnel management matters (Table 9.1).

The survey also attempted to look at the organizational efficiency of the joint ventures. Organizational effectiveness can mean different things to different people and nowhere is the concept more ambiguous than when applied to a joint venture. Each partner is likely to have different motives and objectives and, therefore, the criteria used to assess a venture are likely to be different depending on which partner is being interviewed. A majority of the respondents from Chinese

Table 9.1 Participation in management by foreign partners, organizational efficiency and organizational problems

	Enterprises	
I. Participation in management by foreign partners:		
Heavily involved in all management	3	
Involved in middle and top management	17	
Basically not involved	13	
Total	33[1]	
II. Areas of management involvement by foreign partners:		
Planning decisions	17	(50%)
Marketing channels	12	(35%)
Financial control	11	(32%)
Technology and innovation	10	(30%)
Personnel management	7	(22%)
Others	3	(9%)
Total	60[2]	
III. Organizational efficiency:		
Outstanding	2	
Good	15	
Average	12	
Poor	3	
Very poor	1	
Total	33[1]	
IV. Existing organizational problems:		
(a) Problems acknowledged:		
None	10	
Problems have yet to be discovered	10	
Problems have already arisen	14	
Total	34	
(b) Causes of problems:		
Insufficient consultation	3	
Inadequate understanding on the Chinese side	1	
Inadequate understanding on the foreign side	3	
Mutual misunderstanding	3	
Vague organizational authority	7	
Other	0	
Total	17[3]	

Source: Henley and Nyaw (1990), Table 3, Table 7.
Notes: 1. one firm did not respond;
2. responding firms could select more than one area of involvement;
3. the fourteen firms responding could select more than one reason.

partners rated that the organizational efficiency of the firms was "average" or "above average" ("good" and "outstanding").

As far as organizational problems are concerned, around 40 percent of the Chinese partners said there were substantial problems affecting the venture they were involved with and over 80 percent of the reasons given for difficulties revolved around one form or another of misunderstanding or mutual incomprehension of the other's objectives or methods. Confusion as to who had organizational authority was a particularly common source of friction. By contrast, half of the ventures were considered to function well.

DISCUSSIONS AND CONCLUSIONS

The Chinese authorities, once having made the momentous decision to attract direct foreign investment, selected the joint venture form because of deep-rooted political concerns about losing control of important sectors of the economy to foreigners and the consequences of allowing the establishment of enclaves of free enterprise within a command economy. Foreigners, particularly "off-shore" Chinese from Hong Kong and Macao, have been lured in to form joint ventures on the strength of the attractions of having access to the Chinese domestic market. However, management skills sharpened on the problems of responding to market scarcities do not blend easily with those developed to cope with the market shortages so characteristic of socialist systems.

The instinct of a socialist manager is to hoard whatever resources are available, human or material, against the possibility of future shortages. The foreign manager, by contrast, is used to responding to variations in price signals as indicators of relative scarcity and to minimizing inventories. It is, therefore, hardly surprising that there are problems in establishing joint management principles. After all, conventional wisdom about successful joint venture management is that a venture only works effectively when one partner is clearly dominant. In a command economy, this is clearly impossible by definition, for if the Chinese partners could truly be dominant with respect to marketing and technology then there would be no need for a foreign partner. On the other hand, while the foreign partner may control marketing skills and technology there is no possibility of controlling sourcing where supplies are administered rather than traded in the market. The implication of this is that Chinese joint ventures are indeed joint affairs where neither partner can dominate the organization. Hence deadlock and complaints about "vague organizational authority" are part of the pathology of mixed socialist and capitalist joint ventures. In my view, a cultural explanation for the remarkable obduracy of organizational problems in Chinese joint ventures is inadequate for, after all, most joint ventures actually involve culturally similar partners, namely, "overseas" Chinese and mainland Chinese.

The present industrial relations system of China's joint ventures seems to function well. Although bureaucracy and the indiscriminatory levy of fees not specified in the joint venture contracts are the subjects of common criticism by foreign investors, little has been reported on any malfunctioning of the trade unions. In addition, labor productivity in joint ventures in China is generally far higher than that of state-owned enterprises. This is due to better management of labor in joint ventures. Workers are more disciplined and financially motivated (Henley and Nyaw 1989; Pi *et al.* 1989). Undoubtedly, joint venture has the support of trade unionists. One prominent Hong Kong entrepreneur, who has successfully invested in a joint venture in Shanghai, noted: "I urge Hong Kong entrepreneurs not to oppose establishment of trade unions [as in Hong Kong]; the union has assisted the workers greatly in filling the economic tasks of my enterprise" (Koo 1987).

One of the arguments used to support continued experimentation with joint ventures is that they offer some kind of test-bed from which reform strategies for state-owned enterprises can be derived. This seems implausible if it is accepted that the fundamental problem is the distinction between the logic of the economics of shortages and the economics of scarcity. For example, a clear theme that is emerging from numerous studies of joint ventures in China, is the propensity of higher-level administrative bodies to interfere in and restrict the managerially optimal level of venture autonomy.

Of course, joint ventures are relatively new organizations and so many of the problems encountered are merely a reflection of that newness. Likewise, China is a culturally distant society from Western Europe and North America so there is bound to be considerable scope for misunderstanding within Sino–foreign ventures. Nevertheless it is my contention that the continuing search for solutions to the managerial problems of joint ventures needs to be directed toward the wider political economy of China as much as to the particularities of the internal arrangements of joint ventures.

NOTES

1 The background and development of the open-door policy of China are discussed in Ho and Huenemann (1984), Jao and Leung (1986), Su (1985, 1986), and Chu (1986).
2 The fourteen coastal cities are: Dalian, Qinhuangdao, Tianjin, Yantai, Qingdao, Lianyungang, Nantong, Shanghai, Ningbo, Wenzhou, Fuzhou, Guangzhou, Zhanjiang, and Beihai.
3 Cooperative venture, or "contractual joint venture" as it is sometimes called in China, is a loose form of enterprise where Chinese and foreign partners cooperate in operations and management in line with the contract but without forming a unified organ of authority. The Chinese side usually provides the land and labor but not equity. Under cooperative ventures, profits are split according to a ratio that both parties agree upon.
4 For a detailed discussion of the authority and responsibilities of the workers' congress, see Henley and Nyaw (1986).

REFERENCES AND BIBLIOGRAPHY

Chan, J.C.M., N.Y. Li, and D. Sculli (1989) "Labour relations and foreign investors in Shenzhen special economic zone of China," *Journal of General Management* (Summer), Vo. 14, No. 4, pp. 53–61.
Chen, S.F. and P.K. Li (eds) (1987) *The Management of Chinese–Foreign Joint Venture*, Kexue Puji Publisher (in Chinese).
"China's unions feeling a chill," *South China Morning Post*, November 13, 1988.
Chu, Baotai (1986) *Foreign Investment in China: Questions and Answers*, Foreign Languages Press.
Constitution of the Trade Unions of the People's Republic of China, adopted by Tenth National Congress of Chinese Trade Unions on October 23, 1983.
Daniels, J.D., J. Krug and D. Nigh (1986) "US joint ventures in China: motivation and management of political risks," *California Management Review* (Summer), 27(4), pp. 46–58.
Davidson, W.H. (1987) "Creating and managing joint ventures in China," *California Management Review* (Summer), 29(4), pp. 77–94.
Henley, J.S. and M.K. Nyaw (1986) "Introducing market forces into managerial decision making in Chinese industrial enterprises," *Journal of Management Studies*, 23(6), pp. 635–56.
—— (1987) "The development of work incentives in Chinese industrial enterprises," in Malcolm Warner (ed.), *Management Reforms in China*, Frances Pinter (Publisher), pp. 127–48.
—— (1990) "The system of management and performance of joint ventures in China: some evidence from Shenzhen special economic zone," in *Advances in Chinese Industrial Studies*, Vol. 1, Part B, JAI Press, pp. 277–95.
Horsley, J.P. (1984) "Chinese labor: foreign firms are learning how hard it is to negotiate realistic labor contracts in China," *China Business Review* (May–June), pp. 16–25.

Ho, Samuel P.S. and R.W. Huenemann (1984) *China's Open Door Policy: The Quest for Foreign Technology and Capital. A Study of China's Special Trade*, University of British Columbia Press.

Jao, Y.C. and C.K. Leung (eds) (1986) *China's Special Economic Zones: Problems and Prospects*, Oxford University Press.

"Joint venture enterprises have full autonomy," *Hong Kong Economic Journal*, June 28, 1987.

Koo, S.K. (1987) "Understanding business relationships between China and Hong Kong." Speech presented to a seminar organized by the Chinese Executives Club, Hong Kong Management Association, December 12, 1987.

Ku, Sutong (1984) *Survey of Shenzhen Special Economic Zones and Study of Economic Development Regions*, Nankai University Press (in Chinese).

Law of the People's Republic of China on Chinese–Foreign Joint ventures, July 8, 1979.

Littler, C.R. and M. Lockett (1983) "The significance of trade unions in China," *Industrial Relations Journal* (Winter) 14(4), pp. 31–42.

"Moody's set to review China risk," *South China Morning Post*, June 10, 1989.

National Council for US–China Trade (1987) *US Joint Ventures in China: A Progress Report*, Washington, DC.

Nelson, J.A. and J.A. Reeder (1985) "Labour relations in China," *California Management Review* (Summer), 27(4), pp. 13–32.

Nyaw, M.K. and G.S. Lin (1990) "Wage models of joint ventures in China: a preliminary study," unpublished mimeograph (in Chinese).

Pi, J.S., J. Chang *et al.* (1989) "Management of foreign enterprises: problems and thinking," *Jingji Lilun and Jingji Kuanli*, 3, pp. 63–8 (in Chinese).

"Positive aspects of union organizations in foreign enterprises," *Shenzhen SEZ Daily*, April 16, 1987.

Provisions for Trade Unions of Special Economic Zone Enterprises in Guangdong Province, adopted on May 8, 1985.

Provisions of PRC for Labor Management in Chinese–Foreign Joint Ventures, July 26, 1986.

Regulations for the Implementation of the Law of the PRC on Chinese–Foreign Joint Ventures, September 20, 1983.

Shenkar, O. (1988) "International joint ventures' problems in China: culture, politics, or organizational structure?" Paper presented for the APROS Conference on Firms, Management, the State and Economic Culture, Hong Kong: April 6–9.

Su, Wenming (ed.) (1985) "The open policy at work," *China Today, 10, Beijing Review*, Special Features Series, Beijing Review Publications.

Su, Wenming (1986) "Opening the doors: 14 coastal cities and Hainan," *China Today, 12, Beijing Review* Special Feature Series, Beijing Review Publications.

Tang, F.C. (1988) *Practice and Enquiry of Shenzhen's Utilization of Foreign Investment*, Hai Tien Publisher (in Chinese).

Xu, Dixin (1982) "To build up special economic zones progressively and steadily," in *An Enquiry into the Problems of Special Economic Zones*, Fujian People's Publication, pp. 1–10 (in Chinese).

Zamet, J.M. and M.E. Bovarnick (1986) "Employee relations for multinational companies in China," *Columbia Journal of World Business* (Spring), 21(1), pp. 13–19.

10 The cultural context of negotiations

The implications of Chinese interpersonal norms[1]

Oded Shenkar and Simcha Ronen

INTRODUCTION

Effective negotiation depends on, among other factors, understanding the other side's negotiation practices. Conduct during negotiations is influenced by attitudes and customs, which to a great extent are embedded in a negotiating team's cultural and social traits. Different attitudes and customs can yield significant differences in psychological processes such as selective perception and interpersonal attraction. The growth of international trade, commerce, and industry indicates that cross-national negotiations are increasing, therefore making differences in negotiating behavior a timely issue.

A recent review of research on cross-cultural values (Ronen and Shenkar 1985) concludes that various societies can be assigned to clusters on the basis of the relative similarity and differences among their attitudes and values related to work. These differences were associated with the societies' distinctive cultural identities, and varied along dimensions such as religion, language, geographical location, and level of industrialization. For pragmatic reasons, most of the studies reviewed used a country as the unit of analysis thereby allowing for a convenient – though not entirely justified – delineation of national attitudes. Therefore, we were not surprised that researchers of international bargaining behavior found nationality to be one of the more important determinants of differences among negotiators' attitudes (e.g. Graham 1983). For example, American executives were found to take more risks, to believe more strongly in self-determination, and to be more trusting than were their counterparts from Greece, Japan, South Africa, Spain, Thailand, Central Europe, and Scandinavia (Harnett and Cummings 1980). Understanding such differences may help negotiators separate content (i.e. the substance of what is being negotiated) from process (i.e., style, speed, development, and other extrinsic characteristics) of negotiations. Although differences among negotiation practices are always relevant, they become especially salient when the parties to negotiation come from sharply differing backgrounds – for example, from the United States and China. This chapter examines differences in cultural values and ideology between the two nations, and among various Chinese countries. Following this examination is a detailed description of underlying Chinese interpersonal norms and their implications for negotiation practices.

Unless otherwise noted, this chapter's references to negotiating behavior and interpersonal norms relate to predominantly Chinese countries. This clustering of countries is based on expert assessments (e.g., Eberhard 1971; Metzger 1977), particularly empirical studies, which have noted a significant similarity in work-related values among Taiwan, Hong Kong, and Singapore (Hofstede 1980; Redding 1976) and between these countries and the People's Republic of China (PRC) (Shenkar and Ronen 1986). This similarity largely has roots in the cultural traditions common to all of these countries (Dawson, Law, Leung and Whitney 1977). The perseverance of tradition particularly affects interpersonal norms, which are considered more resistant to change in general, and particularly so for the Chinese (Bond and Wang 1983; Eberhard 1971; Metzger 1977; Pye 1968, 1982; Solomon 1964).

INTERPERSONAL NORMS IN CHINESE SOCIETY

The stability of interpersonal norms suggests their probable perseverance in the PRC, despite the influence of Mao Zedong. Maoist ideology has challenged only some of these norms, while frequently using the very practice of kinship allegiance it officially opposes (Parish and Whyte 1978), thus leaving intact a major basis of traditional interpersonal relations. Furthermore, the volatility associated with applying Maoist ideology and subsequently withdrawing it seems to have strengthened the position of traditional Chinese values and norms as a stable "anchor" (Bond and Wang 1983).

Although Maoist ideology was greatly emphasized during some periods in the PRC – such as the Great Leap Forward and the Cultural Revolution, during which cultural tradition, especially Confucianism, was attacked – in other periods a more pragmatic approach dominated (Laaksonen 1984; Skinner and Winckler 1969). Today, most of those in the PRC administration who support the Maoist line seem to have been replaced by "technocrats": practical persons who are not only less sensitive to ideological appeals, but who have also learned to distrust volatile proclamations and policies. Lindsay (1983) suggests that frequent changes in the PRC led to so much uncertainty that they undermined the effectiveness of any proclaimed ideology. The resultant return to traditional values, which remained entrenched among the masses, heightened the similarity of the PRC to other Chinese countries. Recent findings suggest that differences in work values among the Chinese countries, including the PRC, are relatively minor compared to such differences between these countries and non-Chinese countries (Shenkar and Ronen 1986). This similarity, and the scarcity of data on the PRC, allow us to treat the Chinese countries as generally similar, even as we remain attentive to differences among them.

Indeed, we advise caution in this regard. Chinese countries vary to some extent along the variables of geography, language, religion, and level of industrial development. For example, Singapore is the only Chinese country located in Southeast Asia. This location, caused by immigration, would not in itself be significant except that the Chinese represent only 76 percent of the country's population, and the Chinese language is only one of Singapore's four official languages. One of these languages, English, is also an official language of Hong Kong, but not of Taiwan or the PRC. Moreover, although determining exact figures is difficult – especially for the PRC – one can safely assume that differences in religious affiliation prevail among the Chinese countries. For example, according to one report, 36 percent of the Taiwanese practice Buddhism *vis-à-vis* only 20 percent of those in the PRC (*The Economist* 1980). With respect to industrial development, the gross national product per person in the PRC was US$234 for 1984, compared to US$7,206 in Singapore (National Westminster Bank 1984). In 1980, per-capita income varied from US$566 in the PRC, to US$2,570 in Taiwan, to US$4,100 in Singapore (Lane 1985). This, combined with differences in their economic and political systems, level of foreign influence (such as England's previous rule of Singapore and current rule of Hong Kong), and modern social ideology, should lead one to keep in mind the potential for varying negotiating behavior among the Chinese countries.

Negotiations between Chinese and Americans

Interaction between Chinese and American negotiators poses a special challenge because of the unique combination of opportunities and obstacles involved. Trade with the Chinese presents obvious opportunities for Americans. The East Asian economy is growing rapidly. In addition to Taiwan, Hong Kong, and Singapore – longtime major trade partners with the West, and emerging financial centers – the PRC has recently emerged as the United States' largest communist trading partner. The PRC's rich natural resources and vast market potential offer bright prospects for increasing trade between the two nations (Wu 1982).

Trading with the Chinese, however, involves several major obstacles. The Chinese and American cultures diverge widely in their perceptions of the individual, society, and their interrelationship, which produce significantly different attitudes and behavior. For example, the Chinese, particularly in the PRC, perceive law and the nature of the legal system much differently than Americans commonly do (Eberhard 1971; Pye 1982). Extrapolated to the interpersonal level, these differences create a challenge that American negotiators – individual or team – must address when dealing with their Chinese counterparts.

This chapter endeavors to provide negotiators – particularly Americans – with a rudimentary understanding of interpersonal norms in Chinese countries and the cultural antecedents of these norms. Evidence suggests that these cultural variables significantly affect the success or failure of American–Chinese negotiations. Pye (1982, p. 20), after interviewing US managers who have negotiated with those in the PRC, concludes that "unquestionably the largest and possibly the most intractable category of problems in Sino–American business negotiations can be traced to the cultural differences between the two countries." Another study of American firms that had negotiated with the PRC found that most of these companies perceived major differences in negotiation styles (Tung 1982). Familiarity with Chinese business practices and social customs were noted as factors responsible for the success of business negotiations, and factors considered responsible for their failure include communication breakdown, differences in business practices and negotiation styles, and – to a lesser extent – differences in social customs, culture, and ideology. This chapter discusses below the influence of traditional Chinese heritage and modern ideologies on the development of interpersonal norms and negotiation styles in various Chinese countries.

The influence of Confucius

The culture of traditional China encompasses diverse and competing philosophies, including Taoism, Buddhism, Legalism, and a host of local "little traditions." Nevertheless, Confucianism is most clearly identified as the foundation of China's great cultural tradition, and Confucian values still provide the basis for the norms of Chinese interpersonal behavior (Dow 1973; Metzger 1977; Nivison and Wright 1959; Pye 1972). Thus, Bond and Wang (1983, p. 59) write that "a Confucian analysis has continuing validity toward an understanding of Chinese interpersonal behavior."

Of the basic tenets of Confucian philosophy, four seem particularly relevant to interpersonal behavior. The first is the principle of *harmony*, which reflects an aspiration toward a conflict-free, group-based system of social relations. This principle has not been challenged by modern Chinese ideologies, either in the PRC or in the non-communist Chinese countries, and seems to have persisted in modern Chinese communities in Western countries (Bond and Wang 1983).

The second principle is *hierarchy*, which emphasizes that each individual should be conscious of her or his position in the social system (Eberhard 1971). Maoist ideology fiercely attacked this principle (Andors 1974; Eberhard 1971; Whyte 1973; Willett 1975), with the attack reaching a climax during the Cultural Revolution. This did not, however, have lasting consequences for the management of enterprises in the PRC (Laaksonen 1984).

The third principle is that of *developing one's moral potential* within the legitimate group framework by fulfilling social obligations. This has not been directly challenged in modern Chinese societies (Eberhard 1971; Metzger 1977). The fourth is *reliance on kinship affiliation* as the coherent model for governing interpersonal relations. Sun Yat-sen (1929), whose teachings form the formal basis for ideology in Taiwan, explicitly endorsed reliance on kinship. In the PRC, Mao's efforts to foster rejection of the kinship system incurred only limited success (Watson 1973), and the party and state continued the kinship framework for their own purposes (Parish and Whyte 1978). A central ingredient of kinship affiliation, emphasis on the collective, has not been challenged in any of the modern Chinese countries, and has even been reinforced (Eberhard 1971; Whyte 1974).

These four tenets of Confucian values designate which interpersonal norms are considered acceptable or desirable in the various domains of social interaction. The following three norms have crucial implications for negotiating behavior; basic communication patterns, social obligations, and relationships among different life domains. The Confucian influence means, for example, that communications should be harmonious, that the principle of moral potential obliges one to restrain oneself for the sake of harmony, and that hierarchy designates the different obligations of each party to the communication process. Achieving harmony also depends on fulfilling one's social obligations as required by one's hierarchical position in the kinship system. Kinship affiliation has governed the interrelationship between the realms of work and non-work activities, and the modes of behavior expected for each (Bond and Wang 1983; Fei 1939).

We discuss below these three interpersonal norms in some depth. Understanding them may not only increase American negotiators' effectiveness and success rate in dealing with the Chinese, but – equally important – may also contribute to the development of the mutual respect necessary to building long-term business relationships that benefit both countries involved in the negotiations.

BASIC COMMUNICATIONS PATTERNS

The manifestations of moral potential include the ability to control overt expressions of thoughts and emotions. Showing restraint is the responsibility of the "gentleman," who, in the Confucian hierarchy, is the cultivated and learned person situated above all others. The cultivated person strives to maintain self-control regardless of the situation and thus conform to the ideal of *xinping qihe* – "being perfectly calm" (Silin 1976). Furthermore, to promote harmony, one must carefully curb one's emotions in public as a symbolic expression of selflessly enhancing the general welfare and avoiding the gratification of improper personal desires (Eberhard 1971; Metzger 1977). Raw emotions (even righteous indignation), once expressed, threaten the Confucian principle of harmony (Eberhard 1971) and tend to arouse strong distrust, if not antipathy. Although the PRC does not support the principle of hierarchy, the concept of selflessness is upheld, even strengthened, in Maoist ideology (Mao 1977), and stress on non-emotional behavior also remains unchallenged. Therefore, no one expects the PRC to depart significantly from the norm of self-control, particularly because emotional control has persisted in other modern Chinese communities (Bond and Wang 1983).

When harmony is important, politeness means more than showing common courtesy – it approaches a formal, stylized behavior. Such behavior does not depend on individual discretion, but is fixed according to social position and norms. Polite behavior is both expected and easily recognized, for example, in elaborate preparations for invited guests, or in the way one personally escorts one's guests beyond the front door either part way to their homes or to their next destination. Similarly, impoliteness is considered not merely a simple oversight, but an insult not easily forgiven.

The Chinese preference for restrained, moderate behavior suggests that one should avoid overtly aggressive behavior. The American task-oriented approach, which allows for the admission of differences in the positions of the parties to a negotiation so as to promote "honest confrontation," is viewed by the Chinese as aggressive, and therefore as an unacceptable mode of behavior. Thus, emotionally charged attempts at persuasion are likely to fail when directed at the Chinese, and negotiators should consider other modes of persuasion. Moreover, the American style of accentuating the gap in positions during the first stage of negotiations is inappropriate when dealing with the Chinese, and may lead to early breakdowns in the negotiation process (see Pye 1982).

Chinese emotional restraint may complicate American efforts to judge the reactions of their Chinese counterparts. Pye (1982, p. 80) suggests that "possibly the most striking personal characteristic of Chinese negotiators is their ability to separate whatever emotions they may show from the actual progress of the negotiations." The Chinese tend to prefer to make decisions behind the scenes, as observed in negotiations between the US and the PRC, and this contributes greatly to Americans' anxiety as to where they stand as discussions progress (Tung 1982). This particular norm is common to most East Asian societies, and American negotiators are usually observed to be more animated and emotionally "visible" than their East Asian counterparts. As they move toward final agreement, Americans tend to make decisions more publicly and sequentially, whereas East Asians tend to make their decisions privately ("behind the black curtain") so that they may preserve both harmony and "face", and seem to make concessions as the negotiating process nears conclusion.

Americans negotiating with the Chinese must learn not to interpret silence or the lack of direct eye-contact as either simple disapproval or disinterest, and they should not necessarily respond to such behavior by making additional concessions. One must be patient (Pye 1982) and, perhaps, suggest brief recesses more frequently so that upon reaching an apparent impasse the negotiating parties may make decisions in private.

The limited degree of overt expression by the Chinese means one must pay particular attention to whatever expression is made, so as to interpret it accurately. American negotiators should make genuine efforts to learn Chinese manners of expression. Interpreters familiar with both cultures may fill a new role by translating not only verbal statements, but also non-verbal responses. Americans must learn to observe their Chinese counterparts carefully, prepare to take longer to negotiate with them, analyze – ahead of time if possible – the intricate workings of the Chinese bureaucracy as it relates to their projects, and better anticipate necessary delays (Pye 1982). One should distinguish both the source and probable reason for a delay so that one can sense the point at which waiting becomes significant (Hall 1960).

SOCIAL OBLIGATIONS

Four principles govern the norm of social obligations: the credibility of the individual *vis-à-vis* one's significant reference groups, the emphasis on the collective entity, the pivotal position of the leader, and the indebtedness incurred through interpersonal interactions. We discuss each of these principles separately with respect to their cultural antecedents and implications for negotiations.

Credibility

The Chinese emphasis on the collective, which is tied to reliance on kinship affiliation as an ideal mode of relations, means each person has "human obligations" to a group of identifiable, known others. One's social status derives substantially from one's fulfilling these human obligations, as perceived by the group. Human obligations are considered "social capital" that one may draw upon, if necessary, but which must be repaid (Eberhard 1971). Fulfilling social obligations affects one's moral potential and one's professional and personal *xinyong*, or credibility. Preserving credibility as perceived by the group is important to the success of any undertaking.

The principle of credibility has important applications for negotiations. Americans, who may feel more comfortable with one-to-one situations, may find it difficult not to single out one member of a Chinese negotiating team for special rapport or persuasion. Such a strategy would not be considered acceptable to the Chinese, who expect the group as a whole to be addressed.

Collective emphasis

In contrast to the American emphasis on individual rather than group success, the Chinese emphasize the success of the group, whether this group represents a kinship entity or a modern administrative unit (Whyte 1974). This does not mean that individual action is never appropriate, but that individualism is restricted to certain well-defined areas (Eberhard 1971). Anyone desiring personal aggrandizement threatens established group hierarchies (Pye 1981), and risks being accused of wild ambition (*yexin*). The Chinese generally take a negative view of any group member who actively seeks attention (*chu fengtou*). The ideal behavior of a Chinese negotiating team member is to separate public from private – that is, personal – interests (*gongsi gen siren de fenming*). Often individual group members feel the need to reassure their colleagues that they do not seek personal gain at the group's expense. Conversely, social or organizational failure to cooperate is frequently attributed to personal jealousy. An American who tries to influence a Chinese counterpart by suggesting that this person will accrue personal benefits will soon discover that such an approach will fail – if not backfire.

Leadership

Whyte (1974) states that whereas Western small groups are driven primarily by internal processes, Chinese groups are driven by internal and external political processes. The political environment of the Chinese small group generates its authority structure, suggesting a pivotal position for the leader, who informs the other members as to what is socially and politically appropriate (see Confucius 1983, 12:19, 13:4; Hsiao 1979). Group members are expected to show deference to the leader so as to maintain the Confucian principles of harmony and hierarchy (Bond and Wang 1983; Metzger 1977). In non-Communist Chinese countries such as Taiwan, the perception of leadership and group processes produces strongly paternalistic managerial styles (Negandhi 1973). In the PRC, "cadres" serve as "linking pins" between the political leaders and the masses, producing strong deference to political office holders (Pye 1981; Schurmann 1973). Subjected to pressures from the political system to conform and to internal pressures from the group, the Chinese leader fulfills a double, expressive-instrumental role (Cartwright and Zander 1968). That is, the leader is responsible for maintaining harmony within the group while simultaneously carrying out the policies issued by the political hierarchy.

Despite the leader's pivotal position, American negotiators cannot easily identify the leader of a Chinese negotiating team (Lindsay and Dempsey 1983; Pye 1982). One reason is the perception, shared by both Confucianism and Maoism, of the leader as a morally superior person whose position is supported by broad virtues rather than technical qualifications (Metzger 1977; Shenkar 1984). In contrast to the American practice of senior managers formulating a policy and middle-level managers executing it, in Chinese countries senior managers consistently become involved in the details of daily operation; this has been found in both Taiwan (Negandhi 1973) and the PRC (Laaksonen 1984; see also Lindsay and Dempsey 1983). Thus, the senior member of a Chinese negotiating team may become engaged in even the most minute details of the negotiation rather than concentrating only on the central issues, leaving others to finalize the agreement. Indeed, an American negotiating team faces the challenge of approaching its Chinese counterparts as a group while simultaneously realizing that the leader of the group plays an important role.

Indebtedness

Traditional Chinese values encourage formality as a means of protection against socially ambiguous situations and supporting strict group control over egocentric tendencies. The Chinese are uniformly cautious, at times reluctant, to request assistance from those outside their kinship groups. Reliance upon persons outside one's primary kinship group creates anxiety that one will incur obligations requiring real, yet unspecified future repayment (Eberhard 1971). Paradoxically, one's filial debt to one's immediate family is considered so massive and encompassing that one can never fully discharge it, leading to an absence of any pressing need to worry about repaying this debt. In contrast, smaller debts accrued through requesting help from one's extended family, colleagues, or friends potentially become the hardest to bear.

This perception of indebtedness may influence the negotiation process. The Chinese may fear that any concession by the other party on a given issue represents a "debt" that must eventually be repaid, perhaps at a higher cost. Adding to this fear is the traditional perception of social relations as a "zero-sum" game (*li-hai guanxi*)– that is, one party's gain (*li*) means the other's loss (*hai*). Because indebtedness may be manipulated (Eberhard 1971), Americans negotiating with the Chinese should avoid any "orchestrated" accumulation of seemingly minor debts (Pye 1982), and should instead repay perceived debts immediately (Eberhard 1971).

INTERRELATIONSHIPS AMONG LIFE DOMAINS

The domains of work, family, and friendship are delineated in any society. For the Chinese, however, the interrelationships among these domains take on a special form, influenced by the Confucian emphasis on the kinship system and on hierarchy, and on the concomitant designation of persons as either "insiders" (familiar acquaintances) or "outsiders" (strangers) (Eberhard 1971). The two main principles stemming from this distinguishing between insiders and outsiders are (a) the differentiation between friends and intimates and (b) the necessity of "mutual attraction" for both individual and professional relationships.

Friends versus intimates

Unlike Americans, who generally seek equality and informality in their peer relationships, the Chinese view these relationships as structured and hierarchical. Among the five sacred relationships specified by Confucius, only relationships between friends may use equality rather than hierarchy as their basis. Even with friendship, however, the Chinese distinguish between levels of friendship, separating acquaintances from intimates. Whereas relationships with one's colleagues are traditionally restrained by considerable formality and distance, one is permitted more free and open expression with one's intimates. Mao's (1977) fierce attack on formality and distance at work suggests that this pattern remains entrenched in the PRC.

The Chinese usually attempt to separate affective from economic associations, preferring to do business with friends but not intimates. Valued business colleagues or acquaintances are those with whom one interacts regularly, whose behaviour has become predictable, and against whom one may apply limited sanctions without destroying relationships with them. Chinese business has the norm of keeping relationships involving self-interest amiable, if somewhat distant (De Glopper 1972).

This Chinese perception of friendship as a distinct non-affective relationship determines the Chinese outlook on the informal phase of the negotiation process. In contrast to Americans, who may view breaks in the negotiation process as mere relaxation or social gatherings, the Chinese regard behavior away from the negotiation table as having importance equal to that during negotiations. The Chinese feel extremely uncomfortable chatting about personal habits, family life, and meeting their social obligations to their friends.

Therefore, not only are an individual's private beliefs not open for discussion, but family problems and personal desires are delicate subjects that the Chinese may also mask. Because the Chinese develop close friendships slowly, a negotiator – who is essentially an outsider – must remain keenly aware of both the limits of familiarity and the specific social obligations appropriate to the type of contact being made. When in doubt, one should always remain politely formal.

Mutual attraction

The Chinese prefer to do business with individuals and/or firms that they consider "known quantities," especially those that have established publicly acknowledged exemplary records over a significant number of years. Once a sense of mutual attraction (*bici ganqing*) has been established, it must be carefully nurtured and developed. A regression analysis of a sample of trade negotiations between PRC and US firms shows that incidents of success were associated with years of trade experience and the number of previous negotiations conducted (Tung 1982). A similar preoccupation with mutual attraction and *xinyong* (credibility) has been observed in field studies of local markets in Hong Kong and Taiwan (De Glopper 1972; Silin 1972).

The lesson for US companies is obvious. The first to establish a business relationship with Chinese companies will gain benefits far exceeding the advantages usually associated with market primacy. Such firms can thus establish themselves as known quantities and assume the best position for taking advantage of additional opportunities as they become available. American firms should take a long-range view and enter negotiations even when they cannot determine immediate returns. Similarly, during negotiations American firms may find it worthwhile to forego some advantages for the sake of establishing a long-lasting mutual attraction.

IMPLICATIONS

This chapter identifies some primary characteristics of Chinese interpersonal behavior: emotional restraint and politeness as basic requirements for communication, an emphasis on social obligations, and dependence and cooperation among various life domains. These have numerous implications for US managers conducting negotiations. Keeping in mind the variations among the different Chinese countries, we offer some major recommendations.

Preparing for negotiations

In preparing for negotiations with the Chinese, we recommend that Americans do the following:

- Choose interpreters familiar with both American and Chinese culture, if possible the culture of overseas Chinese.
- In preparing an agenda for training and preparations, include negotiating style.
- Enter negotiations even when no immediate benefit is apparent.
- Select negotiators whose style will be more acceptable to the Chinese – that is, more restrained.

Carrying out the negotiations

In carrying out negotiations with the Chinese, we recommend that Americans do the following:

- When beginning the negotiations, accentuate the similarities rather than the differences between the two parties' bargaining positions.
- Emphasize the strategic, long-range process of negotiation and the gradual accumulation of mutual trust.
- Plan for long negotiation sessions and allow for frequent recesses for private consultation by the negotiation teams. Do not set a deadline for concluding negotiations, and expect continuous delays.
- Avoid aggressive behavior, and practice patience.
- Minimize expressions of emotions, and instead act politely formal.
- Remember that behaviour outside negotiations is as important as behavior during the formal process of negotiations.
- Assess non-verbal responses and do not interpret silence as an expression of either approval or disapproval.
- Address the group as a whole and do not attempt to convince the Chinese to accept a position because it will bring one or more of them personal gain.

Concluding the negotiations

In concluding negotiations with the Chinese, we recommend that Americans do the following:

- Before offering or accepting concessions, carefully weigh the short-term benefits versus the long-term debts they cause a party to incur.
- Be willing to forego some advantages and details so that a lasting mutual attraction may develop.

- When negotiations approach the final stage, allow for a short delay before concluding them.
- At the successful conclusion of the negotiations, show your appreciation to the Chinese team by thanking them for concluding the negotiations to the satisfaction of *both* sides.

CONCLUSIONS

The above recommendations are made on the basis of interpersonal norms alone, and thus do not refer to other factors related to the negotiations, such as the transfer of technology or disclosure of data – both quite sensitive issues – or knowledge of the intricacies of Chinese bureaucracies. The recommendations do suggest, however, that to build a relationship based on mutual trust and respect – which is essential to successful negotiations – negotiators should learn their counterparts' underlying cultural and social traits. Negotiators must also be aware of the differences and nuances among countries with seemingly similar cultural heritages, and of the diversity occurring within a country's borders. Such variations may call for varying negotiating styles.

For example, because the PRC has had relatively limited foreign influence *vis-à-vis* Hong Kong, Singapore, and Taiwan, its legal system has remained quite different from those of its Western counterparts – and frequently is unable to address many of the details and complexities entailed in modern trade negotiations. In this context, an appropriate negotiating style is not merely a prelude to a successful contract. Rather, because of the tendency in the PRC to draft preliminary "letters of intent" using general terms (Pye 1982), a negotiating style may determine the outcome when contingencies not specified in the contract occur.

As an interdisciplinary field, negotiation research can draw valuable information from cross-cultural research in psychology, sociology, organizational behavior, and other related domains. Empirical research is needed to examine the negotiating styles of various countries and cultures. Such research can help us determine which elements of negotiation are culture bound and which are related to other contextual, structural, or personality variables, and therefore further enrich our understanding of the negotiation process.

NOTE

1 This chapter was first published in the *Journal of Applied Behavioral Science* (1987), Vol. 23, No. 2, pp. 263–75. Reprinted with permission.

REFERENCES AND BIBLIOGRAPHY

Andors, S. (1974) Hobbes and Weber vs. Marx and Mao: the political economy of decentralization in China. *Bulletin of Concerned Asian Scholars*, 6, pp. 19–34.

Bond, M.H. and Wang, S. (1983) China: aggressive behavior and the problem of maintaining order and harmony. In A.P. Goldstein and M.H. Segall (eds), *Aggression in Global Perspective*. New York: Pergamon Press.

Cartwright, D. and Zander, A. (1968) *Group Dynamics: Research and Theory*. New York: Harper and Row.

Confucius (1983) *The Analects* (A. Waley, trans.). New York: Vintage Books.

Dawson, J.L.M., Law, H., Leung, A. and Whitney, R.W. (1977) Scaling Chinese traditional–modern attitudes and the GSR measurement of important versus unimportant Chinese concepts. *Journal of Cross-Cultural Psychology*, 2(1), pp. 1–37.

De Glopper, D.R. (1972) Doing business in Lukang. In W.E. Wilmott (ed.), *Chinese Economic Organization* (pp. 297–326). Stanford: Stanford University Press.

Dow, T. (1973) Some affinities between Confucian and Marxian philosophical systems. *Asian Profile*, 1(2), pp. 247–60.

Eberhard, W. (1971) *Moral and Social Values of the Chinese – Collected Essays*. Washington, DC: Chinese Materials and Research Aids Service Center.

The Economist (1980) *The World in Figures*. London: Macmillan.

Fei, H. (1939) *Peasant Life in China*. London: Kegan Paul.

Graham, J. (1983) Brazilian, Japanese and American business negotiations. *Journal of International Business Studies*, 14(1), pp. 44–61.

Hall, E.T. (1960) The silent language in overseas business. *Harvard Business Review*, 38(3), pp. 87–96.

Harnett, D.L. and Cummings, L.L. (1980) *Bargaining Behavior. An International Study*. Houston, TX: Dome Publications.

Hofstede, G. (1980) *Culture's Consequences: International Differences in Work Related Values*. Beverley Hills: Sage.

Hsiao K. (1979) *A History of Chinese Political Thought*. Princeton, NJ: Princeton University Press.

Laaksonen, O. (1984) The management and power structure of Chinese enterprises during and after the Cultural Revolution: with empirical data comparing Chinese and European enterprises. *Organization Studies*, 5(1), pp. 1–21.

Lindsay, C.P. (1983) China: motivational systems in flux. In R.M. Steers and L.W. Porter (eds), *Motivation and Work Behavior* (3rd ed.) (pp. 623–32). New York: McGraw-Hill.

Lindsay, C.P. and Dempsey, B.L. (1983) Ten painfully learned lessons about working in China: The insights of two American behavioral scientists. *The Journal of Applied Behavioral Science*, 19(3), pp. 265–76.

Mao Tse-tung (1977) Twenty manifestations of bureaucracy. *Joint Publications Research Service*, pp. 40–3.

Metzger, T.A. (1977) *Escape from Predicament*. New York: Columbia University Press.

National Westminster Bank (1985, September–October) *An Economic Report*. Westminster, England.

Negandhi, A.R. (1973) *Management and Economic Development: The Case of Taiwan*. The Hague, The Netherlands: Nijhoff.

Nivison, D.S. and Wright, F. (eds) (1959) *Confucianism in Action*. California: Stanford University Press.

Parish, W.L. and Whyte, M.K. (1978). *Village and Family in Contemporary China*. Chicago: University of Chicago Press.

Pye, L.W. (1968) *The Spirit of Chinese Politics: A Psycho-Cultural Study of the Authority Crisis in Political Development*. Cambridge, MA: MIT Press.

Pye, L.W. (1972) *China: An Introduction*. Boston: Little, Brown.

Pye, L.W. (1981) *The Dynamics of Chinese Politics*. Cambridge, MA: Oelgeschlager, Gunn & Hain.

Pye, L.W. (1982) *Chinese Commercial Negotiating Style*. Cambridge, MA: Oelgeschlager, Gunn & Hain.

Redding, G. (1976) Some perceptions of psychological needs among managers in South-East Asia. In Y.M. Poortinga (ed.), *Basic Problems in Cross-Cultural Psychology*. Amsterdam: Wets & Zeitlinger.

Ronen, S. and Shenkar, O. (1985) Clustering countries on attitudinal dimensions: A review and synthesis. *Academy of Management Review*, 10(3), pp. 435–54.

Schurmann, F. (1973) *Ideology and Organization in Communist China* Berkeley: University of California Press.

Shenkar, O. (1984) Is bureaucracy inevitable? The Chinese experience. *Organization Studies*, 5(4), pp. 289–306.

Shenkar, O. and Ronen, S. (1986) *The Workgoal Structure of Chinese Employees*. Working paper, Tel Aviv University, Israel.

Silin, R.H. (1972) Marketing and credit in a Hong Kong wholesale market. In W.E. Wilmott (ed.), *Chinese Economic Organization* (pp. 327–52). Stanford: Stanford University Press.

Silin, R.H. (1976) *Leadership and Values: The Organization of Large-Scale Taiwanese Enterprise*. Cambridge, MA: Harvard University Press.

Skinner, G.W. and Winckler, E.A. (1969) Compliance succession in rural communist China: A cyclical theory. In A. Etzioni (ed.), *A Sociological Reader of Complex Organizations* (pp. 410–38). New York: Holt, Rinehart and Winston.

Solomon, R.H. (1964) *The Chinese Political Culture and Problems of Modernization*. Cambridge, MA: MIT Press.

Sun yat-Sen (1929) *The Three Principles of the People*. Shanghai. China: Commercial Press.

Tung, R.L. (1982) *U.S.–China Trade Negotiations*. New York: Pergamon Press.

Watson, A.J. (1973) A revolution to touch men's souls: the family, interpersonal relations and daily life. In S.R. Schram (ed.), *Authority, Participation, and Cultural Change in China*. Cambridge, MA: Cambridge University Press.

Whyte, M.K. (1973) Bureaucracy and modernization in China: the Maoist critique. *American Sociological Review*, 38, pp. 149–63.

Whyte, M.K. (1974) *Small Groups and Political Rituals in China*. Berkeley: University of California Press.

Willett, F.J. (1975) The development of administrators in the PRC. *Current Scene*, 13, pp. 1–7.

The World Almanac & Book of Facts. Lane, H.U. (ed.) (1985). New York: Newspaper Enterprise Association.

Wu, F.W. (1982) The political risk of foreign direct investment in post-Mao China: a preliminary assessment. *Management International Review*, 22(1), pp. 13–25.

11 American business people's perceptions of marketing and negotiating in the People's Republic of China[1]

Kam-Hon Lee and Thamis Wing-Chun Lo[2]

Brunner and Taoka (1977) conducted a survey in 1975 in which they studied American business people's perceptions of marketing and negotiating in the People's Republic of China (PRC). It was a comprehensive review of various aspects of US–China business, based on the experience of American business people who attended the 1975 Canton Fair. They predicted that there would be increasing business opportunities between the two countries, although the US–China trade at that time was limited in both volume and value. They were absolutely correct in their prediction, and their study results remain as an important reference point to facilitate mutual understanding between the two countries.

THE BUSINESS SITUATION AFTER 1978

Subsequent to the Brunner and Taoka (1977) study, there were many positive moves on the part of China. The basic change was to adopt an "open-door" policy to facilitate the transfer of new technology into China in order to speed up the process of modernization. Economically speaking, the US had been the undisputed driving force in the free-trade world after the Second World War. She had more advanced technology to offer than the other developed countries and was constantly searching for alternative production bases and additional markets. China, on the other hand, wanted to acquire new technology, and was ready for more "give and take". In fact, even in the long "closed-door" period, China had been exporting to Hong Kong, which in turn had been mainly exporting to the US (Lee 1986a).

Implementation of the *open*-door policy after 1978 took several forms. It was reflected in the expanding import and export trade figures. According to the 1986 *Almanac of China's Foreign Economic*

Relations and Trade, the total value of foreign trade (imports plus exports) for China increased from US\$20.6 billion in 1978 to US\$60.2 billion in 1985. US–China trade increased from US\$992 million to US\$6 billion during the same period. In terms of *absolute values*, the US closely followed Japan and Hong Kong as one of China's three most important import and export trading partners. In terms of *growth*, US–China trade was even more spectacular than Japan–China trade and Hong Kong–China trade during the same period.

The implementation of China's open-door policy also brought about a change in the foreign investment situation. After 1978, industrial cooperation activities such as processing trade, compensation trade, contractual joint venture, equity joint venture, and wholly-owned foreign subsidiaries began to emerge, and these new forms of trade expanded very rapidly, especially in the special economic zones of China (Lo 1986). A total of US\$4.6 billion of foreign capital was invested in contractual joint venture enterprises, equity joint venture enterprises, and wholly-owned foreign subsidiaries in China during the period from 1979 to 1985 (Chu 1986). The US was only second to Hong Kong in terms of investment amount committed during this period. If the situation in the Shenzhen special economic zone (SEZ) was indicative, there had been an upward trend throughout these years (Lo 1986).

This implementation of China's open-door policy was *also* reflected in the way of concluding business deals in China. Previously, foreign business was mainly handled in a specific place and in a specific period of time, such as the Spring or Autumn Canton Trade Fairs. After the open-door policy, different units gradually had more autonomy, and business dealings became year-round events at different government levels. To cope with this new situation, the Bank of China was upgraded to an independent status in 1979, directly responsible to the State Council, so that there would be a suitable financial mechanism to facilitate ongoing trading and investment activities (Jao 1983).

US–CHINA TRADE NEGOTIATION LITERATURE

Scholars were not slow to follow-up the new developments. Specifically, they paid special attention to the issue of negotiation, which was particularly important in China trade. Significant work was done by DePauw (1981), Pye (1982, 1986), and Tung (1982a, 1982b). Much of the contribution was based on in-depth case studies and discussions. DePauw did a thorough investigation based on the experience of Control Data Corporation. Pye synthesized various observations and presented succinct recommendations. Tung assembled various related secondary documents, reported a number of in-depth interviews, and summarized the result of a survey of member firms of the National Council for US–China Trade in the States. Although all the writings are instructive, only Tung's survey is based on the experiences of a large group of American business people. However, even Tung's survey is not a good reference point for comparison purposes with the previous study by Brunner and Taoka. First of all, although Tung used a nineteen-page, seventy-two-item questionnaire, the items were not designed to match with those in the Brunner and Taoka study. Also, Tung only reported a portion of the data analysis results, which further minimized the possibility of having a comparative investigation. Second, Tung's study was conducted in 1979, the beginning of China's open-door policy. It was still too early for American business people to experience any changes, if any. (However, it should be noted that it was not Tung's intention to conduct her survey as a follow-up study.)

In order to facilitate better mutual understanding and attain more effective negotiation between the US and China, it has become increasingly important to do such a follow-up study in order to establish a picture of American business people's perceptions of marketing and negotiating in the PRC.

METHOD

This present follow-up survey was conducted in late 1985 among American firms who were members of the American Chamber of Commerce in Hong Kong. As long as China still adopted her closed-door policy, as correctly implied in Brunner and Taoka's study, American business people who had front-line experience in China Trade were those attending the Canton Trade Fair.

After China adopted the *open*-door policy, it was quite clear that American business people who had such front-line experience in China trade now were those actively working in Hong Kong (Forsell 1986). The mode of China trade operation changed from a one-time event to a continuous business interaction throughout the year. Hong Kong became an ideal bridge because of her well-established infrastructure and her geographic, cultural, and relationship proximity to China. The middlemen's role of Hong Kong in US–China trade became indisputable (Ho 1986; Mun and Chan 1986). Firms who were keen in China trade in the old days were those attending the Canton Trade Fair. Firms who are keen in China trade nowadays are those setting up their China offices in Hong Kong. By studying the perceptions of American China traders stationed in Hong Kong, we might be closer to the idea of comparing "like" with "like" (Green and White 1976).

Sample

The survey was conducted among corporate members who were voting members of the American Chamber of Commerce in Hong Kong (AMCHAM) in 1985. Since only *American* companies were voting members, this survey covered all American companies who were AMCHAM members. Since all reasonably large American companies were, in fact, AMCHAM members, this survey effectively covered almost all American companies in Hong Kong. Each voting member had a designated company representative who would vote for the company in AMCHAM. Thus, these representatives became qualified spokesmen for their respective companies, and the ideal informants in this survey. There were a total of 397 such firms in 1985.

Questionnaire

The research instrument in this study was virtually the same as the questionnaire used in Brunner and Taoka's study. The thirty-eight attitude statements constituted the core of the instrument. Since four of the original thirty-eight items were written in the context of Canton Trade Fair, four new items were developed to serve as comparable counterparts in the questionnaire of this study. The four items were statements 13, 19, 20, and 23. Other questions in our questionnaire included the nature of the company, the importance of China trade to the company and the informants' experience in China trade.

Data collection method

Since the questionnaire was relatively straightforward, and chief executives were very busy, it was decided that a mail survey would be most appropriate. The questionnaire was sent to each company representative of the 397 firms in early December 1985. In order to raise the response rate, there was a mail follow-up and a telephone follow-up. A total of 136 useful questionnaires were received before the cut-off date, which was January 15, 1986. (Questionnaires were considered useful only when they were completed by informants who had China trade experience and/or whose companies were involved in China trade. There were seven non-useful responses.) Mail service in Hong Kong is highly efficient. Addressees receive the mail the day after it is sent. Also, according to past experience of mail surveys in Hong Kong, it does not pay to suggest a deadline for returning the questionnaire longer than one week after the addressee has received it. Thus, a mail survey with a second wave and a telephone follow-up can be completed in six weeks in Hong Kong.

RESULTS

The products these companies handled mainly fell into four categories. They were chemicals (20 percent), light industrial products (19 percent), textiles (19 percent), and machinery (13 percent). Other categories included metals and materials (8 percent), cereals/ oils (7 percent), native products and animal byproducts (7 percent). These companies were involved in four main types of business activities. They were export to China (60 percent), import from China (36 percent), equity joint venture (12 percent), and contractual joint venture (12 percent). (Companies might be involved in more than one type of business activity. Thus, summation of the percentages exceeded 100 percent). the above categories reflect the variety of activities of the respondent firms. It also gives some idea about the background of the respondents. Since the purpose of this chapter is to identify the *modal* pattern of American business people's perceptions, there is no separate treatment for each category in the subsequent discussion.

The future of China trade

As reported in Table 11.1, China business was quite important to these companies, and respondents perceived that the degree of importance would be increased in the course of time. In fact, 35 percent of the firms surveyed by this present study expected their trade with the PRC to be extremely important to their companies over the ten-year period. (Please note that the Brunner and Taoka study did not survey their respondents' perceptions over the ten-year period.) Compared with the Brunner and Taoka study, the percentages of firms which expected their trade with the PRC to be

Table 11.1 Respondents' perceptions of the importance of PRC trade to their companies

Time period	Not important (%)	Somewhat important (%)	Moderately important (%)	Very important (%)	Extremely important (%)
Right now (n = 134)	6	30	25	26	13
Two years from now (n = 130)	2	9	36	39	14
Five years from now (n = 127)	1	6	21	52	21
Ten years from now (n = 123)	2	4	16	42	35

either extremely or very important to their marketing plans had increased from 18 percent to 53 percent over the two-year period, and from 26 percent to 73 percent over the five-year period respectively. These results presumably came about because of China's adoption of the present open-door policy and the optimism of the respondents to this present study towards China's commitment to this policy over at least the next decade.

Compatible with the above findings, and as reported in Table 11.2, respondents expected that there would be an upward trend of sales increase in the years to come. Thus, the promise of US–China business is as positive as what was reported in Brunner and Taoka's study ten years ago.

Review of overall perception

As in Brunner and Taoka's study, there were thirty-eight statements used to reflect the respondents' attitudes towards the various aspects of US–China business. Five-point scales were utilized ranging from "strongly agree" (a value of 5) to "strongly disagree" (a value of 1). The mean values of these statements were computed to facilitate comparisons with the figures obtained in the previous study. Also, ranks were assigned to the thirty-eight statements according to the mean values obtained in the two studies respectively. Because of page limitations, it is impossible to include an appendix and report the details. Interested readers may obtain a copy of the appendix from the authors.

As an initial step in comparing the results of these two studies, a Spearman rank correlation coefficient (r_s) was computed to check the

Table 11.2 Expected increase in PRC trade of respondents' firms

Time period	Median increase (%)	Decrease or no increase (%)	Increase by (%)							
			1–25	26–50	51–75	76–100	101–150	151–200	200+
Two years (n = 131)	1–25	8	45	24	13	9	–	–	1
Five years (n = 127)	26–50	5	25	24	20	9	9	4	4
Ten years (n = 123)	51–75	6	20	17	15	16	3	2	20

consistency of these two ranking patterns. The coefficient is 0.59, which is significant at 0.001 (t test and $N = 38$). Thus, the American business people's experience in China business today is very much in line with the American business people's experience ten years ago. In order to have a detailed investigation, a changeover table is constructed to screen the thirty-eight attitude items. The statements are first classified into three categories according to the results of Brunner and Taoka's study. The *first group* of statements are those with ranks from 1 to 12, representing the statements the respondents basically agreed with. The *second group* of statements are those with ranks from 13 to 26, representing the statements with which the respondents basically neither agreed nor disagreed. The *third group* of statements are those with ranks from 27 to 38, representing the statements that the respondents basically disagreed with. This allocation of statements generally followed a normal curve.

Following the same rationale and the same method, the statements can also be classified into three categories according to the results of this study. A changeover table is constructed as Table 11.3 based on these two classification results. There are nine cells in Table 11.3. The upper number in each cell indicates the number of statements in the category. The lower numbers in each cell refer to the numbers of the respective statements as reported in the Appendix. The alphabetical classification is used for easy reference to a particular cell.

Out of the nine cells, four deserve special attention:

- Cell A represents statements which were basically agreed with both in 1975 and in 1985. Thus, they should be regarded as persistent perceptions in China trade.
- Cell I represents statements which were basically disagreed with both in 1975 and in 1985. Thus, they should be regarded as groundless perceptions in China trade.
- Both Cell C and Cell G represent statements which show significant *switches* of respondents' positions between 1975 and 1985. They may serve as starting-points from which to investigate the differences in business operations in these two periods of time.

Persistent perceptions in China trade

Statements in Cell A (persistent perceptions) include the following:

1 In establishing a good business relationship with the People's Republic of China, some knowledge of China's history and culture is helpful (Statement No. 1)

Table 11.3 A changeover table showing the shifts of American business people's perceptions of marketing and negotiating in the PRC from 1975 to 1985

		Statements in this study		
		Basically agree	Neither agree nor disagree	Basically disagree
		A 8	**B** 2	**C** 2
	Basically agree	Statements 1, 4, 6, 7, 8, 11, 25 and 27	Statements 13 and 24	Statements 9 and 12
		D 2	**E** 9	**F** 3
Statements in Brunner and Taoka's study	Neither agree nor disagree	Statements 10 and 29	Statements 2, 3, 14, 15, 17, 20, 22, 28 and 29	Statements 18, 26 and 37
		G 2	**H** 3	**I** 7
	Basically disagree	Statements 31 and 33	Statements 16, 23 and 32	Statements 5, 19, 21, 34, 35, 36 and 38

2 Foreign firms provide US firms with very stiff competition for the People's Republic of China import trade. (Statement No. 4)
3 The Chinese take a longer time to reply to foreign trade proposals than do Europeans. (Statement No. 6)
4 The People's Republic of China negotiators require more

interaction than is expected in the US before fully trusting an American firm. (Statement No. 7)

5 The People's Republic of China representatives are extremely "tough" (smart and firm) negotiators. (Statement No. 8)

6 Group decisions are preferred to individual decisions by PRC negotiators. (Statement No. 11)

7 In order to prevent merchandise quality disputes, it is essential to specify the nature of inspection tests and product standards in contracts. (Statement No. 25)

8 When a contract dispute arises, the Chinese prefer to negotiate settlements rather than employ the arbitration provided in their contracts. (Statement No. 27)

Statement No. 1 indicates a way to establish a rapport in initial contacts. Statement No. 4 indicates that the Chinese know the way to uphold their bargaining power by establishing more alternatives.

Statements No. 6, 7, 8 and 11 reflect the heart of the matter in China trade negotiations. The Chinese tend to emphasize *"relationships"* and classify people into *insiders* (people belonging to the same group) and *outsiders* (people *not* belonging to the same group). If a person is regarded as an insider, all dealings become easy. If a person is regarded as an outsider, it becomes very unlikely that a significant business relationship can be established. Since the insider–outsider dichotomy is a discrete rather than a continuous phenomenon, one would feel that it takes much longer and more effort to enter into a rewarding relationship in China than in the Western world. However, once the relationship is established, the long-term payoffs can be significant. This cultural inclination is further reinforced by the centrally planned government system. Because of the bureaucratic structure and the lack of an incentive reward system, negotiators are not eager to conclude a deal and they can afford to wait. Also, people in charge of different units have to consult each other and reach a group consensus before taking any significant steps. Thus, the interaction process will take even longer, but at the same time, an established relationship will not be easily dismissed.

Statement No. 25 refers to the fear of lacking common understanding of the terms in contract. Statement No. 27 reflects the Chinese reluctance to go to court, which is considered a disgrace (losing face). At the same time, China is a nation, which, in general, is stronger than an individual company (even a big one). It is to the advantage of China to have negotiated settlements.

Groundless perceptions in China trade

Statements in Cell I include the following:

1 Because we are late arrivals on the trade scene, it will be difficult to establish a trade relationship (as the Chinese show great loyalty to suppliers of long standing). (Statement No. 5)
2 Night life in China provides social interaction between the Chinese and the foreign businessmen. (Statement No. 19)
3 In order to make a favorable first impression, US firms are wise to quote low prices initially, with the intention of making up lost profit later by raising prices. (Statement No. 21)
4 The economy of the People's Republic of China will, in the foreseeable future, become very productive and begin to compete internationally with American companies. (Statement No. 34)
5 Because of its low-cost labor supply, the People's Republic of China will flood markets with low-cost, labor-intensive products. (Statement No. 35).
6 The trade of technological goods to the People's Republic of China will erode the US advantage in technology. (Statement No. 36)
7 Opposition by labor, consumer, and political activist groups will deter the development of trade with the People's Republic of China. (Statement No. 38)

Statement No. 5 is not true because China only recently adopted an open-door policy, and a lot of her business partners are newcomers. As there are always many more areas to be newly-explored, opportunities are always growing rather than diminishing. Statements No. 19 and 21 reflect the danger of applying business practices in the free-trade world to China trade. Night life as it is known in the West does not exist at this time in China. An initial low-price deal will become a reference point for demanding low prices in future deals. That will become an unfavorable rather than a favorable factor in future negotiations.

Statements No. 34, 35, 36 and 38 reflect a gap between business reality and public conception in America. While the American public may agree with these statements, the American business people perceive differently, according to both the Brunner and Taoka study and our survey. It thus becomes a challenge for American companies to convince the American public of the realities, so that the companies may have more room to maneuver and conclude more deals in China trade.

Changes of the business environment

Statements in Cell C are statements that respondents *agreed with in 1975*, but *disagreed with in 1985*. They include:

1 The officials of the People's Republic of China trade corporations are technically well trained regarding the products they represent. (Statement No. 9)
2 During negotiations, trade officials of the People's Republic of China are reluctant to reveal their positions or titles. (Statement No. 12)

Statements in Cell G are statements that respondents *disagreed with in 1975*, but *agreed with in 1985*. They include:

1 The language barrier makes communications between the People's Republic of China and US representatives very difficult. (Statement No. 31),
2 The People's Republic of China imposes financial requirements on import trade forming definite obstacles to increased trade. (Statement No. 33)

The above changes are basically the results of system changes in order to expand the scope of foreign business in China. Since the country adopted an open-door policy, and many units at different levels had more autonomy in concluding business deals with outsiders, it became unnecessary (and in fact impossible) for the trade officials to hide their positions or titles. However, it still requires great skill for foreign business people to learn the *meanings* of those positions and titles. Also, since the scope and nature of foreign trading activities are expanding and emerging so rapidly, there is not enough qualified personnel. This is especially true in complicated joint venture projects which involve millions of dollars. Thus, it is natural to notice the problem of technical incompetence and language barriers. At the same time, for a developing country with foreign exchange control that wants to import a lot of advanced technology and to expand the scope of foreign business, it would not take long for the country to encounter the problem of foreign exchange shortage. Thus, activities such as "countertrade" are becoming important in China business.

MANAGEMENT IMPLICATIONS AND RESEARCH NEEDS

Results of this study confirmed the potential and increasing strategic importance of US–China business to American firms in the coming decade.

At the same time, when reviewed together with the results of Brunner and Taoka's study, results of *this* study also confirmed that a *high degree of stability* in US–China business seen from a perspective of cultural and bureaucratic factors, exists at this time, and is likely to remain for the foreseeable future. The significant "changes" experienced were not actual changes as such. They appeared mainly because the scope and nature of business operations with China had become larger, more varied and increasingly more complicated than they were ten years ago.

Thus, American business people could view Brunner and Taoka's study and this study as two important reference points, since the results of these two studies reveal a relatively consistent picture of the China business environment. They can use this information and exercise their wisdom to map out appropriate marketing and negotiating strategies.

For illustration purposes, this chapter adopts the framework developed by Graham and Sano (1984, 1986) to discuss the management implications of these findings in the various steps of business negotiations.

Selection of negotiating teams

It has been said that American executives (the "John Wayne" style) do not mind (or even prefer) going alone to negotiations with foreigners, rather than being accompanied by colleagues. This would be a mistake in the China context because they would be at the mercy of the interpreters recruited in China, where the quality of the interpreters is not highly reliable. The language barrier was not important in the 1975 study, however it was in 1985.

In order to prepare the American negotiators with an adequate background on Chinese history, culture, and customs, it is important to include at least one "Chinese" executive on the negotiating team. (By "Chinese" executives, we mean ethnic Chinese. They may be North American Chinese, or Hong Kong Chinese.) It was confirmed in a recent survey that Chinese executives of transnational corporations made significant positive contributions in China trade marketing negotiations (Lee 1986b). They play a key role in behind-the-scenes (informal) persuasion. According to the experience of a world-class soft-drink company, whenever the PRC officials had queries or wanted to settle some issues, they would send representatives to talk to the "Chinese" executives of the soft-drink company; they never approached the American executives informally.

Negotiation preliminaries

American business people should do their homework before they go to the PRC. *First, it is important to identify the relevant parties they should approach.* It is not unusual to discover that the end-user of the products is located in a southern province, the ministry responsible for negotiation is in Beijing, and the deal is finally settled in a special economic zone. It takes a lot of time to identify the concerned parties and organizations on the Chinese side and their interrelationships. Because of the recent policy towards more autonomy, the related parties in a particular deal involving the same products may be quite different. Relevant parties will depend on the size of the deal and whether the end-user is located in a special economic zone, in one of the fourteen open coastal cities or in a province other than Fujian and Guangdong. In a China business orientation session hosted by the American Chamber of Commerce in Hong Kong, an American industrial distributor said to one of the authors, "Just tell me who I should approach in the PRC". Such an impatient mentality may only generate unnecessary frustration.

Second, it is equally important to find out the foreign exchange limit of the concerned parties in the PRC. Different ministries, cities, or units may vary a lot in terms of their foreign exchange availability and spending capability. Published foreign exchange information is scarce, although occasionally, useful data can be obtained from the Trade Development Council in Hong Kong. If the related parties have a foreign exchange shortage problem, American executives may have to decide whether they want to enter into countertrade arrangements, postpone or cancel the business dealings.

Lastly, since it takes a much longer period of time to close a deal in China trade than Americans are accustomed to, the American business people may have to adjust the time horizons accordingly before they initiate the business contracts.

At the negotiating table

In the course of China trade, there will be a lot of time and expense spent in non-task sounding (talking about things not directly related to business). A typical American executive may get annoyed and feel time and effort is wasted. However, this is necessary to establish and intensify relationships.

Task-related exchange of information is very crucial. Since the

China side is making a group rather than an individual decision, it becomes necessary to make sure that relevant considerations related to all parties involved are clearly communicated and understood. Persuasion is primarily accomplished behind the scenes. American business people may depend on their Chinese colleagues to interact informally with PRC officials or representatives on the China side. Different Chinese units may have different queries and requests. It is important to make sure that these issues are dealt with properly *before* the two sides have a formal meeting.

Concessions and agreements should be handled very differently from the way that American business people are usually accustomed to. The Chinese, like the Japanese, normally only make concessions towards the end of negotiations, a holistic approach to decision-making. Quite a number of China trade executives have had the experience of finally getting their contract at the airport . . . while just a short while ago, they had thought that their mission was a complete failure. This is quite different from the sequential approach that American executives are familiar with. Also, it is not wise for the US firms to quote a low price initially, because it will become a reference point (even a ceiling price) for all subsequent potential transactions. On the other hand, it is important to reserve a margin for final price deduction when the business deal is about to be closed. By so doing, the American firms will do a favor to the China side, who can show their superiors that they managed to get a very good deal indeed.

After negotiation

Although the China side places more emphasis on "relationship" than "contract," it is nonetheless true that when there are disputes and when they think that the American side has breached the contract, the Chinese are not slow to make use of the terms stated in the contract to work for their advantage. On the other hand, American firms may want to learn to appreciate the Chinese logic of compensating the damaged party in a past deal by more favorable treatment in a future deal. Negotiated settlement is preferred to arbitration, which may hurt the long-term relationship.

Future research needs

There is enormous potential in US–China business. Some efforts, though far from adequate, have been made to understand the

American business people's perceptions and related aspects of marketing and negotiating in the PRC. However, business deals are joint efforts of two involved parties. In order to facilitate more effective and efficient business transactions, it is equally important to understand the Chinese perception of business and the process of business negotiating. It will help the Chinese side to work more effectively and make an equally important contribution to the much coveted success of US–China business deals.

NOTES

1 This chapter was first published in *International Marketing Review* (Summer 1988), Vol. 5, No. 2, pp. 41–51. Reprinted with permission.
2 The order of authorship is alphabetical, since both authors contributed equally to the preparation of this manuscript. The authors are grateful to Neil Holbert, Johny Johansson, David Ricks, Kenneth Simmonds, the *IMR* editors, and two anonymous reviewers, for their constructive comments on earlier drafts of the manuscript.

REFERENCES AND BIBLIOGRAPHY

Brunner, J.A. and Taoka, G.M. (1977) "Marketing and negotiating in the People's Republic of China: perceptions of American businessmen who attended the 1975 Canton fair," *Journal of International Business Studies*, Fall/Winter, pp. 69–82.
Chu, Bao-Tai (1986) *Foreign Investment Situations in China*, a paper presented in a seminar on PRC foreign investment and technology transfer, organized by the Hong Kong General Chamber of Commerce (15 July).
DePauw, J.W. (1981) *US–Chinese Trade Negotiations*, Praeger Publishers, New York.
Forsell, J. (1986) "China windows–why so many American managers call Hong Kong home," *Journal of the American Chamber of Commerce in Hong Kong*, October, pp. 45–7.
Graham, J.L. and Sano, Y. (1984) *Smart Bargaining, Doing Business with the Japanese*, Ballinger, Cambridge, MA.
Graham, J.L. and Sano, Y. (1986) "Across the negotiating table from the Japanese," *International Marketing Review*, Autumn, pp. 58–71.
Green, R.T. and White, P.D. (1976) "Methodological considerations in cross-national consumer research," *Journal of International Business Studies*, Fall/Winter, pp. 81–7.
Ho, Suk-ching (1986) "Entering the China market–via Hong Kong?" *Asia Pacific Community*, Winter, pp. 45–54.
Jao, Y.C. (1983) "Hong Kong's role in financing China's modernization," in Youngson, A.J. (ed.), *Hong Kong and China: The Economic Nexus*, Oxford University Press, Hong Kong, pp. 77–103.
Lee, Kam-Hon (1986a) "International marketing: environmental factors and

managerial perspectives," in Bagozzi, R.P. (ed.), *Principles of Marketing Management*, Science Research Associates, Chicago, pp. 617–60.

Lee, Kam-Hon (1986b) "The TNC Chinese executives in China trade: the impact of culture on marketing negotiation," a paper presented in the International Conference on Transnational Corporations in the World Development and China's Open-Door Policy, held at Nankai University, Tianjin, the PRC, October 26–30.

Lo, T.W.C. (1986) "Foreign investment in the special economic zones: a management perspective," in Jao, Y.C. and Leung, C.K. (eds), *China's Special Economic Zones: Policies, Problems and Prospects*, Oxford University Press, Hong Kong, pp. 184–200.

Mun, K.C. and Chan, T.S. (1986) "The role of Hong Kong in US–China trade," *Columbia Journal of World Business*, Spring, pp. 67–73.

Pye, L. (1982) *Chinese Commercial Negotiating Style*, Oelgeschlager, Gunn & Hain, Publishers, Inc., Cambridge, MA.

Pye, L. (1986) "The China trade: making the deal," *Harvard Business Review*, July–August, p. 74, pp. 76–80.

Tung, R.L. (1982a) "US–China trade negotiations: practices, procedures and outcomes," *Journal of International Business Studies*, Fall, pp. 25–38.

Tung, R.L. (1982b) *US–China Trade Negotiations*, Pergamon Press, New York.

12 International business in China

Gao Guopei

Marketers sometimes feel frustrated or even indignant about their experiences in China. They take part in lengthy negotiations, which often run on like endless marathons; they write letters and send catalogs which fail to evoke responses; they make travels to and from China, all without definite results. Therefore, they come to the conclusion that it is very difficult, if not impossible, to enter the Chinese market.

Why such exasperating experiences? Many attempts have been made, both in China and in other countries, to explore this pheno-menon, and explanations offered. These explanations vary, but they can be classified into two categories. According to one category of explanations, trade with China is difficult because there exists in the country serious bureaucracy, which is related to China's management system; according to the other, the Chinese are masters of stalling, a cultural tradition which dates back to ancient times.

Based on the explanations, researchers of China write out a prescription – patience. They say that patience is important because it will help a marketer survive Chinese bureaucracy and outlive the stalling tradition of the Chinese. In their view, patience is a cure-all and the key to success.

Is this sound advice? Before answering this question, another question has to be answered – are the above explanations correct? This is because it is on these explanations that the advice is based. It is perhaps a little paradoxical to say that the explanations are partly right and partly not right. However, this answer fits in well with the reality of China. Any marketers who want to be successful in China should try to seek a true picture of the country instead of a false one. To see China as it is, is the first step towards success.

The explanations are correct, for in China there do exist serious bureaucratic tendencies. For instance, there are overlapping lines of authority and competing ministries and commissions, which means that rounds and rounds of approval must be sought before a decision can be made. More important still, when a marketer sits down to talk to a Chinese trade official, he faces not only the person opposite him, but also the whole hierarchical system behind him, involving hundreds of officials, whom we may call invisible negotiators. It often happens that any decision, important or unimportant, cannot be made by the Chinese negotiator sitting alone across the table. The decision has to be reached by common approval by the units and committees in the hierarchical system, and any objections raised by any unit or committee will greatly prolong the decision-making process. The tragedy is that most likely the marketer will never know where the objection comes from. All this naturally constitutes an obstacle to the marketer on his way to his goal, and makes trade an experience both time-consuming and exasperating.

The cultural tradition also plays a part. Once in contact with the Chinese businessman, a marketer will find that his attitude is quite different from the make-or-break attitude prevailing in the West. The typical response a Chinese businessman gives to a proposition is "I will take it into consideration." This is indeed an elusive answer, for it can be interpreted in different ways. It may mean a very positive attitude towards what has been proposed; it may be a truthful statement of the fact that the offer needs time to be considered; or it may be just a euphemistic way of saying "No." This kind of answer often puts a marketer in a lurch, making him at a loss to know whether he should go ahead or back out.

This attitude comes from the Chinese tradition of playing safe, which in turn has been developed from the "doctrine of the mean" preached about 2,500 years ago by Confucius.

There is no need to elaborate on this attitude here. However, at this point it will be of interest to tell a story widely circulated in China. The story will serve as a vivid illustration of the attitude of the Chinese businessman. Once upon a time, there were three scholars who went to the capital to take part in the imperial examination. Not knowing what fate awaited them, these scholars went to a fortune-teller, and asked him whether or not they could pass the examination. The fortune-teller, after much affectation, held out one finger by way of reply. This was the kind of answer which actually covered all possibilities. If one scholar passed the examination, the finger would mean one scholar would pass; if two scholars passed the examination, the finger would mean that one would fail; if three scholars passed, the finger would mean that one whole lot of them would pass; if three scholars all failed, the finger would mean the whole lot of them would fail. In short, whichever possibility turned up, the fortune-teller was always infallible. This story may enlighten those interested in China on the methodology of understanding the country. Current researchers advocate a quantitative approach, showing great interest in all sorts of figures. While there is no doubt that this is a good method to use, the researchers may as well devote some time to the study of China's legend and folklore, which sometimes tell a lot more about the country's basic philosophy and cultural traditions than a heap of figures.

Now we come to the question why the explanations are not correct. A theoretical exposition may be of interest, but it is not called for. To know the answer, one needs only to know one simple fact – China's foreign trade has been on the increase over the years. Take 1988 for example. In that year China imported goods worth more than US$40 billion. This was a pretty large sum in view of the fact that all the buying was done in one short year. To import goods worth so much, the Chinese businessmen could not afford to lose much time. They had to act fast, and they did act fast, for they knew well that if they failed to do so, they could not possibly import all the things needed within a comparatively short time. In fact, there are numerous examples of the rapidity of the Chinese in taking action. For instance, people often find Chinese purchasing-missions buying things abroad worth millions of dollars within a couple of weeks. Evidently, in this process neither bureaucracy nor the cultural tradition has any role to play. That is why the above explanations are considered incorrect; they fail to give a convincing account of things in China.

Then what is the real situation in China? There is one very essential fact which marketers may do well not to forget – China's is a planned economy. Many researchers tend to ignore this fact. They get bogged down in details when studying the country. They have committed the mistake of failing to see the wood for the trees.

The fact that China's is a planned economy will not become less important because of the many reforms being carried out in this country. Efforts are now made to build up a new economic model. However, this is something which cannot be accomplished in one move; it needs time. While the new economic system is not in place, the old one, the centralized planned economy that has dominated China for decades, is still a reality a marketer has to face. Even if the new econmic model is completed, it will be different from the market economy of the West in that it will retain the basic features of socialism, and that the state will exercise a much greater control over the economy than the government of a market economy, and the control is effected through plans. That is why the new economic model China intends to build is given the name "the planned market-oriented economy."

Under the old economic system, there is a plan for everything. Take import for instance. All China's purchasing activities are guided by an annual plan. This means that there is little likelihood for China to buy anything that is not included in the plan. Should it happen that there is a need for a product not envisaged in the plan, the need will be subjected to a long process of examination. The end-user interested in the product has to apply for permission to buy the product from abroad through various levels of the local government; occasionally, he has to go a few steps further until he reaches somebody in the central government who has the power to say the final word. What is noteworthy is that waiting at the end of the long process is not always a "Yes," and as often a "No" can be expected. If there is any bureaucracy, it is felt in processes like this. However, if a product is included in the plan, it must be bought quickly, because it is not permissible not to fulfill the plan, which is a mandate. So here we have two conflicting sides of a picture: on the one hand, there is a lot of stalling; on the other, there is a lot of quick buying. This is a picture which cannot be satisfactorily interpreted other than by the fact that China's is a planned economy.

Would it be possible, then, for a marketer to know the specific contents of the plan? Unfortunately, there is no way of knowing them. The Chinese see the plan as a kind of commercial secret; it is perhaps just common sense not to let the cat out of the bag until one knows where it will jump. Sometimes even a national foreign trade corporation (FTC) does not know the details of the plan at the initial stage. For instance, a plan may allocate a few million dollars for hospital equipment, which may mean anything from small pincers to sophisticated medical apparatus. It is only when the Ministry of Public Health comes up with a detailed order list that the FTC concerned knows what the term "hospital equipment" refers to.

Faced with this reality, what is the sensible course of action for a marketer to take? As the first step, he should recommend his products to the FTCs. This is necessary for business to get started. Then, if the product happens to be included in the annual import plan, and if it is good in quality and competitive in price, the marketer can expect very quick results; if, however, what he recommends happens not to be included in the plan, he will have to wait for possibilities to turn up at a later time. People say that trade with

China is like lottery-drawing, and a marketer cannot take any initiative since everything is left to pure chance. While this view is not justified, it raises a very interesting question: does a marketer necessarily have to be in a state of inertia when he deals with a reality which he is not in a position to change? The answer is "No." A serious businessman will not simply make the contact and then sit back and relax, waiting for the results. He will go further by conducting in-depth studies of the country's economic development, which usually determines its demand pattern and import strategy, as is the case with other countries.

As has been pointed out, China's is a planned economy. To study its economic development means first of all studying its economic plans. It is the practice in China, as in many other socialist countries, to make a plan every five years for its economic construction. So far, China has gone through seven five-year plans, with the first extending from 1953 to 1957, the second from 1958 to 1962, the third from 1966 to 1970, the fourth from 1970 to 1976, the fifth from 1976 to 1980, the sixth from 1981 to 1985 and the seventh from 1986 to 1990. Take the first five-year plan for example. A study of the plan will reveal that it gave a lot more emphasis to the development of heavy industry than to the development of light industry and agriculture, and this order of priority would actually provide people with the clues as to the demand pattern of the country in that period. As it turned out, the proportion of the means of production imported rose from 89 percent of the total import in 1950 to 92 percent in 1957, and the proportion of the means of livelihood imported fell from 11 percent of the total in 1952 to 8 percent in 1957. This is of course a very rough picture. When such a study is conducted, a lot more details will have to be taken into consideration, but even this rough picture will suffice to show that it is not true to say that a marketer cannot do anything when he tries to enter a market such as China's. He can always chart out his course of action in the light of the prospects of the economic development provided by the plan under study.

Another point to note is that a five-year plan of China is always conditioned by the basic thinking prevailing at the time of its formulation. Therefore, it is important to study the plan in conjunction with significant policy changes, if any. For instance, during the fifth five-year plan period from 1976 to 1980, a conference was held in China – the third plenary session of the Eleventh Central Committee of the Communist Party of China – at which three important decisions were made: (1) the focus of work will be shifted from class struggle to economic construction; (2) the people's livelihood will be gradually improved; (3) China will open its door to the outside world. These decisions were important because they represented a new basic thinking, which was a complete breakaway from the practice of the past thirty years of launching one political campaign after another, of branding economic construction as a sin, of requiring people to sacrifice their personal interests for the state interests, and of closing the door of the country to the outside world more and more tightly. This drastic change in basic thinking was bound to manifest itself in the five-year plan under execution, and called for adjustments of some of its original targets. For instance, to improve the people's livelihood, it became necessary to restructure the economy which had laid too much emphasis on heavy industry. Since the economic restructuring could not be accomplished in one move, the logical step would be to import consumer goods from abroad to meet the long pent-up demands of the people while the restructuring was underway. This was why consumer goods were the fastest-growing category in the period between 1978 and 1980, accounting for about 60 percent of the total import of the country. During this buying boom, China imported large quantities of watches, radios, television sets and refrigerators.

It is therefore not impossible for marketers to explore trade potentials and develop trade with China through a study of its economic plans and policy changes. In the late 1970s, Japanese manufacturers of household electrical appliances were quicker than others in conducting such a study and in responding to business opportunities available in China by developing products suited to its actual conditions. Consequently, they succeeded in entering the market earlier than others. Japanese products still enjoy an advantage over others even today, as exemplified by refrigerators. The Japanese refrigerator manufacturers were the first to enter the Chinese market, and have been able to maintain their position ever since by offering a design which better meets the needs of the Chinese – it consumes less power, thus keeping electricity consumption of the Chinese low; it is of a slim size, which blends well with the small room of a Chinese. Refrigerator manufacturers of other countries have failed to be equally successful because they were slow-starters in the first place, and their products look like white elephants in the eyes of the average Chinese, with their automatic defrosting feature, which means higher power consumption, and with their large size, which is simply not in scale with the crowded living place of a Chinese.

Marketers often complain that they feel like a blind mouse when doing business with China. In the past, it was really very difficult for them to get hold of figures needed for the study of the country, but with the implementation of the open-door policy, data are much more easily accessible now. In fact, there are in China today a wide range of yearbooks and other sources of information for a marketer to choose from. Such being the case, only the marketer who fails to conduct the necessary study of China as a market will become an unfortunate blind mouse. Once, a Canadian businessman approached the author, delighted with the discovery of the possibility of selling tissue paper to China, where he thought the large population must have a great demand on the sanitary, soft and white thing. This was evidently a wrong conclusion, for anyone who studied China's strategic plan for economic development would not fail to see that this possibility simply did not exist. As we already know, according to the strategic plan, China's per-capita national income, which is a little more than US$300, is projected to reach about US$800 by the end of this century, or even less if the population is not kept to an appropriate size. It can hardly be expected that a country with its per-capita national income standing at such a level is a marketplace for tissue paper and similar things which are usually consumed in countries having a much higher per-capita national income.

So far we have focused on China's imports. Yet what has been said of the country's imports is also true of its exports. In other words, by conducting a similar study, the marketer can also identify China's export pattern and strategy. As a large developing country, China cannot hope to get away from its old export pattern of selling primary goods, such as minerals and farm produce, in exchange for foreign exchange needed for its economic construction. As a result of the adjustment of priorities, as can be seen from China's economic plans, China is now vigorously developing its light industry, particularly its textile industry, following the same pattern as Britain in the mid-nineteenth century, and the US in the early twentieth century. This means that for a long time to come, China's major industrial exports will be light industrial and labor-intensive goods such as textiles.

All the above discussions boil down to one essential point – it is not true that a marketer cannot do anything under a planned economy such as China's. He can always find out the country's import and export patterns by studying its plans which usually give clear indications of its level of economic development. If, after the study, a marketer comes to the conclusion that his line of production does not fit in with China's possibilities, the best course of action for him to take would be to quit, for in this case, to wait, no matter how patiently, means just a waste of time. If, however, the answer is "Yes," he should continue to recommend his products, waiting patiently for chances to turn up, if the possibility of immediate sales do not exist. It is only in this context that the advice of patience makes sense.

Marketers may not like a game like this, but this is a reality he must adapt himself to. When dealing with a planned economy, one must play the game by different rules, whether he likes them or not.

NOTES

1 P. Hibbert, (1989) *Marketing Strategy in International Business*, McGraw-Hill.
2 Zhen Jibing, (1988) *Reflections of the Contemporary Chinese*, Guizhou People's Publishing House.
3 Zhou Shulian, Min Jianshu *et al.* (1988) *On the Mechanisms of Business Operations*, Economic Management Press.
4 Gao Zhenjie (1987) *Revelations of Japan's Recent Success*, China Peace Press.
5 Suzane Ogden (1989) *China's Unresolved Issues*, Prentice Hall.
6 Scott D. Seligman (1989) *Dealing with the Chinese*, Warner Books.

13 The preparation of managers for overseas assignments

The case of China

Richard W. Brislin and C. Harry Hui[1]

The preparation of international business people for the special problems they will face during overseas assignments has become an active research area that has many potential applications (Paige 1986; Brislin 1989; Bhawuk 1990; Adler 1991). A major application has taken the form of cross-cultural training programs, or formal efforts to prepare people to live and work in countries other than their own. Topics commonly covered in such programs include the stresses and strains that stem from the pressures of adjusting to another culture, coping with the "culture shock" that results from the need to deal with so much unfamiliarity and with so much that is contrary to expectations, and differences in how important tasks are accomplished in the other country. For business people, such tasks include the establishment of joint ventures, negotiations for the importation of goods produced in other countries, the marketing of products, and so forth.

Helpful resources exist for the preparation of business people contemplating, beginning, or coping with the difficulties of assignments in China (Pye 1982; Tung 1982, 1987; Chesanow 1985; Macleod 1988; Webber 1989). While containing large amounts of very thoughtful and useful information, the material in these books and articles is not presented in a manner suitable for use in formal training programs. Rather, the information is presented in a manner much like this entire book: the written word, placing a premium on reading skills. For busy executives who do not have time to study these materials, or who learn more effectively when methods other than reading are added, attention must be given to various ways of conveying information about their overseas assignments so that they will be able to use it when attempting to achieve their goals. Attention to "various ways" of conveying information is central to good cross-cultural training programs.

One widely-available set of cross-cultural training materials is known as the "culture general assimilator" or "sensitizer" (Brislin, Cushner, Cherrie, and Yong 1986; also described in Brislin 1993). The purpose is to encourage participants in a training program to "assimilate" new information about their cross-cultural assignments so that they are less likely to be negatively affected because of culture shock, stress, and disappointments that business dealings have not progressed according to their expectations. Further, participants are encouraged to become "sensitized" to information about adjustment to other cultures, and to cultural differences, so that they not only *tolerate* but *look forward* to the enrichment to business dealings that cultural differences can bring. The two bases of the training materials are: (a) 100 critical incidents that capture experiences that trainees are likely to encounter on their cross-cultural assignments, and (b) a set of eighteen themes, or concepts, that should become central to how trainees *think* about their cross-cultural assignments in more sophisticated and complex ways. The materials were designed to help people adjust to overseas assignments no matter which country they are from and no matter the country in which they will be working (hence the term "culture general," above). However, in recommendations for how the materials can be used in actual programs (Brislin 1989, 1993), the guideline has always been presented that this general set of materials can be used as an *outline* for a program designed to prepare people for a specific country. The purpose of this chapter is to discuss how the culture general materials can be used when preparing business people for assignments in China.

AN EXAMPLE OF THE 100 CRITICAL INCIDENTS

The uses of the materials in training programs prior to people's overseas assignments can be most clearly seen when specific examples are examined. The following is one example (adapted slightly for use in programs for China) of the 100 critical incidents (Brislin *et al.* 1986, p. 137).

They are talking about me

Alan Burke had been in Shanghai for about six months and had begun work in an organization where 95 percent of the employees were Chinese citizens. Alan had worked all his life in his home country, New Zealand, and had done well in four full years of college-level study of the Chinese language. He was making good progress on the job and had been asked to give formal presentations on organization-related matters to the company as a whole. His language skills were good enough so that he could make formal presentations in Chinese. While he was pleased with his professional development, he was unhappy about informal contacts at work. He did not seem to be included in informal gatherings, such as work-breaks. Coworkers would sit around smiling and laughing and chatting, and Alan overheard his name mentioned often enough to become convinced that these informal groups were mostly talking about him. He became worried that they were talking negatively. He began to lose sleep, and this eventually became reflected in lower productivity on the job.

If Alan asked you to help him sort out his feelings, what would you say to him? Focus on the issue that is almost certain to be affecting Alan:

1 there is a natural tendency for sojourners to feel that they are being singled out for attention in hosts' conversations among themselves;
2 the coworkers should have been more sensitive and should have included Alan in their informal work-breaks;
3 coworkers were jealous of Alan's success as shown by his being asked to address the company as a whole;
4 Alan's formal language studies in New Zealand did not include coverage of casual, social conversation (language as it is used rather than language from a book), and so he was ill-prepared to interact informally with people.

When used in training programs, participants are told that there may be more than one good answer. Life is not a collection of perfectly clear incidents that can be understood after analyzing one precise explanation. Life is more ambiguous, and this fact is captured as participants consider all the alternatives. Participants can discuss the incident and develop a group consensus about the explanations. Once participants have examined a number of the incidents, they often become comfortable with formulating explanations *without* the structure offered through the provision of various alternatives, as in the example above. If the coordinator of the training program has experience in the more "active" training methods such as role-playing and participation in simulations, trainees can play out the roles depicted in the incident (Brislin 1989). After they consider various alternative explanations, participants can compare their analyses with those suggested by the authors of the training materials

(Brislin *et al.* 1986, pp. 145–6). "Sojourners" is a term frequently used when referring to people who accept assignments outside their own country for significant lengths of time. Considering alternative number 1, people read:

1 This is a good answer. Sojourners, all of whom go through some degree of culture shock, are naturally anxious about their relationships with hosts. Most want to make a good impression and want to be well remembered after they return to their own countries. But it must be remembered that the presence of a sojourner is a unique event – with 95 percent of Chinese nationals in the organization, outsiders *are* noticeably different and *will* be the focus of hosts' curiosity and informal conversations. The advice for sojourners is that they will be the focus of people's talks, but this fact should not be over-interpreted. Sojourners should not conclude that hosts are always talking ill of them, are talking about them all the time, or constantly call special meetings to talk about sojourners.

2 While perhaps true, this is not the best answer to help Alan sort out his feelings (which is the focus of the question posed at the end of the incident). People like to be with their ingroup during informal chats, and while this may lead to the exclusion of newcomers and outsiders, informal groupings of people who are similar is a natural tendency.

3 This is a possibility, and unfortunately one about which sojourners should be careful. Especially in periods of widespread uncertainty in a country, such as China after the Tiananmen Square incident, people are concerned with *why* certain individuals seem to receive favorable treatment. While the possibility of jealousy, and the issues stemming from "standing out from others," should be discussed with experienced sojourners and with trusted Chinese colleagues, there is another answer that meets the request to focus on the issue that is almost certain to be affecting Alan.

4 The content of what is taught in college language courses varies widely. Some instructors, realizing the criticism that students once left their classes "talking like books" is valid, now regularly introduce material on informal conversation styles in their coursework. For instance, instructors invite foreign students to come to their classes and to engage in informal chats with students. While this is a good answer, there is another issue that meets the criterion that it is certain to be affecting Alan.

THE EIGHTEEN THEMES DESIGNED TO ASSIST IN THE ORGANIZATION OF INFORMATION

Large amounts of information can be presented during cross-cultural training programs such that the memories of participants can be severely challenged. Eighteen themes, or categories, have been developed and participants are encouraged to relate new information to the content of these categories. Information is less likely to be forgotten, and it is more available when needed, if it is efficiently organized in people's minds. The origin of the eighteen categories stems from interviews with highly experienced sojourners. Before preparing the materials, the developers (Brislin *et al.* 1986) asked experienced sojourners questions like, "What was most memorable about your experiences in the other culture? What difficulties did you encounter? What advice would you give to people going to the other culture for the first time?" There was a great deal of commonality in people's answers, and the eighteen themes were developed by examining the underlying reasons for the memorable stories and the advice for neophytes that the respondents offered. Examples of issues faced by business people in China will be offered to demonstrate the use of the eighteen themes in actual training programs.

The eighteen themes are themselves organized in a three-part framework: (a) people's *emotional reactions* brought about by encounters with cultural differences; (b) *knowledge areas* that incorporate many specific cross-cultural differences that sojourners find hard to understand; and (c) *the bases of cultural differences*, with special attention to how people in different cultures think about and evaluate information.

Emotional reactions

Most people are unprepared for the challenges to their emotional lives that sojourns bring. They often *know* certain facts such as the type of housing they can expect, the differences in food that they will surely encounter, and the upheavals brought on by recent political events. But they are far less prepared to deal with the emotional reactions they will have when adjusting to these and a multitude of other differences.

1. *Confrontation with prejudices and stereotypes.* One emotional challenge is that people will find that their prejudices and stereotypes are not at all useful. Most individuals, deep in their souls and perhaps unconsciously, feel that they are from an advanced culture and that

people in other countries behave in strange, unproductive ways. If sojourners communicate this feeling in China, they will be unsuccessful. The Chinese are very proud, much more aware of their history than people in many other countries, and feel that they have made incredible advances over the last fifty years. Sojourners who can show appreciation for various aspects of Chinese culture, and who are knowledgable about major historical events and intellectual traditions, will have an advantage. Another emotional challenge is that there are few stereotypes that will be useful in all cases. Stereotypes are generalizations about people. While usually thought of when combinations of people and negative words are combined (e.g., sly or inscrutable Chinese), stereotypes can involve any combination of a group label and descriptive words. Examples are, "Americans are concerned with short-term profits"; "Chinese willing to work with overseas business people are forward-looking." Few descriptive words are useful in all cases. We referred to three earlier in this paragraph: the Chinese are proud, know their history, and point to recent advances. One of the frustrations sojourners face (and one shared by preparers of training materials) is that these generalizations will not always be true. Sojourners may encounter individual Chinese who strongly prefer European and American cultural practices, are uninformed about history, and feel that China has lagged significantly over the last fifty years. The sorts of generalizations (which, since they are about people, are stereotypes) that can be presented in a chapter such as this one are reasonable first approximations to what sojourners will find in their specific business dealings. Sojourners must constantly be willing to modify, sharpen, and become more sophisticated as they interact with various Chinese nationals. Chang (1989, p. 36) makes a similar observation:

> Americans typically see China as a political, economic, and sociological monolith. Nothing could be further from the truth. Although under the mandate of a central government, the people and provinces of China are as different from each other as the countries of Europe. And it has always been this way in China, for thousands of years.

2. *Anxiety.* Since sojourners will encounter many unfamiliar demands for which they have not yet learned appropriate behaviors, they will experience anxiety and stress. Anxiety can stem from uncertainty about appropriate behaviors in various business settings, about the future in general, and about the unknown. Business people contemplating investments in China must deal with uncertainty about

the future of the authoritarian figures in government. Many are old and will die within ten years, but who will replace them? Should business people believe the rhetoric of the early and mid-1980s about the vast possibilities for intelligent investment, or should they make conclusions based on the Tiananmen Square disaster? The government's reaction to this disaster has included a set of tight security measures with which many sojourners from America and Western Europe are unfamiliar. Some business people are quite uneasy about their incoming fax messages being monitored.

3. *Disconfirmed expectancies.* Sojourners very frequently experience intense stress because the reality they find in China differed from their expectations. The stress stems from the *difference* between their expectations and reality, not necessarily the reality itself. If they had been better prepared so that they had a more accurate picture of conditions in China, they would not experience the expectations–reality distinction to the same degree. As A.J. Robinson (1989, p. 30) points out,

> Contrary to what some may want to believe, most Western businesses . . . have yet to break even on their investments. It's a myth to think US and other foreign companies are in the China game to make a quick buck. It's simply not happening.

In addition to such general expectations about investment possibilities, disconfirmations can take place during everyday behaviors with Chinese counterparts. Many business people expect to meet tight-lipped factory managers who are unlikely to discuss politics in a candid manner. Some Chinese, however, will make very negative comments about the government if they are assured of confidentiality. Some business people expect the government to be more open about foreign investment as a *sign* that China is still committed to economic development. This will be true in some provinces and some special economic zones, but not in others. There is no substitute for very careful homework.

4. *Belonging.* Sojourners want to feel accepted by others and want to feel "at home," but they often cannot since they have the status of outsiders. There are a number of reasons why Americans and Europeans might not feel accepted or at home among the Chinese. China has had a tradition of closing its doors to foreign influences. On the most basic level, the sojourners' appearance and formal business dress sets them apart from host nationals. Groups function differently in Chinese culture. The collective bonds that tie people together are stronger, and often can be traced back through

many generations, and so accepting a newcomer may not occur as quickly as in America or Europe. The lack of physical space may further restrain people from inviting foreign business people into their homes. Interestingly, the Chinese have recently adopted a set of behaviors that they use with foreign guests that *could* be seen as signals that they want foreigners to feel at home. The Chinese may be *extremely* courteous and charitable to foreign guests. These Chinese may save their Western colleagues the best seats in a cinema or boardroom and may run errands for them. Sometimes, these *overly* generous behaviors may only add to a foreigner's feelings of not being accepted.

   5. *Ambiguity.* Sojourners become upset because the messages they receive from Chinese counterparts are sometimes unclear. The Chinese may feel that they are being very clear in delivering their intent, but the foreigners may feel that the messages are ambiguous. During verbal exchanges, Americans may be surprised at how quickly and seemingly abruptly their Chinese acquaintances end conversations. Leave-taking messages sent off by the Chinese are often short and subtle. "*Hao*" (meaning "good!" in Chinese) is sufficient to end a conversation between two Chinese friends. The same utterance translated into English does not serve a similar function and is seen as overly abrupt or as the sort of utterance a busy superior would use with a subordinate. "*Zai shuo ba*" appears to mean "Say that again" in English. An American responding to that "request" who repeats what he or she has just said will be seen as a pest. A more accurate paraphrase of "*Zai shuo ba*" is "We shall talk about it at some later time." In any particular situation people may wonder if the other party is angry or rude. The stimuli and appropriate reactions are ambiguous and confusing. These sorts of misunderstanding in people's everyday conversations have been analyzed by Carbaugh (1990). A good piece of advice is that when interacting with people from a different cultural background, participants in conversations should *not* make the same sort of conclusions as they would if conversing with someone they know well from their own culture. Aspects of conversations such as rising pitches, abrupt leave-taking, periods of silence, and stock phrases will probably not have similar meanings. When tempted to make a negative conclusion, consider the difficulties people from other cultures probably have with the stock American phrase, "We'll have to have lunch together soon!" This is a polite leave-taking expression. Our advice is to entertain the possibility that the Chinese have similar polite conventions that can be misunderstood.

Knowledge areas

The second major clustering of various cultural differences that affect the adjustment of business people on overseas assignments centers on people's preexisting knowledge about human behavior, ways of doing business, criteria for success, career development, "getting things done," and so forth. Business people will not be allowed to represent their companies on overseas assignments unless they have had considerable success in their own countries. There, they have invested great amounts of time and energy in learning what their own country considers *knowledge* that people need to achieve success. They attend school year after year, obtain college degrees, participate in on-the-job training, and work themselves up through the ranks. When they undertake overseas assignments, they can become very disconcerted when they find that people in the other country consider other facts and ways of doing things to be "proper knowledge." Further, they may find that acceptable knowledge in other countries is the exact opposite of what they have previously learned.

6. *Work.* When the important concept "getting things done in the world of work" is considered, there are many specific cultural differences. Many Americans find that institutions such as offices and schools have a greater significance in Chinese culture. In mainland China, the workplace is often a part of a unit that controls almost all aspects of life: allocation of housing, family planning, whether one can go to visit another province or country, and so forth. While work relations have many implications for other aspects of life, the converse is also true. Often, employees will socialize after work, and it is quite possible that some of the social relations that form outside of the workplace will influence working relationships among people and decisions that are made during office hours. In Chinese, the term *guanxi* means "connections," and it is used to refer to these social relationships that can have far-reaching implications. Work cannot be done outside these connections. The parallel term in English is "network," but in our experience people in China are more aware of the importance of *guanxi* than English speakers are of the importance of a good network.

Especially in small companies of 300 people or less, a good metaphor to keep in mind when examining managerial and leadership behavior is "family" (Hui 1990). The owner and/or manager is much like a father-figure, and he combines sternness, authoritativeness ("I know what is right!"), and a paternal concern for the well-being of workers. All the benefits and weakness of family-run businesses become part of the analysis. Benefits include a loyal set of workers, long-term commitment to the company, and clear goals as long as the workers accept the leader's authoritative views. Weaknesses include feelings of exclusion if one is not considered "part of the family," poor communication with other companies or with other units within large organizations, and inadequate policies to prepare a new generation of leaders as the father-figures grow old.

7. *Time and space.* While the stereotype of Asians may include carelessness about punctuality, Chinese in large cities have become more precise about the use of time given that they have dealt with overseas business people for over a decade. In fact, foreigners may be surprised at how scheduled and organized certain activities are in Chinese culture. Socially, however, punctuality may not have quite the same importance. Friends are accustomed to participating in activities in large groups and people must often wait for others. Foreigners can contribute to the development of positive relationships by waiting for all the people in a group to arrive, chatting pleasantly with those present and *not* displaying signs of irritation. In rural and suburban areas, attention to time is less important than in big cities. One helpful guide is to examine the number of clocks on walls and on people's desks. If there are only a few, a reasonable inference is that people are not too strict about time.

The lack of personal space may agitate Americans who spend large amounts of time in China. The majority of Chinese who reside in cities are accustomed to living in small places surrounded by other people. On crowded city sidewalks, people are much more likely to pass closely, cut off others, and brush by or bump into others. People may stand closer to each other than is comfortable for Americans. Business partners may move their heads so that they almost touch when they discuss confidential matters. Americans may consider these as "spatial invasions" and as signs of rudeness. The Chinese do not mean to convey this message. The difference is cultural: people in China claim and respect far less *individual* space than in the West.

This different orientation to the use of space may relate to the concept of privacy. Generally, privacy is much less respected in Chinese culture. Parents will often question where their adult children have been. Chinese colleagues walk in and out of each other's offices freely. If people keep all their mail, telexes, and fax messages under lock, others may become suspicious. Perhaps those people have something evil or unlawful that they are hiding.

8. *Language.* If an American attempts to learn Chinese, several problems will almost surely occur. The foreigner will encounter the

KING ALFRED'S COLLEGE
LIBRARY

frustration of running into people who only want to practice their English, denying the sojourner the opportunity to practice Chinese. Such experiences will become more and more frequent as people in China become even more aware of the importance of speaking good English in the business world. If foreigners do not speak Chinese, they will very often be speaking with people who are using a second language. Sojourners must develop patient listening skills and must develop the ability to explain complex ideas in simple words. They must also anticipate subtle miscommunications due to nuances in meaning. For example, the English words "may" and "can" are very similar to one Chinese word. But if a Chinese speaker communicating in English uses "may" instead of "can," a native English speaker may unconsciously conclude that the Chinese individual is acting in an aloof manner and is "giving permission" rather than indicating that something is possible. Irritants such as this one when communicating across cultural barriers are frequent (Carbaugh 1990), and sojourners should *not* interpret them in the most negative manner possible.

Speaking English may be a source of great pride for some Chinese. If a native Chinese speaker, perhaps an English teacher or interpreter, speaks to a sojourner in English, it may be considered insulting to respond to that person in Chinese. Americans doing business in China are more likely to encounter Chinese who speak adequate English than to find fellow countrymen who both know Chinese culture and who speak good Chinese. The search for Americans knowledgeable about both the Chinese language and culture may be expensive, but it can be central to business success (Kamsky 1989). Without their help, visiting business people will become overly dependent upon their Chinese counterparts, and the Chinese may demand concessions for agreeing to satisfy the visitors' need for dependence.

9. *Roles.* People engage in various sets of related behaviors, or play various roles, in the course of their lives. Examples are "boss," "parent," "troubleshooter," "leader," and so forth. The exact behaviors associated with these various labels become part of a culture's expectations of how people will behave if they assume these roles. The term "role" is borrowed from the theater. People must behave in certain ways if they accept a certain role. If they agree to play Hamlet, they must be indecisive and cannot kill their uncle in the first act. If they agree to play Willy Loman in *Death of a Salesman*, they cannot earn $35,000 in commissions during the first ten minutes of the play.

Difficulties arise during intercultural interactions when people from one culture expect certain behaviors but when people from another are unwilling to engage in these expected behaviors. For instance, many Americans think that "good workers" should figure out ways to solve minor problems on their own. However, they complain that this is not expected behavior of good workers in China. Richard Holton (1990) carried out interviews with American managers of nineteen joint ventures in China. He found that many Americans noted that

the Chinese employee is trained to take orders, but not to initiate change. . . . It is difficult to push the Chinese manager into taking responsibility for getting things done on his own; he is more inclined only to respond to the specific instructions from his superiors. Thus the Chinese enterprise is likely to be a very static organism, except for changes which are initiated by the authorities to which the unit reports or are required by circumstances which absolutely demand some sort of response.

(Holton 1990, p. 125)

The desire for specific instructions from a higher authority relates to the previous discussion of ambiguity and uncertainty avoidance. Chinese managers dislike ambiguity and uncertainty. They prefer specific written directives from higher authorities both to reduce uncertainty in their own behavior and to have a "paper-trail" of their orders in case policy decisions are later shown to be mistaken.

Other behaviors attached to role-labels are puzzling to foreigners. The "teacher" may be expected to care about and guide the moral, physical, and emotional growth of the student as well as offer instruction in a traditional subject-matter. Some employees in service industries (e.g., cabin crews, store clerks, receptionists, waiters/waitresses) may find it quite difficult to be pleasant when asked to do things looked upon as "lowly" by others. These behaviors may include refilling water-flasks, searching for items required by a potential customer, and having to work while the client is sitting comfortably in a chair and reading or chatting with others. Managers from North America and Europe can avoid creating unpleasant working relations by giving great amounts of attention to the feelings and emotions of Chinese workers; and by showing appreciation and ascribing high status to the work requested from the company's personnel (see Baird, Lyles and Wharton 1990 for other advice for American managers working in China).

10. *The individual and the group.* Large cultural differences exist

that center around people's socialization into their culture. Were they socialized to pursue their own goals and to put the goals of others (e.g., their extended family) in a less important position (called individualism), or were they socialized to consider the goals of others when formulating their own plans for their lives (called collectivism: Triandis 1989)? The answer has very important implications and it can be the underlying reason for many misunderstandings among individualist North Americans and collectivist Chinese. For instance, many business people have commented on the importance of "saving face" among the Chinese (Holton 1990). One reason is that the Chinese identify with their collective (which can include people in one's organization) much more strongly than do Americans. Being embarrassed or "losing face" in front of others, then, leads to a much stronger negative reaction among the Chinese.

A good question to ask in China is, "Will this group of workers be together ten and twenty years from now?" The answer will be "yes" more frequently than in the United States, where people move from community to community and from organization to organization to seek better jobs. But given that the answer will often be "yes" in China, there are many implications. The Chinese will be more familiar with the concept of lifelong employment in the same company (sometimes called the "iron rice-bowl"). It is more important to maintain long-term good relations between managers and workers, since ill-feelings can remain for many years in people's memories *and* in their informal conversations with young workers who assume entry-level positions in the organization. There will be more protection of obviously incompetent workers, given that maintenance of the collective (here, the work group) and protecting a person's "face" may be more important than increasing productivity through the active recruitment of ambitious and capable young workers.

The importance of the group or collective is so important that it is wise to look for various places where its influence can be seen (Triandis, Brislin and Hui 1988). By constantly seeing the workings of the collective, sojourners will be less likely to forget its pervasiveness. The allegiance to the family group helps explain why older, single people continue to live with their parents and why Chinese seem so concerned when they see a foreign friend eating alone. Many subtleties in Chinese culture preserve group unity. At meals, individual dishes are shared by everyone. When people go out to eat together it is customary that one person pays. Splitting the bill after a meal seems to imply a sense of separateness among people.

Another manifestation occurs when Chinese colleagues are asked what they want for dinner. The response will almost inevitably be, "Anything will do." The Chinese prefer not to reveal their preferences because they may conflict with those of the person ordering dinner. Such conflicts have the potential of interfering with interpersonal harmony. Chinese who have not interacted very much with foreigners may frown upon their self-assertiveness and unwillingness to take group feelings into account.

Americans in particular will almost surely be tempted to say, "All this emphasis on the group is inefficient!" However, in the long run they will save time and energy by deciding upon activities in which everyone can and wants to participate. Recall the question about people being together ten and twenty years from now. American business people who will be successful in China have to communicate the fact that they are deeply involved and that they are investing "for the long run." They have to communicate that they want to become part of the Chinese sense of collective feelings and that they are willing to assume the life-long obligations that membership in collectives demands. The "in and out in a couple of years" sort of business arrangement, even if financially successful, is not at all appreciated by the Chinese.

11. *Rituals and superstitions.* The traditional beliefs of the Chinese are endless: don't eat fried food if you have a sore throat; don't sleep with your feet pointed at the door; if you don't finish your rice your husband will have bad skin; and so forth. Many young people still consult Chinese herbalists, and their practices, which make use of the less familiar parts of plants and animals, often work though they may seem strange to sojourners. People's religious beliefs vary from place to place, from time to time, and even from business to business. In southern China, many people believe that the spirits of the wind and the water can influence happiness, health, fortune, or hardship. Geomancy remains an important consideration for choosing sites of plants and offices. Other people believe in gods who are happy to take "bribes." But there are others well-versed in materialist doctrines (mostly Communist Party cadres) who do not have high regard for the worshippers.

Overseas business people will have difficulties empathizing with and planning their work around the many Chinese religious practices. To make matters more complex, different Chinese have different expectations of foreigners. Some want their foreign partners to go through the same religious practices so that good luck is assured. Others tend to hold the view that people from North America and

Europe should be more modern and scientific in their thinking, and they suspect ulterior motives and hypocrisy if sojourners go along with their Chinese colleagues. A good piece of advice is to develop a close relationship (with its long-term obligations: see "individuals and groups," above) with a Chinese colleague who can give advice on attention to religious practices at a specific time, regarding a specific matter, to be carried out or ignored in a particular place, and so forth. Such a person is called a "cultural informant" and can offer advice whenever the possibility of behaviors influenced by people's cultural backgrounds are involved.

12. *Hierarchies: status and authority.* Many Chinese are highly concerned with the relative status of the people with whom they interact. One's high school, year of graduation, university attendance, and company name will often be used in introductions to indicate a person's relative status in a new social group. A new acquaintance will accord a person higher status if that person's uncle or father is known. Conversely, if person A mentions to person B that he or she has interacted with one of B's subordinates, then person A will be treated more like a subordinate than as an equal. Where a person works also gives additional information to people, since the work unit is very closely linked to other aspects of one's life.

Age is another cue that determines relative status. People will go to great lengths to find out someone's age, and perhaps also their tenure with the company they represent. Americans who have moved from company to company every three or four years can be put at a disadvantage. People do not mind telling others their own age. A person with many years of experience in a profession or trade is addressed as "old so-and-so." For example, a sojourner named "Scott" who seems to be sixty years or older will be addressed as *Lao* (old) *Shi* (first syllable of Scott when transliterated). Similarly, if a sojourner is younger than the rest, he or she may be addressed with *Shao* (little preceding the last name). A person addressed as "Old-so-and-so" is often respected. In China, age is not associated with senility. It is a synonym for "wisdom and experience." Women from North America and Europe should not feel offended when addressed as *Lao*.

In government departments, bureaucracy is the fact of life. Because of their relatively low status, Chinese subordinates may not work through the bureaucracy as effectively as a sojourner who has a high-status title and knows how to interact effectively with Chinese officials. If sojourners want something done within a bureaucracy, it is often best to make a personal call. Delegation can often lead to unacceptable delays.

There is more deference to authority in China than in the United States, as long as the authority figures remain visible in the organization. Many American partners in joint ventures have complained that plans were put in place and seemed to be widely accepted, but that these plans were ignored as soon as the American partners left. Discussing the manufacturing of new products, for instance, Americans complained that

> quality control standards are likely to slip unless supervision is vigilant. "The sky is high and the emperor is far away," the saying goes, and it is easy to return to behavior that is easy and convenient unless performance is constantly monitored.
>
> (Holton 1990, pp. 130–1)

13. *Values.* People's views about broad areas such as religion, economics, morality, politics, aesthetics, and interpersonal relationships become internalized. Understanding these internalized views, called values, is critical in intercultural adjustment. Values can affect very basic policy decisions, such as whether foreign businesses should be in China at all, and they can affect day-to-day relations among foreigners and Chinese citizens.

With respect to the most basic decision concerning a foreign presence in China, many business people feel that the Chinese government behaved in such an intolerable manner during the Tiananmen Square episode and its aftermath that further business relations are immoral and unacceptable. The Chinese government ordered that soldiers open fire on unarmed students; after this, dissidents were rounded up and treated in a manner that violates the value of "punishment fitting the crime" and the value that justice cannot tolerate "cruel and unusual punishment." Some business people feel that an absence of business investment in China should be used as a sanction until there are clear changes made in the government's attitude towards democracy.

Other business people feel that changes in government policy will occur with a constant overseas presence that exposes the Chinese to different viewpoints, different values, and different ways of dealing with problems. Wan Runnan (1989, p. 31) feels,

> China has seen enormous changes during the last ten years; the most important ones are the changes in the people and in their way of thinking. This stems from the efforts and contributions made by foreign business people. . . . Without their efforts, there would be no such overwhelming democratic movement in China today.

Arguing from a similar position that foreigners concerned with change can have more impact if they stay in China than if they leave, Kamsky (1989, p. 33) writes:

> In the long run, the greatest contribution American business can make to the development of peace and democracy may well be to do what it knows best – produce and distribute goods in the most imaginative and efficient manner that it can.

Reasonable people disagree about "presence in" or "withdrawal from" China as having the most positive impact on the democracy movement. While it is not a smooth transition to move from this extraordinarily important moral issue to more mundane issues of day-to-day working relationships among people, it is important to understand that values affect these, also. Many Chinese have been socialized to be cautious, risk-aversive, conservative, and resistant to change. Buyers from foreign trading companies may find it difficult to convince some Chinese business people and factory operators to make modifications concerning their products and services. The general manufacturer of a factory that produced dinnerware (specifically, fine china) refused to change the design of its up-market plates from a round shape to a slightly octagonal shape. He explained his decision: "If the original design was well-accepted by consumers in the past, why wouldn't it be in the future? Besides, who else but myself will take the blame if the change flops?"

Many Chinese have been socialized to avoid overt emotional expressions. This is particularly true of negative emotions such as anger. The value of modesty is obvious when Chinese friends receive compliments. Such compliments are rarely accepted with a thank-you; instead, they are often shunted aside or credited to another source. Responding to a compliment about an ability, a Chinese friend may say, "No, not really." If a person compliments a possession by saying, for example, "I like the dress you're wearing," a Chinese woman may respond, "Oh, it's my mother's," or, "My sister gave it to me." Accepting the compliment directly with a statement like, "Oh, thanks, I just bought it yesterday!" is common in the West but may be interpreted as arrogant in China. Just as they do not accept compliments with a "thank you," some Chinese do not acknowledge the help that they receive or show overt appreciation when others go out of their way to help in various ways. Americans who expect people to say "thank you" for various types of help they offer will be both disappointed and perhaps irritated.

The bases of cultural differences

The purpose of analyzing the third major clustering of cultural differences is to help people understand the underlying reasons for some of the very specific behaviors that strike them as strange and odd when they live in another country. No single chapter or book can prepare people for all of the differences that they will find. However, if some of the basic reasons for cultural differences are understood, people are less likely to conclude that "difference" is the same as "inferiority." Rather, differences simply reflect the various ways that cultures guide members toward the attainment of different goals, whether those goals be achievement in the business world, loyalty to one's group, secure employment, a happy family life, and so forth.

14. *Categorization.* People cannot pay attention to every specific piece of information to which they are exposed during any single day. Rather, they group pieces of information together and treat the grouping (called a category) as if its members were more or less the same. For example, if readers of this chapter return to their desks after a two-week trip, they see an in-basket full of work to be done. They would be unwise to give equal attention to the pieces of information in the in-basket. Rather, they develop categories, such as "urgent," "can wait a few days," "delegate to a subordinate," "toss in the wastecan," and so forth. Then, they organize their work around the categories they have formed. The important point to be understood in intercultural contact is that people from different cultures often place the *same* piece of information in a different category. For instance, consider the previous discussion of working with bureaucracies under the heading, "Hierarchies: status and authority." There is a seemingly minor matter that the overseas business person finds in her in-basket involving a visa for a colleague from the home office. She is tempted to put it in the "delegate to a subordinate" category. But if she has a high-status title and is good at making low-status officials in the bureaucracy feel important and respected, she may have far better results if she puts it in the "urgent" category so that she gives it her own, immediate attention. A good question to constantly ask oneself when faced with new information is, "Are there differences in how overseas business people and the Chinese are likely to categorize this information?"

Many times, irritation will be caused when the overseas business people *themselves* are the new pieces of information that are being put into categories. When interacting with Chinese, a business person may be frustrated at being put immediately into the category of "foreigner." In Chinese culture the category of foreigner is well-developed and often resistant to change. Certain stereotypical behaviors are often expected of foreigners and the sojourner may feel frustrated that Chinese hosts do not seem to perceive individual differences. A German engineer hired by an American multinational corporation to work in Shanghai is put into the same category as Americans. To an average Chinese citizen, people from Germany, France, England, the United States, and Canada all look the same and behave the same.

Of course, categories are also part of the thinking that overseas business people apply to the Chinese. There are many commonly used categories that obscure individual differences: Party members, Shanghainese, people from the rural region, cadres, dissidents, and so forth. Overseas business people are likely to be more successful if they go beyond category labels to examine the potential contributions and insights of individuals within these broad groupings. If they dismiss new information with the overly quick use of a familiar category, they may miss opportunities that would help in their work.

15. *Differentiation.* When information is combined, it is placed in various categories that people carry in their minds. When information is taken apart, it is differentiated and people then respond to more specific bits of information than is contained in a large category. One result of increased interest in, or importance of, a certain topic is that more and more information is differentiated within that topic area such that new and smaller categories are formed. Examples are the *many types* of obligations that accompany various interpersonal relationships in China, and the *various* ways to overcome red tape. If sojourners do not differentiate information in the same manner as hosts, they may be treated as naïve or ignorant. The question sojourners should ask, then, is "What distinctions do hosts make when thinking about a certain topic." Then, sojourners should learn to make the same distinctions. For example, overseas business people studying the American garment industry have to learn to make many fine distinctions when "markets" are considered. As a class exercise, American college students in big cities can easily distinguish ten status levels of retail stores where new clothes might be bought, ranging from "low"-status warehouse-like discount houses to "high"-status boutiques. Business people from other countries should learn to make similar distinctions.

Business people in China often fail to notice distinctions that *could* be of use to them. Because of the somewhat "monotonous" color scheme and "simple" design of Chinese people's clothing, many sojourners have mistakenly thought that the Chinese wear more or less the same clothes to work in factories, to eat in a canteen, to attend a business meeting, or to be served at a sit-down dinner. The sojourners have missed subtle distinctions. The result is that the sojourners may use their *image* of Chinese dress standards as a guide and as a result show insensitivity in what they choose to wear. In actuality, the style, cutting, and material of the Chinese people's clothing inform the "insiders" concerning the wearer's social status, the importance being attached to an occasion (e.g., a business meeting), and their view of the others who are attending the same function.

16. *The ingroup–outgroup distinction.* Ingroups refer to people with whom interaction is sought. Outgroup members are held at a distance and can become the targets of rejection. People entering another culture have to be sensitive to the fact that they will often be outgroup members from the hosts' point of view, and that there will be some behaviors associated with ingroup membership in which they will never participate.

In China, it is a well-accepted practice to take care of those whom one knows well and to treat them as ingroup members. In contrast, the Chinese are far more reserved with outgroup members. Ingroup members can be from the same work unit, from the same region of the country, may have attended the same school, can know someone who is a relative of a relative, or have some other link considered important in China. When a choice is to be made between people who do and who do not have this type of link, then the people who have some kind of ingroup ties will be favored (Hui 1990). This type of ingroup membership is not readily available to the sojourner. A foreigner can be part of only one or a few of these linkages (e.g., same work group) but will not have the strong relationships based on childhood friendships that go back to attendance at the same grade school. In addition, people share problems only with ingroup members. Such problems as disappointments in the school performance of one's children, marital difficulties, and disagreements with one's boss will rarely be shared with sojourners who have not had the same cultural experiences that permit a full understanding of these problems. But if personal problems are not shared, limits are placed on the development of close relationships between sojourners and the Chinese.

To make this topic even more complex, ingroups are often arbitrarily defined to meet the needs of the moment. One Chinese person may regard a fellow regional (an individual from the same province or county) as an ingroup member, and will go out of the way to help the individual secure the supplies necesary for completing assigned tasks. Similarly, it is possible that if people from different regions of China are employed by IBM, they will treat each other as members of their ingroups when working in the same Chinese subsidiary of IBM. However, those same people may treat each other as outgroup members when they find themselves among a large group of fellow regionals who went to the same school. At a social gathering where many IBM employees are in attendance, for example, one of the ingroups that forms may be "Shanghainese working for IBM." This group may temporarily exclude other Chinese who did not come from Shanghai.

17. *Learning styles.* People acquire new information in different ways, and they also approach new learning opportunities with different attitudes. When different ways of acquiring information and different attitudes toward examining new opportunities are widely shared in a culture, they can cause frustration if not well understood by outsiders. When examining the possibility of joint ventures in China, various analysts have suggested that Americans go about their learning tasks in ways different from people in other cultures (Macleod 1988; Takeichi 1989). Americans sometimes approach the possibility of doing business in China with romantic and idealistic notions such as "millions of potential consumers," or "these people need our technology," or "we are spreading a superior way of life." These attitudes lead to the acceptance of rosy forecasts and unrealistic time-frames. Business people from other countries, such as Japan, are considered to be more pragmatic. Takeichi (1989, p. 40) argues that:

> US companies . . . approach China more idealistically or in a more venturesome manner. Japanese companies are quite pragmatic in their decisions to choose where and with whom in China they will do business or create joint ventures. . . . Large Japanese corporations are very cautious about business in sensitive countries. They have enough corporate resources already invested to judge and act reasonably, based on both Japanese thinking and a global perspective.

On a scale less grand than decisions about the possibility of doing business in China, there are differences involving approaches to learning that may be encountered in face-to-face encounters. In meetings where overseas companies are presenting proposals,

Chinese business people will often devote hours and hours to grilling the presenters about the technology behind the proposals (Pye 1982). This is done to allow the Chinese to learn about technologies to which they have not had access over the last forty years. Further, they may play one company off against another. If company A is unwilling to go into details about recent technological developments because they are considered proprietary, the Chinese may claim that company B has demonstrated more goodwill because its representatives shared their technology graciously.

18. *Attributions.* People observe the behavior of others, and they also reflect upon their own behavior. Especially if the behaviors do not live up to expectations, people feel the need to develop explanations for why others are behaving in certain ways. Judgments about the explanations that people develop concerning the *causes* of behavior are called "attributions." Difficulties are likely to arise in those cases where the *same* behavior is explained differently in one culture compared to another. For example, a friendly suggestion from another concerning how to improve one's work may be attributed to "helpfulness" in one culture. This same behavior might be attributed to "a desire to embarrass me in front of my group" in another culture.

When people engage in extensive intercultural interactions, it is almost always best to withhold the tendency to make quick attributions. Instead people should examine the behaviors of others carefully to determine what attributions *they* are making about *their own* behavior. When sojourners learn to make attributions that are the same as those made by hosts, then this is a major indicator of a successful adjustment to life and work in the other culture. For example, many Americans have made the attribution that the "Chinese do not live up to the specific agreements we carefully negotiated together." In contrast, the Chinese have made the attribution that "Americans do not live up to the spirit of agreements." The resulting set of charges and countercharges might be avoided if cultural differences were understood and if each side momentarily took the other's viewpoint to see if underlying reasons for the difficulties could be identified. Here, the difference is the relative emphasis placed on general principles versus specific details. Pye (1982, pp. ix–x) argues that:

> The Chinese reject the typical American notion that agreement is best sought by focusing on specific details and avoiding discussions of generalities. They prefer instead agreeing on the general

principles of the relationship before dealing with the troublesome details. The Chinese use the occasion of such preliminary exchanges on generalities to size up the other party and to determine how vulnerable he may be, especially whether he lacks patience. For Chinese officials, displaying impatience is a major sin, and they are masters of the art of stalling while keeping alive the other party's hopes.

Realizing this differential emphasis on general principles versus details, American negotiators will be more likely to make the attribution that the Chinese are "pragmatic business people according to their own practices" rather than to conclude that they are "devious." They will also be able to negotiate in ways that may satisfy both sides, for instance, by pointing out how attention to a certain set of very specific details contributes to the general principle identified by the Chinese.

THE NEED FOR CULTURAL INFORMANTS

This chapter has dealt with the difficulties that business people face when working in China. Many of the problems stem from the human rather than the economic or technical aspects of the business world. Learning about issues that stem from individual and cultural differences is admittedly difficult. People spend years and years *in their own country* learning about the human side of business, such as leadership, selection, training, helping subordinates with their problems, negotiations, decision-making, and so forth. It is a massive task for these same people to learn new approaches and to adapt to new demands in China. No one chapter such as this one, or even a set of books (e.g., in the bibliography to this chapter), can provide enough information to guarantee success.

Of course, chapters and books can provide people with enough information to ask good questions and to provide a basis for further learning. A good recommendation is to identify one or more "cultural informants." Such people can answer questions about cultural differences between overseas and Chinese business people that can affect negotiations, goal accomplishment, the long-term success of joint ventures, and so forth. Good candidates for the cultural informant role are people who themselves have spent a significant length of time in a culture other than their own. Given that they have spent time outside their culture, they have had the experience of adjusting to another way of life. In the language of this chapter, they have had disconfirmed expectancies, challenges to preexisting stereotypes and prejudices, frustrations when trying to meet their need to belong, misunderstandings concerning expectations about work, and so forth. Given their past experiences, they understand that cultural differences have major impacts and can answer questions about them. They can be expected "to advise, to guide, even to lead at times" (Kamsky 1989, p. 31). In working with these informants, however, it is often unwise to ask general questions about cultural practices in China that might lead to difficulties. Questions at this level of generality are unlikely to draw out specific advice that is useful in specific business dealing. It is better to review a systematic approach to learning about another culture, such as the eighteen themes presented in this chapter and in the longer, original treatment (Brislin *et al.* 1986). With the examples provided in the 100 critical incidents in that collection and the analysis exemplified in the eighteen themes, cultural informants can then search their memories and suggest specific applications that are applicable to a specific business proposal in China.

RECOMMENDATIONS

When doing business in China, the following steps are recommended:

1 Become acquainted with the cultural differences brought on by the individualist versus collectivist background of the people involved. Many Americans are socialized into an individualist culture where they value the pursuit of their own goals. Many Chinese are socialized into a much more collective orientation in which the value of goals set by a group is more important. This distinction has many very specific implications for business dealings (Triandis, Brislin, and Hui 1988). One implication is that the Chinese value long-term commitments. When they offer friendship, they are offering membership in their collective, and this demands life-long obligations.

2 Participate in formal training programs organized by experts well-versed in the issues people face when doing business in cultures other than their own. The program designed by Brislin and his colleagues (1986) was discussed here. If this does not seem suitable, other programs are described in various published sources (Paige 1986; Fowler and Mumford 1991). Make sure that the wide range of issues people face are covered, not just those dealing with the business world. The adjustment to all aspects of life in China,

not just to one's business dealings, can affect success. Finding cultural informants who can answer specific queries about differences and about factors influencing success in business is a good investment of resources.

3 Most readers of this book will probably not need the advice that they should do their homework carefully. Business in China should probably be looked upon as high risk, and should only be considered by people who can afford to postpone even the anticipation of returns for many years.

4 Generalizations about business in China are very difficult to make because of the vastness of the country and the large number of cultures summarized by the general term, "Chinese." The suggestions made in this chapter and in others by authors such as Pye (1982) and Tung (1982) should be viewed as starting-points that must be open to modifications based on people's own experiences in different businesses, different years, different parts of China, and so forth.

5 When doing business in China, there will inevitably be frustrations. As a consequence, there will be temptations to become angry, upset, and to view the Chinese as the causes of problems. Instead of becoming visibly angry, it is often best (with the help of cultural informants) to focus on cultural differences that might be causing difficulties. This focus ("I have ways of doing things that I learned in my culture, and I wonder if there are differences") takes the sting away from perceived attacks on individuals. Reviewing a systematic approach to cross-cultural interactions, such as that provided by the eighteen themes reviewed in this chapter, can help identify culturally-based reasons for difficulties.

NOTE

1 The authors would like to thank Karen Eastman for her help in the preparation of this chapter.

REFERENCES AND BIBLIOGRAPHY

Adler, N. (1991) *International Dimensions of Organizational Behavior* (2nd edn), PWS-Kent.
Baird, I., Lyles, M. and Wharton, R. (1990) "Attitudinal differences between American and Chinese managers regarding joint venture management," *Management International Review*, 30 (Special Issue), pp. 53–68.
Bhawuk, D. (1990) "Cross-cultural orientation programs," in R. Brislin (ed.), *Applied Cross-Cultural Psychology*, Sage, pp. 325–46.

Brislin, R. (1989) 'Intercultural Communication Training', in M. Asante and W. Gudykunst (eds), *Handbook of International and Intercultural Communication*, Sage, pp. 441–57.

Brislin, R. (1993) "A culture general assimilator: preparation for various types of sojourns," in M. Paige (ed.), *Education for the Interculture Experience*.

Brislin, R., Cushner, K., Cherrie, C. and Yong, M. (1986) *Intercultural Interactions: A Practical Guide*, Sage.

Carbaugh, D. (ed.) (1990) *Cultural Communication and Intercultural Contact*, Lawrence Erlbaum.

Chang, D. (1989) "Heaven is high, and the emperor is far away," *Harvard Business Review*, 67(6), pp. 33–6.

Chesanow, N. (1985) *The World-Class Executive*, Rawson.

Fowler, S. and Mumford, M. (1993) *Intercultural Sourcebook: Cross-Cultural Training Methodologies*, Intercultural Press.

Holton, R. (1990) "Human resource management in the People's Republic of China," *Management International Review*, 30 (Special Issue), pp. 121–36.

Hui, C.H. (1990) "Work attitudes, leadership styles, and managerial behaviors in different cultures," in R. Brislin (ed.), *Applied Cross-Cultural Psychology*, Sage, pp. 186–208.

Kamsky, V. (1989) Comment on "The case of the China diary," *Harvard Business Review*, 67(6), pp. 31–3.

Macleod, R. (1988) *China Inc.: How to do Business with the Chinese*, Bantam Books.

Paige, M. (ed.) (1986) *Cross-Cultural Orientation: New Conceptualization and Applications*, University Press of America.

Pye, L. (1982) *Chinese Commercial Negotiating Style*, Oelgeschlager, Gunn & Hain, Inc.

Robinson, A.J. (1989) "China is not monolithic," *Harvard Business Review*, 67(6), pp. 28–30.

Runnan, W. (1989) "Maintain a presence but halt expansion" (Comment on "The case of the China Diary"), *Harvard Business Review*, 67(6), pp. 30–1.

Takeichi, S. (1989) "US companies are idealistic; Japanese, pragmatic," *Harvard Business Review*, 67(6), p. 40.

Triandis, H. (1989) "The self and social behavior in different cultural contexts," *Psychological Review*, 96, pp. 506–20.

Triandis, H., Brislin, R. and Hui, C.H. (1988) "Cross-cultural training across the individualism–collectivism divide," *International Journal of Intercultural Relations*, 12, pp. 269–89.

Tung, R. (1982) *US–China Trade Negotiations*, Pergamon.

Tung, R. (1987) *The New Expatriate: Managing Human Resources Abroad*, Ballinger.

Webber, A. (1989) "The case of the China diary," *Harvard Business Review*, 67(6), pp. 14–28.

Index

KING ALFRED'S COLLEGE
LIBRARY